Design T

London Busine
Design Management
Seminars

Edited by
Peter Gorb with Eric Schneider

The Design Council

First published 1988 in the United Kingdom by
The Design Council
28 Haymarket
London SW1Y 4SU

Typeset in Singapore by Colset Private Limited
Printed and bound in Great Britain by
Biddles Limited, Guildford and King's Lynn

British Library Cataloguing in Publication Data

Design talks.
1. Design. Management aspects
I. Gorb, Peter II. Schneider, Eric.
III. London Business School IV. Design Council
658.5'7

ISBN 0–85072–218–7

Contents

Introduction
Peter Gorb   1

PART 1: Design Identity and Corporate Strategy

Design as a Corporate Strategy
Robert Blaich   9
The New Design Dimension of Corporate Strategy
Christopher Lorenz   27
Corporate Commitment to Design
David Maroni   35
Identity — The Corporation's Hidden Resource
Wally Olins   54
Current Business Trends and Corporate Identity
Donn Osmon   74

PART 2: Design, the Product and Product Innovation

The Importance of Design
Sir William Barlow   85
Design and Innovation at Novo
Mads Øvlisen   104
Design and Product Innovation on London
Underground
Dr Tony Ridley   112
Design as a Management Tool for Innovation
Dr Günther Zempelin   121

PART 3: Design, Retailing and the Business Environment

The Advancement of Design Awareness
Sir Terence Conran   135

Contents

Information Technology and Office Design
Dr Francis Duffy   141
The Impact of Design on the Retail Landscape
Rodney Fitch   153
Design and the Service Industries
Helen Robinson   162
Observations on Architecture
Richard Rogers   174

PART 4: Design, the Country and its Culture

On Design and our Industrial Future
Stephen Bayley   193
The Design Mind
David Bernstein   202
Design and the National Interest: 1
John Butcher MP   217
Design and the National Interest: 2
Sir Simon Hornby   226

PART 5: Design Case Studies

Design and the Building of Storehouse
Sir Terence Conran   241
The Columbia-Presbyterian Medical Center,
Identity Program
Colin Forbes   247
Design Management Policy at British Rail
Jim O'Brien   258
Micro-encapsulation: The Special Delivery System
Donn Osmon   288
Design Management at Ford
Uwe Bahnsen   292
Index   303

Introduction
Peter Gorb

Design Talks! is a collection of papers which originated from a series of seminars held at London Business School between 1983 and 1987. The subject of these seminars was design and its management. Their objective was to bring together an audience of both designers and managers to hear the views of people whose work and reputation spanned the two fields.

This book is intended to present those views to the growing audience with an interest in the relevance of design to the management world.

Although fast growing, interest in this subject is still relatively recent, and a seminar series of this kind in a business school remains unique. London Business School, which pioneered teaching design to managers in the mid-1970s, is still the only business school anywhere in the world with a full-time staff wholly devoted to the teaching of design.

Nevertheless, it is gratifying to report that teaching of this kind is beginning to happen elsewhere in the UK, at the universities and the polytechnics, and that our leadership in this field is being followed elsewhere in Europe, and also in the USA. Furthermore, the design community as well as management is showing increasing interest in the subject. Design teaching institutions are beginning to incorporate management studies into their programmes, the Chartered Society of Designers has given formal recognition to the profession of design management, and it and others are beginning to run discussions, seminars and teaching programmes in design management.

Much of the impetus for this growing interest has come from government which, since 1982, has not only made a financial commitment to design, but has either directly or indirectly, through the activities of the Design Council, promoted the importance of design to industry and committed funds to

1

support the work of others in this field. In a small way this book would not have been possible without both encouragement and financial support of this kind.

The success of the seminar series has depended, of course, on the quality of the speakers. Of the twenty-one represented in this book many are well known in either the design or business communities or both. A few, like Sir Terence Conran, are household names. Others, particularly those from overseas, are perhaps less well known. A short introductory note on each of them is included at the beginning of each paper. What follows are some comments on their collective backgrounds. Of the twenty-one, six are from overseas. One, Mads Øvlisen, is a Dane. Of the two Americans, Bob Blaich works in Holland and Donn Osmon in the USA. There are two Germans: Günther Zempelin, who has worked mainly in Holland, and Uwe Bahnsen, who now works in Switzerland. One of the Britons, Colin Forbes, now works in the USA, and many of the others operate internationally.

An international viewpoint may have helped to develop their awareness of the importance of the links between design and management. Of more interest is the extent to which their backgrounds and careers have also contributed.

Eight of them have design backgrounds, and of these four work in design or design consultancies (Duffy, Fitch, Rogers and Forbes), and four have crossed over to other fields: Blaich to design management, Conran to retail management, Bahnsen first to design management and recently to education, and Bayley to running a museum. Eleven of them have business backgrounds. Of these seven have remained in the management world: Osmon, Øvlisen, Ridley, Zempelin, O'Brien, Barlow and Hornby. The latter two are respectively the past and present Chairman of the Design Council. All of them have strong design interests. The other four (Maroni, Olins, Bernstein and Robinson) have now crossed over to work mainly in design or design-related fields. The last two, Butcher, a politician, and Lorenz, a journalist, are well known for their interest in design.

There is no doubt that if design is to continue to occupy a

key position in the business world, then the career 'crossovers' of the kind that some of our speakers have experienced will help to make it happen. The growing profession of design management both here and in the USA has so far been made up mainly of designers who have crossed over to management. One of the objectives of teaching design at business schools is to encourage career crossovers in the other direction.

When the seminar series was planned the backgrounds of the speakers determined their sequence, alternating where possible between designers and managers in order to emphasise this cross-fertilisation. This pattern has not been followed here. It seemed more appropriate in a book to choose a subject classification for the papers. Such a classification had of course determined their nature in the first place, with the objective of giving representation to as many aspects of design as possible.

Work in the mid-seventies at London Business School suggested that, if a classification of design subjects for management were to be meaningful, it needed to be stated, not in terms of the specialisation of designers (graphics, textiles, interiors, industrial design and so forth) but in terms of the use that organisations make of design. Furthermore, that use needed to be quantifiable in business terms. A classification was developed, which is now in general use and which falls under the following headings:

— Product design
— Environmental design
— Information design

It is important to describe each of these in detail. Like any simple classification each has become popular and their meaning tends to be eroded over time.

Product design means the design of those products that manufacturing industry makes in order to sell, and which distributors and retailers buy in order to sell; those which constitute the main purpose of the business. The value of those products, and so the design value, is calculated in the gross margin of the business.

Environmental design means those things which all businesses use to help them to achieve their main purpose — buildings, of course, including offices and shops, but also machines and machine tools and even other pieces of capital equipment, from vehicles to computers. The value of environmental design is a contribution to fixed assets and so to the key business ratio: return on capital employed.

Information design means the design of those things by which the business communicates its purposes to all of its audiences: customers, employees, shareholders and so on. It covers the design of management information systems, promotion and advertising, annual reports, company videos and many other similar products.

Information design is an expense cost and, although easy to evaluate financially, it is a relatively trivial cost in terms of its importance to the business. This is particularly the case for corporate identity design which has its origins in information design but spreads widely into the other two areas.

Corporate identity design is intimately concerned with the strategy of the business, and is almost certainly the most complex and the most cerebral aspect of the design contribution to business performance — the one which most concerns top management. Nearly all the other aspects of information design flow from decisions made in this field.

These three 'user' classifications determine how managers think about design irrespective of the nature of the products involved, many of which can fall into two or more of the classifications. For example, a calendar in a calendar factory is designed as a *product*. Hung on an office wall it becomes part of the *environment*. Since it is used to determine work schedules it needs to be designed for *information* purposes. Obviously the inevitable conflict between these three user classifications becomes a design management task.

The user classifications are the basis on which this book has been planned, but not exclusively and by no means comprehensively. Exclusivity would have constrained the speakers, whose freedom to range over the whole design field was an important part of their contribution. Comprehensiveness would have required far more than one book. However, the first three of the five sections are devoted to one or more aspects of the user classifications.

Part 1, Design Identity and Corporate Strategy, is devoted entirely to that key aspect of information design described above. Each paper explores an aspect of corporate identity design and leads on to a discussion of other aspects of information design. Some reach out further into areas of product design to discuss aspects of corporate culture which have more tenuous design connections.

Part 2, Design, the Product and Product Innovation, is devoted in the main to the innovation process in manufacturing industry. In today's economic climate the importance of innovation is the aspect of product design which dominates our thinking and each of the speakers uses it as the main element of his or her paper, although once again each of them has a wider design concern and design interest.

Part 3, Design, Retailing and the Business Environment, takes a more general view of environmental design, although three of the five papers are principally concerned with retailing design. This dominance reflects the leadership role of the UK retail sector in using design effectively. The other two papers are about building — one about the impact of information technology on offices, and the other a more general statement about the built environment.

In the fourth part, Design, the Country and its Culture, two of the four papers are very wide ranging, and two give differing viewpoints on the same subject. All of them affirm the proposition that design influences much more than the bottom line of a collection of business profit and loss accounts. The speakers argue that it is of direct concern to the nation, its culture and the individuals it is educating to shape its future economic and social well being.

The final part comprises five case studies each of which illuminates a practical aspect of the design process and its links with management. Two of them are by people who treated the cases as part of their paper when they originally gave it at London Business School. Their case studies have been separated out to appear in this book because they are easier to read in this way. And so the contributors' names appear twice in the list of contents.

I should like to start my acknowledgements by thanking all twenty-one contributors. They worked assiduously to prepare a paper and came to London Business School (some of them travelling long distances) to talk to and discuss their views with lively, appreciative and sometimes critical audiences. They have all done this for no reward other than perhaps the pleasure gained from helping to promote a good cause.

May I also acknowledge the important contribution of my co-editor, Eric Schneider. He undertook the initial task of ensuring that each text was as acceptable to a reader as a listener, and painstakingly prepared detailed summaries of each text on the basis of which the editorial work on the book could proceed.

Finally, may I thank all those people without whose help, advice and encouragement this book might not have happened. First, the Department of Trade and Industry which not only provided funding for the book, but actively encouraged its preparation. Second, the Design Council which has undertaken its publication, and particularly Stephanie Horner who has helped to ensure publication without tears. Thanks are also due to the members of the Advisory Committee which guides my work at London Business School, and especially its Chairman, Sir Peter Parker, whose help and encouragement over many years has been particularly valuable.

It was the members of this Committee who first had the idea for this book, and who urged me to go ahead with its preparation. I hope that readers will feel that their enthusiasm for it is justified.

Peter Gorb
January 1988

PART 1
Design Identity and Corporate Strategy

Design as a Corporate Strategy
Robert Blaich

Robert Blaich is an American. He trained as an architect and, after working as a consultant, he was for many years the Vice President of Design of Herman Miller, the office furniture and office systems manufacturer which has an international reputation for innovative design.

He is now Managing Director of Corporate Industrial Design, a subsidiary of Philips, the Dutch-based international electronics company. As such he is responsible for the design of all their products world wide. His job is probably the biggest and the most international design management job there is.

His paper describes how the design management process works at Philips, and discusses the international harmonisation of products which he sees as vital to the company's success, but he also recognises the need to take account of local and individual needs — a major design challenge.

There is not very much mystery about what the function of research and development is. What engineers do, or what we expect those in marketing to do. But there is still a great deal of mystery, it seems, about exactly what *design* is, what *really* is the role of the industrial designer, and how the design function fits into the spectrum of activities involved in the management process.

The confusion about exactly what design is is understandable. If you ask 50 people, you might get 50 different definitions for design. The dictionary doesn't offer much help.

English —
Industrial Design
'Art of making designs for objects which are to be produced by machines.'

American —
Industrial Design
'Design concerned with the appearance of three-dimensional machine-made products: (also) the study of the principles of such design.'

French —
Esthétique Industrielle
'Technique related to the creation of products developed by a company by subjecting them to the criteria of suitability for use, beauty, ease of production and reduction of costprice.'

Italian —
Disegno Industriale
'Giving industrial products a beautiful attractive form.'

German —
Industrielle Formgebung
'Design of the external appearance of products used in industry.'

Dutch —
Industriële Vormgeving
'Giving industrial products a good attractive form.'
'Design of the external appearance of products used in industry.'

Russian —
Promyslennji Dizajn
'Art/design activity in industry concerning the product of a designer.'

Japanese —
In-da-su-to-ri-a-ru de-za-in
'Design which, taking both usefulness and attractiveness into account, is intended for industrial products in all areaas.'
Also: Kô-gyô, i-shô
'New ideas for embellishment relating to form, external appearance and colour, or combinations of these, for industrial products, including inventions for ways of making them.'

Chinese —
Gongyè Shèji
The term does not exist in Chinese dictionaries.

But it is apparent to me that within the last few years, as I have attended various forums of discussion about design in industry and the management of design, design professionals who represent industries from all over the world and a wide range of product activities are increasingly in agreement about the role of design within the management process.

And increasingly also, the industrial design function is being discussed well beyond professional design publications. The management page of the *Financial Times* frequently presents articles about design as a component of strategic planning; *Time Magazine* considered design important enough as an element of today's lifestyle to establish a new section devoted to the subject. And articles frequently appear in such publications as *The Economist*, *Fortune*, *Wall Street Journal* and other publications.

The result of this attention in the media, and of discussions about design will perhaps be to demystify the subject.

I would like to try to clarify what industrial design is and to strengthen the case for design management as a corporate strategy.

There is general agreement in the design profession — and it must be assumed with some general support from the enterprises they represent — about some very basic functions of design.

Some of these important concepts are:

The process of design is becoming less and less something that has a beginning and an end. It is evolutionary, and ongoing. Thoughtful designers have moved from an emphasis on the single object and a preoccupation with its aesthetics to an awareness that the designed environment must be viewed holistically if it is to be genuinely humane.

11

There is a recognition that design is crucial to industrial and commercial competitiveness. If this is true, then it is certain that designers should be given greater influence in management.

It is essential that design be an early part of the product planning and development process. The past practice of handing over a product for final 'styling' — some colour decisions, graphic placement, a little tinkering with knobs or buttons — is outdated, and in general opinion, such practices are doomed to commercial failure.

One definition of creativity is thinking up new things. While innovation is *doing* new things, I believe innovation typically occurs in the interface of multiple disciplines and the industrial designer is one of these disciplines available to business in the struggle to remain successful.

The product is the most important statement a company can make about its image. It *is* the image. And in an increasingly competitive market with growing consumer sophistication, the skills of the industrial designer are critical to the definition and solution of problems involved with products that meet consumer needs and demands.

People often link 'taste' with design as the domain of the designer. However, 'taste' is an arbitrary and subjective basis for making decisions. Instead, designers at Philips, for instance, use these criteria to judge the success of their work:

1. Is the product ergonomically designed to satisfy human factors; is it intelligible?
2. Does it not only meet minimum safety standards, but extend to anticipate potentially dangerous situations?
3. Does the product successfully solve a consumer need, not only in itself but as an element of the environment in which it is being used?
4. Is the product designed to utilise materials, production processes and energy in the most efficient way?
5. Are the aesthetic elements such as form, colour and texture as well as graphic information integrated in an appropriate manner?

Now, if indeed there is some consensus that designers can contribute importantly to the product development and marketing process, it is fair to ask what special skills designers bring into the product programme.

Industrial design has become fully interdisciplinary. It must, therefore, include training not only in engineering and aesthetics, but also in graphic design, computer science, market research and ergonomics, because of its anthropometric and psychological aspects. Because product intelligibility has become of such critical importance, industrial designers must also know how to communicate clearly.

The traditional debate about where the function of the engineer ends and the industrial designer's role begins obviously still requires some clarification. This seems clear after the discussion on that subject held here during Christopher Lorenz's presentation (see p. 27).

With my years of experience acting as liaison between designers and engineers, I would agree with the American writer and design critic Ralph Caplan, that the difference between the two are as follows:

An engineer customarily works from the inside out. That is, he is trained to solve problems by thinking in terms of technical details. But the industrial designer normally works from the outside in. His thinking starts with the complete product as it would be used by someone, and works backwards into the details required to make the concept work.

The engineer is charged with seeing to it that the shaver will work. The industrial designer is charged with seeing to it that someone will — and conveniently can — use the shaver. The engineer's main concerns have to do with the interaction of components and materials. His job is to develop the best products consistent with the state of technology and the anticipated market price. The designer's job is to make sure that the product is one that will be bought and used.

The object of design and engineering attention is not invariably a discrete product, for both in engineering and design the emphasis on product has often given way to an emphasis on systems.

But the two disciplines differ in approaching systems design too. The engineer must see a system as a series of products and components that can be related to each other in various configurations. The designer is concerned with those possible configurations. But he is also concerned with the related systems of graphics, packaging, marketing and above all, the mechanics of operation by users and groups of users.

However, even though the approach between designer and engineer differs, it is unproductive to carry on a debate about whether designers and engineers are invading each other's turf. Instead, it is our emphasis at Philips to consider the work of designers and engineers as a collaboration, with each contributing importantly to the product development process.

The various activities in which a designer must be knowledgeable and actively involved are numerous.

The designer's concerns may also be different from those of other management disciplines, since, as I pointed out earlier, the designer is concerned with whether the product is bought, and how it is used.

For example, the retailer is often seen as the customer by marketing managers. For the designer, however, the customer is always the end user. The difference is that the retailer's image of the perfect product is something that keeps moving off the shelves, while the user's concern has to do with direct value and performance. Working for the retailer will rarely lead to innovation whereas thinking abut the needs of the user almost always opens up the possibility of improvement. Manufacturers spend a lot of time keeping their dealers happy: what the designer does is bring in a comparable concern for the buyer.

Because of the designer's link with this area of activity, he is increasingly seen as the connector between commercial and technical disciplines, as well as the end user. Professor Christopher Freeman, head of the Science Policy Research Unit at Sussex University and recognised as the foremost academic in the field of economics and technical innovation, in a *Financial*

Times article went so far as to call the total process of planning, co-ordinating and managing the broad product innovation process 'design management'. It explains, he said in a paper on design and British economic performance, why more companies have given their industrial designers a central role in the product development process.

With this discussion of how the role of design is being perceived in at least some quarters, I would like to acquaint you with how in fact it now functions at Philips.

Allow me briefly to preface this examination with some background information.

Industrial design started at Philips in 1925 as part of Philips' Advertising Department. Its main activity seemed to be to provide art services — including the design of the emblem. In 1960 the Board of Management recognised industrial design as a special function, establishing 'Concern-bureau Vormgeving'.

In 1966, Knut Yran, my predecessor, joined Philips and the department became known as the Concern Industrial Design Centre — CIDC — with its director reporting directly to the Board of Management.

In 1980, I came to CIDC as managing director. In the past few years the major change is one of attitude — that the company now views design as part of strategy instead of merely a service — this change in perception was, in my opinion, critical since I had established such a perceptive change as my mission.

My training was in both architecture and industrial design, but my career has encompassed the diverse activities of industrial design management and corporate communications. These have included management responsibilities within Herman Miller, Inc., and international manufacturer of living, learning, working and healing systems, in marketing product design and development, facilities design and corporate communications. At Herman Miller we had the freedom to take risks — we often 'bet-the-company'. For this you need a fertile ground. We had it at Miller and I am finding that the cultivation to produce fertile ground is also possible at Philips.

15

Philips, founded in 1891, is the 28th largest company in the world — fifth in electronics and second in consumer electronics. We have national organisations in 60 countries with 350,000 employees. The company has eight research labs in six countries with a total staff of 4,000. In addition there are 17,000 employees involved in product development with 7 per cent of its turnover being spent on R&D. Part of this R&D is the Concern Industrial Design Centre. CIDC has the responsibility for all industrial design including packaging and graphics and the company house style.

We have design offices in 30 locations in 20 countries with the centre in Eindhoven, the Netherlands. There are over 200 people of 20 nationalities in the design organisation. CIDC is commissioned by product divisions for the design work of new and existing products. National organisations also request design assistance for locally developed, produced and marketed products.

A few examples of the scope of our design activities are:

Home entertainment and information systems

TV	Video recorders
Cameras	hi-fi
Radio recorders	Video and audio digital disc players

Domestic appliances

Cooling	Cooking
Washing	Cleaning
Personal care	Time

Professional products

Data systems

Dictation	Small business equipment
Word processors	Banking terminals
Computer systems	

Telecommunications

Telephones

Communication
 systems

Teletext

Traffic and emergency
 controls

Medical systems

Diagnostic and treatment products

Science and industry

Testing, measuring, diagnostic equipment

Electroacoustics

Television cameras, Intercoms

Public address and conference systems

Packaging and graphics

In addition, CIDC is responsible for developing and evaluating house style standards which are intended to give consistency to all visual communications and products. I serve as
chairman of the house style council.

The basic centre of competency is the CIDC in Eindhoven,
responsible for design policy, design research, information,
selection and training of designers, administration and house
style. The Product Divisions — Audio, Video, Lighting and all
Professional Product Divisions are served from Eindhoven.
Additional satellites in Drachten and Groningen, in the
Netherlands, serve Small Domestic Appliances. Major Domestic Appliances is served from Cassinetta, Italy. Other European
units in the UK, Belgium, France, Germany, Austria, and Spain
are located in production centres.

In addition to satellite design staffs throughout the world,
we make designers available for special projects. In the past year
personnel from CIDC have worked on refrigerators and domestic appliances in Mexico; radio recorders, hi-fi and portables in
India and shavers and small domestic appliances in Japan.

Organisationally, CIDC is currently structured to parallel
the product division structure of Philips. Teams of product and

17

graphic designers, under the leadership of design managers, carry out the basic work of CIDC. The teams include Professional Products and Systems; Small and Major Domestic Appliances; Personal Care; Audio and Video Products; Lighting; Packaging and Graphic Design. The seven design managers work with the director in developing and evaluating design policy.

The design teams are served by such staff design services as model making, research and information gathering and distribution, computer-aided design and general administrative services.

In the past year a number of CIDC-designed products have received some important awards. The 660 Pocket Memo has received awards from the US, Austria and Germany; and 15 design awards were made at the Gute Industrieform, Hannover, for Lighting, Data Systems and PTI products. Our Compact Disc was included in *Time Magazine*'s 'The best of 1983'.

With this background information about the Philips industrial design organisation in mind, we come to the question: does it operate as an integral part of the corporate strategy?

I would like to describe several examples in which industrial design has a significant role in developing product strategy. In Europe we have instituted several Design Steering Committees, where members of the product division and CIDC work together to ensure harmonisation, integration and standardisation of products and systems.

One example of how industrial design participates very effectively in the total product management is in the professional products and systems area. A professional products harmonisation programme was initiated by CIDC. With regard to this programme, Mr Jeelof, a member of Philips Board of Management, said in the foreword to the harmonisation-professional equipment brochure:

Corporate identity is increasingly important in the competitive marketplace, and management of the identity is a task that requires the active, serious attention of those involved within the concern. This activity is the result of such teamwork, in which professional product management and representatives from CIDC and Concern Standardization Department came together to address the question of developing a coherent image for Philips professional products.

The problem was one of a previously uncoordinated design programme — and a wide divergency of design solutions existing in Philips and our associated companies prior to 1980.

The task was to create a harmonious programme so that products and systems for our various organisations would be compatible within a working, healing and scientific environment while providing a consistent image for Philips as a professional company.

The goal of the harmonisation committee, which I chair, was to underline to the customer the ability of Philips to handle the complex solutions, networks and systems of which the products form a part. Secondly, harmonisation could lead to standardisation, which could serve an economical goal by preventing duplication of products or systems.

Our first task was visual harmonisation, including colours and finishings, identification and product graphics and, finally, form. The policy considerations were those of a long-term nature, dealing with:

— International market requirements
— Different life-span of product ranges
— Compatibility of product ranges
— Philips professional image — one that is contemporary, evolutionary and has continuity.

As 'universal' products and systems become more important, it has become necessary to reorient our own industrial design policies from individual products to systems and co-ordinated programmes, from local-for-local design activities in national organisations to world market concepts.

The first such programme was Eurorange television. Prior to 1977 there was a very broad range of TV designs — with special products for each country. When market tests proved

19

this was not necessary, the Product Division organised a European video programme policy. A European product team was set up to establish specifications and allocation of development and production. CIDC was commissioned to co-ordinate and control the scattered industrial design activities.

These data show the tremendous progress made in the past six years in the rationalisation of TV products for the European market:

European colour TV before 1977
Separate programmes in 12 countries
90 basic models
23 industrial designers working in 7 countries

Eurorange 1
45 basic models
16 designers

Eurorange II
40 basic models
16 designers

Eurorange III
25 basic models
 6 designers from CIDC
 4 designers from Italy, Sweden, for follow-up

Of course the basic models referred to still have small variations for other brands and special local market requirements.

Another example of design as a strategic activity is the ongoing collaboration between Major Domestic Appliances and Small Domestic Appliances as exemplified in the Philips 'Kitchen of the Future' which was exhibited at the Köln Domotechnica. The task was to present new ideas for complete kitchening. It presented a co-ordinated design for:

— Built in major appliances
— Storage of small appliances

— Optimum lighting
— Integral A / V system.

The basic concept was a service rail and storage zone to be utilised within the standard European norms.

This positioned Philips as an appliance manufacturer, not only for the kitchen but also for home entertainment and lighting. It opened a dialogue with manufacturers of kitchen cabinets and it became a vehicle for the development of new appliances.

What do we know about other companies and the relative importance of design in their product planning processes? There are a number of companies that have a strong and well-known reputation for their commitment to design. These are companies such as IBM, Olivetti, Braun, Ford and Sony.

It is now legendary that Thomas Watson, former president of IBM, simply issued an edict that design must be an important part of IBM's management mentality. The order to accomplish this was short and to the point. It said

Good design is good business. Imaginative use of design helps to sell our products. Pleasant, efficient work areas contribute to better morale and productivity. Dramatic design in printed material increases its message impact. The V.P. for design is responsible for coordinating company design activities in architecture, interiors, display, products, packaging and printed material. Since design excellence concerns all areas of the business, you should make certain that all your people are aware of its importance.

Thomas Watson, 26 January, 1961

This is still the policy at IBM. A recent *Wall Street Journal* article on the Ford Motor Company provides a rather dramatic example of how Ford listened to its designers — the following was reported

Shortly after he was named president of Ford Motor Company in 1980 Donald Petersen asked Ford designers if the cars on their drawing boards from 1983 and beyond were what

21

they really wanted to be designing. When he got back a resounding 'No' he pushed through authorization for the designers to give far more emphasis to designing the kind of cars they wanted to drive and own themselves: they then designed cars that had less drag, gained fuel efficiency and minimum mechanical changes.

The results are the new Sierras.

Certainly design plays a major role in the industrial policy of Ford.

The Olivetti design programme is well-known for its reinforcement of excellent product design with the hiring of respected graphic designers and architects to build a total image of quality. The design-integrated programme culminated in an award by the American Institute of Architects. The citation said

For a history of excellence in communicating its image through product design, corporate communication, architecturally distinguished working and merchandising facilities and sponsorship of numerous social, educational and cultural programs for both its employees and the public at large.

Apple's computer, renowned for its flexible management style, points to how design will be integral to tomorrow's corporate success stories.

Steven Jobs, co-founder of Apple, observes that design at Apple is not just the company's logo but everything from advertising to the idea of building an 'Apple Community'. A design council meets monthly and includes Jobs, the VP of corporate communications, all senior designers and the head of Apple's advertising agency.

When I recently visited Sony, Yasuo Kuroki, head of their product planning centres, said

Designers should not be artists — particularly industrial designers who should be the creators who understand fully all the facilities available for them within the company. They should be market creators who can make new products by combining the social trends and the inner factors of their own corporation.

The dynamism which organizes all these factors effectively is what I call 'Design Management'.

The catalogue for Sony's 1983 exhibit at the Victoria and Albert Museum in London, says

Sony is highly conscious that design is an image of corporate attitudes; thus the change from 1946 when engineers had the job of deciding what a machine looked like, to 1982 when the design process has become a fundamental part of corporate strategy.

The exhibit showed that the design division is at the core of the total marketing activity of Sony with a responsibility for market research, corporate identity, product planning, design of R&D products, package design and display design.

The world today is characterised by information sharing and the symbiosis of different cultures. This is a trend that we must recognise and be prepared for.

In this homogenising trend, industrial design has succeeded through its quest for 'design for the masses' and 'international design' to establish a common vocabulary. The more this succeeds, the less able it is to satisfy individual and local needs.

In the book *Megatrends*, one of the most widely read books today in the US, author John Naisbitt discusses globalised industry and as an example states, 'The 30 auto companies now competing on an international scale, will by the end of the '80s be reduced to as few as seven or eight companies or alliances of companies.'

In another chapter on multiple options he states that homogenised tastes are no longer satisfied by a few product choices in what he calls the Baskin-Robbins society, where everything comes in at least 31 flavours. As an example, while the number of car companies is shrinking, the options within lines are increasing. There are 752 different models of cars and trucks sold in the US — not counting the choice of colours they come in.

This dichotomy, or what Naisbitt calls counter-trends between homogeneity and cultural diversity, can be accomplished within the context of overall systems. This in itself is a 'design' opportunity.

While this is a trend to which product policy should pay close attention in developing strategy, there are always some exceptions that do not fit the rule. We will still also need to pay attention to some individual products to satisfy cultural diversity.

Some observers of change contend that the great breakthroughs in technology are behind us, that we are in the post-industrial era, moving from manufacturing to service economies, and that technological innovation will be based on incremental knowledge and add-ons. I doubt this. As new technology emerges, the sophistication of future innovation is likely to challenge the comprehension of even the most informed layman.

What does this mean for design and designers in the future? You may be certain that the fundamental shapes of most of our common products will change radically. New products will have new shapes. These future products will be different, more complicated, and the designer as the connection between technology and the consumer will have an increasingly important and difficult role. Therefore the designer must combine knowledge of materials and processes with skill and craftsmanship and a basic integrity.

Fifty years ago industrial design was largely about fitting hardware forms to functions that grew up with mass production. Today it is more and more about fitting software forms to new functions.

Let me give you some examples of software versus hardware. In data and information processing, software has been a major determinant in the design of the products. Now with the video and audio disc we have the same phenomenon and in the future with the integration of office and home communications we will have new configurations.

Miniaturisation and the black box signal that the physical requirements of electronics product design are diminishing. Shapes are no longer dictated so much by mechanical components. Fewer constraints will leave more latitude in the design process. With the dematerialisation of hardware, new attitudes about form will emerge. As products become smaller and smarter we will see a great deal of innovation, both visual and technical.

Product intelligibility is an increasingly important concern for industrial designers. Many of the products that will be developed will be able to do things that people have not encountered before. Important new criteria for designers will be built around how to respond to consumers' demands for 'How quickly can I learn to operate this product: how easily can I understand it?' Consumers must cope with the problem of time (lack of it), absorption of information and exasperation when that information is confusing or non-existent. It will be an increasingly important challenge to the designer to make a product self-explanatory.

Ergonomics and product intelligibility are very closely linked. Ergonomics has been extremely important for professional products and will continue to be a major factor in their design. Today we are finding an increasing ergonomic requirement in consumer products, from shavers where hand to face operations are carefully studied, to hi-fi with the emergence of flat panel technology.

As mentioned earlier, there is a clear move towards more system thinking. This has in the past been limited at Philips to professional products such as computers, word processor and medical equipment. Today we find systems in home environments, the links between hi-fi, television, video or comprehensive home entertainment and information systems are with us today, not just a dream for the future. In the area of food storage and preparation there is system thinking being reflected in consumer products as previously shown in the 'Kitchen of the Future'. Whether or not the consumer buying kitchen appliances, a stereo set or a small computer relates these to a concern for 'total environments', it is important

25

for the design process to encompass the whole of the human environment.

I hope that I have succeeded in 'de-mystifying' design, especially product design at Philips. The products we produce are the most important things we can say about ourselves. The purchasers of both consumer and professional products and systems are more aware than ever before of everything that comprises a good product — and aware, in short, of good design. They do not simply accept good design, they expect it, and in the future will most likely demand it.

This is an idea, completely without mystery, whose time has come.

The New Design Dimension of Corporate Strategy[1]

Christopher Lorenz

Christopher Lorenz is a journalist and the Management Editor of the Financial Times, *in which influential newspaper he writes regularly about design matters.*

He has recently published a seminal work The Design Dimension *which deals with the recent revolution in product design and its effect on corporate strategies in a wide range of international companies.*

In his paper he develops some of the arguments made in the book, quoting examples from Ford, Sony and IBM, among others, and showing in each case how design acts as a bridging and co-ordinating activity between the many management functions involved in bringing a product to the market.

Even by the extraordinary standards of Hollywood, it was one of the most lavish parties ever thrown. To the tune of 'Happy Days are Here Again', more than 1,000 guests from the worlds of movies, TV and high society were wined and dined amid rampant luxury in the historic MGM studio where 'Gone with the Wind' had been filmed.

The occasion of this $1.5m extravaganza was not a film première, but the 'roll-out' of the 1986 Ford Taurus and Mercury Sable, two sleek new cars on which the Ford Motor Company was pinning its hopes for a competitive revival against the massed ranks of General Motors, the Germans and the Japanese.

[1]This paper is developed extensively from a talk given at LBS by Christopher Lorenz when he was researching his book *The Design Dimension — the new competitive weapon for business*. Published by Basil Blackwell, Oxford and New York, 1986 (hardback), 1987 (paperback). © Christopher Lorenz.

The launch also had a wider significance. It marked the conversion of the world's second largest motor company to a strategy of competing through adventurous, aerodynamic product design. Gone was the traditional policy, common to all American motor manufacturers, of cladding a lacklustre and unimaginative vehicle in an unwieldy, boxy, battering-ram shape, garnished with all sorts of ritzy, angular radiator grilles, tail fins and chromium strips.

In its place was a policy of integral design, in which the car's uncluttered shape was heavily influenced by its function, and particularly by the need to reduce wind drag in order to improve its fuel consumption.

Sparked off by Ford's European offshoots in the late 1970s, the new strategy had taken time to convince conservatives back home in Dearborn, Ford's headquarters in the heart of mid-west Michigan. But stung by the company's poor sales, and its plunge into heavy financial losses between 1980 and 1983, its top brass were now committed. As Donald Petersen, Ford's new chairman, told the gathering of celebrities, the company's 'dynamic vehicle philosophy' (the motor industry just loves hyperbole) encompassed not only the virtues of performance, handling and aesthetics, but also a galaxy of characteristics like quality, function, safety, comfort, reliability and cost of ownership.

In shifting to this unusually deep commitment to product design, Ford had to undergo a conversion of Galileo-like proportions. Conventional wisdom in the automobile industry had always put a company's interests before those of its customers. 'But that has changed', declared Petersen. 'Now the driver and passengers, not the company, are the centre of Ford's universe.'

If the result was a set of products that made Ford markedly different from its competition, that would no longer be a worry — in fact, so much the better. Never mind if their low noses, high tails and smooth shapes quickly earned them the nickname of the 'jellybean look'.

Ford's courage was well-justified. During 1986 the Taurus became America's best-selling car. The *New York Times* commented that 'aero' design had not only put Ford back on the right track, but changed the look of the entire American car industry.[2]

In down-to-earth terms, Petersen was saying that Ford's use of design as a competitive weapon formed part of its belated conversion to a broader cause: the concept of marketing first promulgated more than a quarter of a century ago by Theodore Levitt and others, in which the imaginative satisfaction of customer needs and wants, whether active or latent, takes over as the company's driving force from the traditional approach to trying to sell whatever the company happens to produce.

Remarkably, this shift from 'sales' to 'marketing' is one which many companies have been slow to make. They may have given their sales chief a grand new 'marketing' title, but they continue to lack the ability to think long term, to think in terms not of an amorphous mass market but of particular market segments, and to be imaginative in the identification of potential new segments and products and markets.

Only in the early 1980s did things really start to change. From Tokyo to Detroit, Milan to Munich, London to Los Angeles, companies large and small belatedly began to embrace a new approach, in which product design is used as a key competitive weapon. For those involved in competition on a global scale — a rapidly increasing proportion of companies — the design dimension is becoming a particularly important factor. It is being exploited more and more to create competitive distinctiveness for products of all kinds, whether it be Minolta cameras or Sony hi-fis from Japan; Philips compact disc players or shavers from the Netherlands; Wilkinson razors from Britain; Audi automobiles from Germany, or the 'Swatch' watch from Switzerland.

Differentiation by design is, of course, a familiar strategy in premium products, such as Rolex watches, Braun shavers, Porsche cars and Herman Miller office furniture. But it is now spreading to the world of mass marketing. In the words of Theodore Levitt's fellow marketing guru, Professor Philip Kotler, 'one of the few hopes companies have to "stand out

---

[2]*New York Times*, 24 May 1987.

from the crowd" is to produce superiorly designed products for their target markets'.

Design is no longer a luxury, in other words, but a necessity.

To some of the latest design converts this is merely a matter of styling: the original $30 Swiss 'Swatch', for example, was essentially a stripped-down and zappily restyled version of the much more expensive Concord Delirium, which was the thinnest watch in the world when it was launched in 1979. The new cars which in 1982 and 1983 heralded Ford's initial shift to aerodynamics in the United States — the Thunderbird, Lincoln Continental Mark VII, Tempo and Topaz — and which boosted its market share dramatically, were also re-skinned versions of existing models. So, among Ford's European range of cars, was the Escort. But like the Sierra and Scorpio/Granada, its more recent US models reflect a radical redesign of what lies under the skin.

As Kotler argues, in order to succeed, companies must 'seek to creatively blend the major elements of the design mix, namely performance, quality, durability, appearance and cost.'[3]

Each of the elements affects the other, and it is becoming unacceptably expensive, in competitive as well as financial terms, to decide them separately — they have to be specified in parallel, with all the necessary trade-offs settled at the start. Yet many companies persist with the conventional pattern of leaving decisions about the various aspects of industrial design until last.

It is through their recognition of the need to manage product development along Kotler's lines that the more enlightened companies have begun to realise that they must stop treating design as an afterthought, and cease organising it as a low-level creature of marketing — whether marketing 'proper', or sales masquerading under a grand name. Instead, they have elevated it to fully fledged membership of the corporate

[3]'Design: a powerful strategic tool', P Kotler and G A Roth, *Journal of Business Strategy*, Autumn 1984.

hierarchy, as it has been for decades in design-minded firms such as Olivetti and IBM. (Coincidentally — or is it? — both of these companies rely at least in part on outside design consultants, rather than just on in-house teams. But the consultants are so well integrated by now that they are treated as insiders — with the difference that their external experience wins them extra respect.)

Other companies have gone even further. They have recognised that design is so central to the company's purpose, and such a multi-disciplinary skill, that industrial designers can play a uniquely catalytic role in the product development process, and even, through product strategy, in helping to form market strategy. Again, this applies not only to premium products, but to the world of mass marketing. Sony, Olivetti, and even the much larger Philips can all boast successful products which were conceived by industrial designers working informally as product planners and project leaders.

Usually this happens behind the scenes, but in some cases they have taken on this role officially. Early in 1985, for instance, Sony's design chief was given the additional role of co-ordinating the development of products which combine the expertise of the company's various organisational groupings, such as its audio, video and television divisions. In the electronics industry this sort of integration role is becoming especially crucial, in the light of the growing popularity of home video 'systems' which combine innovative audio techniques (such as the compact disc) with top-class video, and with interactive home computer systems.

Even in the most unlikely of industries, industrial designers are becoming co-ordinators of the product development process. The chief executive of Baker Perkins, a leading international process machinery maker (now subsumed into the APV group), has described his industrial designers as 'translators, bridges and catalysts' between marketing and the various types of engineer: design engineer, development engineer, production engineer, and so on. In common with top managers in a number of other companies, he uses his industrial designers as an extra arm of general management.

31

In the arcane but descriptive language of behavioural science, industrial designers who are given such pivotal roles display a combination of several skills which are generally considered necessary to the success of any management team. At one and the same time they seem to be acting, alone or in conjunction with the official project team leader, not only as an invaluable source of ideas, but as 'facilitator', co-ordinator, evaluator and completer. This is a very far cry from the stereotype of 'designer as stylist', and much closer to the all-round role of co-ordination and integration which, in many countries, an architect plays in the building process.

That sort of project management is just as important in the process of designing, developing, making and launching a manufactured product, but it is seldom managed successfully. Co-ordination of all the different specialists is either left to a very formalised but inefficient procedure of inter-departmental communication, or is concentrated in the hands of a project team leader or product manager who probably lacks imagination and has an inadequate understanding of the various specialist skills at his or her command. In the words of one senior manager within the sprawling Philips organisation, 'good product managers are a very rare breed'.

Underpinning the ability of many designers to play a full part in the development team, and the potential of some even to become the team's co-ordinator, is a set of unusual personal attributes and skills. Some are inborn, others are learned. They include imagination; the ability to visualise shapes and the relationship between objects, in three dimensions; creativity; a natural unwillingness to accept obvious solutions; the ability to communicate, through words as well as sketches; and, finally, the designer's stock-in-trade — the ability and versatility to synthesise all sorts of multidisciplinary factors and influences into a coherent whole.

This is a pretty demanding combination — even more so when the successful designer in industry must also possess all the usual executive virtues of determination, drive and discipline. But many architects possess it: not those notorious individualists with massive artistic egos, but the more level-headed, co-operative and business-like variety.

So do a good number of industrial designers. Contrary to popular myth, these latter-day versions of Renaissance Man (and Woman) do not all hail from Milan and the other design-rich parts of Italy. Ettore Sottsass, Mario Bellini, Rodolfo Bonetto, Giorgetto Giugiaro and other famous Italian consultants are undoubtedly international masters of design, but so are Germans such as Richard Sapper and Hartmut Esslinger, as (respectively) IBM and both Apple and Sony have recognised in the form of lucrative contracts. A number of less well-known Britons, too, deserve the same accolade: not only consultants such as Kenneth Grange and Nick Butler, who have worked, respectively, for Kodak and Minolta cameras, among many other clients, but also a bevy of unsung heroes who work as insiders at world-scale companies such as BMW and Olivetti. British and German designers seem to take more easily than their Italian counterparts to the culture and discipline of working within a large company. So do Americans — which is just as well, since many of the top US product designers are anonymous members of in-house teams. With a few exceptions, such as Niels Diffrient, a former partner of the late Henry Dreyfuss, most of the great American product design consultants are names from the past.

Whatever their nationalities, few other sorts of professional can be expected to possess such a broad combination of characteristics and skills, be they planners or accountants, engineers or even marketing executives. Indeed, it is the very paucity of vision on the part of many so-called 'marketing' departments which often torpedoes the application of Levitt's formula of 'the marketing imagination'.

The clear message of all this is that, for a company to develop a fully fledged 'marketing imagination', and to exploit it to its utmost, it needs to upgrade its use of design. As Levitt himself argues, 'the search for *meaningful distinction* (my italics) is a central part of the marketing effort'.[4] Yet, in a crowded and increasingly global marketplace, the achievement

[4]Levitt, T, *The Marketing Imagination* New York and London: Free Press, 1983.

of meaningful distinction requires the company to make all sorts of new connections.

In the broadest of senses, it must make new connections between itself and the consumer. To do this it must be able to establish more effective links within its own organisation, between the various elements of the company's 'value chain' (or 'business system', as it is sometimes called), namely: technology which is either available on the market or is coming out of research; development; production; marketing; sales and distribution; and service. And it must make new connections between the market and the various elements of Kotler's 'design mix': performance, quality, durability, appearance and cost.

For these connections to be made successfully requires a team effort in which the industrial designer's imagination, synthesising skills, and entrepreneurial drive are given equal weight to the tools of the engineer, the financial controller and the marketer. The design dimension is no longer an optional part of marketing and corporate strategy, but should be at their very core.

Corporate Commitment to Design

David Maroni

vid Maroni is a Director of British Olivetti where, for many
irs, he has helped to establish his company's world-wide
putation for using design effectively in the development of
eir business. A former Chairman of Governors of the Central
:hool of Art & Design and a leading promoter of design
irough industry, he received the bicentennial medal of the
SA in 1983 and honorary fellowship of the Chartered Society
f Designers in 1985. Most recently, he has steered a committee
to establish a Centre for Design Studies in the UK.

In his paper he argues the case for reforming design
education to make it more relevant to business needs and he
describes half a dozen ways in which Olivetti has made use of
relevant design.

I assume that the purpose behind asking representatives of
companies like IBM and Olivetti to speak is that we tend, like
Chaucer's parson, to practise what we preach. However, the
acid test is whether a company actually makes some change in
the way it manages design, or even in its *attitude* to design. If
nobody does, then such talks will add yet another mountain of
ineffective verbosity to the existing Everest of constantly
regurgitated design pronouncements. If, on the other hand, it
makes any company take a fresh look at its policy on design, it
will all have been worth while.

You probably all know the radio game where you are asked
to find out what three totally obscure names have in common.
I am going to ask you the same question and the three names
are: Jonathan Swift, Goethe and Harold Macmillan. The only
difference is that, being a decent sort of chap, I'm not going to
ask you for the answer, I'll tell you: all three said something very
relevant to design without knowing it. Goethe said: 'Everything

has been said before, but as no-one was listening it is worth saying again.' Swift said: 'Everybody talks about the weather but nobody does anything about it', and Harold Macmillan talked about 'the wind of change'. The last quote is here because I looked up a speech that I made 18 years ago and, apart from the very real and hefty support from the Government for the design industry (epitomised by that patron saint of design John Butcher), we have talked a great deal but not changed very much. All wind and little change. If you think that I am exaggerating you should know that even in 1867 a government committee reported that it appeared that a great deal more could be done for design. All wind . . . no change.

If I were asked to put the problem in a nutshell, I would say that industry, on the whole, has not *truly* understood how more attention to design could help it prosper. We may pay lip service to the saying of the great pioneer of design Raymond Loewy, who said that design is the art of making the cash till ring — but we don't really believe it. Perhaps the only positive change, apart from the Government's own attitude, is a general feeling that after all design should be looked at. I notice, for example, that a few years ago, if I spoke to the Chairman or Chief Executive of a large industry about design, he would listen patiently and a glazed look would come over his eyes. I would know that he was thinking: 'I mustn't be rude but I have not the faintest idea what this chap is talking about.' Now, he will listen patiently, the same glazed look will come over his eyes but he will say quite openly: 'I don't know the first thing about design, but I do know that I ought to be involved in it in one way or another.'

Among other things, I am going to touch on a number of aspects relating to Olivetti's approach to design. It is not a sort of underhand commercial. You have paid too much money for that, but the title given to me *is* 'Commitment', and our commitment goes back a long way.

I personally have been with British Olivetti for 35 years. It would be silly and, in fact, wasteful, therefore, not to use our company as a point of reference for some of the design issues that I would like to address briefly. However, I am also a consultant on corporate image to some large companies and I am very involved in design education. My comments, therefore, are not solely based on my experience of Olivetti. Since we are one of the many companies represented here with some kind of design commitment, I believe that one of the reasons for including us on this distinguished platform is precisely because of our very long history — possibly *the* longest — of dedication to, and belief in, the value of design. In fact, the first design manager — in the truest sense of the word — was Adriano Olivetti himself, while the first official appointment to head the design management function was made more than forty years ago.

An inkling of the shape of things to come was a statement made at the beginning of the century by the founder himself — Camillo Olivetti — when he launched the first typewriter in Italy. He said

The aesthetic side of the machine has to be carefully studied. A typewriter . . . should have an appearance that is elegant and serious at the same time.

Camillo Olivetti, 1911

This is the first testimony I can find from an industrialist of the indivisibility of beauty and function.

Before I comment on Olivetti's long-standing attitude to design I would like to deal with a related question that I am continually being asked: 'Why are so many Italian designers acknowledged internationally and why is Italian design so successful throughout the world?' If you asked ten different people you would get ten different answers; I can only give you a personal view. There is, of course, one standard answer, namely, the embarrassment — almost the bombardment — of visual stimuli which have permeated the whole of Italy since well before the Renaissance. Such stimuli are highlighted by the climate, which sharpens everything, especially colour contrasts. But then Greece has even greater visual stimuli and an even better climate, so that's not a totally satisfactory explanation. Less obvious, but I believe more fundamental, is the Italian

37

attitude towards the established order which is very different from that of the UK and Germany.

In the UK, thank goodness, there is an underlying respect for authority, for institutions, for government — or at least for the system of government — even a sneaking respect for the Civil Service. In Italy, the tendency is the exact opposite: the bureaucratic machine is despised, government often ignored, and any institutional approach disliked. The result is that the very same force that creates a certain element of disorder, also fosters an entrepreneurial spirit and an individualism which makes people act *in advance* — and often in opposition to — any official policy statement. This entrepreneurial spirit is strengthened by a number of factors: the strong family unit which, after the war, spawned thousands of very hard-working family businesses; the so-called black economy; the deficiency in raw materials that turned manufacturing and exports into expedients for survival. Especially after the war, the design element found a fertile soil, not only because of the cultural inheritance already stated, but because of the reaction to 20 years of Fascism, with the inevitable straitjacket that goes with a dictatorship. Couple to this the need to add flair — the u.s.p. as the advertisers would say — to promote exports in competition with countries with more credibility, such as Germany, and you have all the ingredients for a well-designed, top-selling cake. The Latin blood with its tendency to be less cautious, and therefore take more risks, provided the final element for the Italian design phenomenon. British designers — as shown by the design brain drain and by the general demand for their services — have to be *at least* as good in order to survive in the far less fertile design soil of the U K. The fact that they do is a tribute, not only to their skills, but to the design education system of the UK.

I would now like to comment on a number of long-standing attitudes and practices in the field of design within Olivetti and relate them to the design world in general. These are:

1. The total co-ordination of all visual aspects (corporate design/corporate image)

2. The priority and high regard given to design inside the company
3. The significance of ergonomics as a selling tool
4. Long-term design research (not project-related)
5. Continuous innovation
6. The high status of designers employed as consultants

CO-ORDINATION OF ALL VISUAL ASPECTS

First then, the importance, not only as Wilde would say, of being earnest, but of having a clear identity and very high standards; remembering that whether on purpose or by default, we all have some kind of identity, whether as companies or as individuals. Having given you an overview of the Olivetti corporate identity, I will start on the subject of visual co-ordination with a slightly mischievious quotation which I am sure my friend, Tony Cleaver, the Chief Executive of IBM, won't object to. It actually comes from Tom Watson Jnr, President of IBM many years ago, who wrote:

> I think IBM designs and architecture are really lousy. I've collected a lot of Olivetti brochures and pictures of their buildings . . . The Olivetti material fits together like a beautiful picture puzzle . . . We (therefore) took all the top level people in IBM to a hotel and considered IBM design in contrast to that of Olivetti and other companies.

Obviously, if I were not a fervent admirer of IBM's current design management practice I would not have dared to quote you that particular piece.

The co-ordination so well stated by the IBM President has been maintained in our group ever since and is, in a sense, duplicated at national level where the relevant director (myself in the case of the UK) is responsible for all visual aspects including architecture, advertising, sponsorships of all kinds and anything which might affect the visible corporate image. I might add here, that in the UK over the years I have employed many local designers as consultants for literature, for lithographs, for showrooms, for exhibitions, and so on. There are also examples where Olivetti in Italy has used British design consultants for international purposes. One that comes to mind is Alan Irvine — a British Royal Designer for Industry — who is responsible for all our major international art exhibitions. They come under the responsibility of Paolo Viti, head of corporate image and design for the group. The only common factor in all this is not, as you might think, some rigid style set in a design manual but the maintenance of an accepted standard below which none of us will go.

People often say that design cannot be managed. As Wally Olins says in his admirable book on the subject: 'You could say the same about financial matters, marketing, or any other corporate function. Design *is* a corporate resource like any other.'[1] However, as has been said innumerable times, in order to achieve a sensible design management strategy you always, I stress always, need total commitment at the very top and the appointment of a totally committed person at a reasonably senior management level. What matters most is dedication and enthusiasm coupled with a willingness to seek expert advice.

In the case of Olivetti there is no doubt whatever that the reason why design management has had such a high priority for such a long time and is acknowledged as a leader in the field throughout the world, is the dedication of Adriano Olivetti himself, the son of the founder, to the cause of design, a dedication recognised by the unique award given to the company by the respected American Institute of Architects. The award had never previously been given to a company. It read

For a history of excellence in communicating its image through product design, corporate communications, architecturally distinguished manufacturing and merchandising facilities, and sponsorship of numerous social, educational, recreational and cultural programmes for both its employees and the general public.

[1] *The Corporate Personality*, London: Design Council, 1978.

There are many other examples of intelligently introduced design-based corporate identities. British Airports and British Rail are two of them. British Rail is interesting because of the life cycle of some of the products. A locomotive designed by Ken Grange or David Carter now, has to last for 30 years and its design remain valid. British Rail is also interesting because of its huge size and its huge problems. But 'God is in the detail' said the great architect Mies van der Rohe, and it is not surprising therefore to find that painting red 10,000 lamp posts has had the effect of making the staff much more visually aware and conscious of the need to do something about all aspects of design. It's a tiny first step but significant.

Going back to Olivetti, I take particular pride in Waterloo because some ten years ago we were asked if we could do anything about improving the station by a mixture of an advertisement and some form of art, and we commissioned the Belgian artist Jean Michel Folon to produce what turned out to be the biggest canvas in Europe and for a year or so it graced and certainly livened up the far end of the station. That was before any of the renovation projects had actually started.

But the big change at the top in British Rail came when the current Joint Managing Director, Jim O'Brien, personally took charge of the design advisory panel and brought on to it the directors of the main operational sectors — ensuring that the advice given by the panel was translated into fact with enormous speed. Another concrete example of the need to have commitment at the top.

On the commercial side there are dozens of excellent examples of intelligent corporate identity, like that of Coventry Panels, Baker Perkins or Clark's Shoes. All of them have in common the commitment at the top. It goes without saying — if you will forgive yet another cliché — that the successful visual change in corporate identity *must* reflect the change in *all* company attitudes.

HIGH REGARD FOR DESIGN

The second priority on my list of commitments within Olivetti is the high regard given to design inside the company, evidenced by the fact that design is on the same level as other main functions like finance or planning, responding direct to the world-wide Chief of Operations. In many companies that I know, design is, at best, a sub-function of some other department. This is because the standard of visual understanding in the UK is on the whole much lower than in France, Italy, Scandinavia and Germany. It has something to do with not understanding the nature of design and how it could help the economic health of companies. Maybe it is some kind of streak which, in some strange way has been passed on as a gene that carries design blindness, like dyslexia or colour blindness, or it may be a relic of puritanical Britain that connected design with art, art with pleasure and pleasure with something that must, on no account, be enjoyed. I really don't know.

Whatever the truth, there must be a reason or we wouldn't have a situation where fortunes are spent on advertising second-rate products and relatively little on product design and development — or a situation where design, in most companies, is relegated to the third division, or a situation where some of our best designers emigrate, or a situation in which, when things go wrong, we look at price, marketing, discounts and — if at all — look at design last. Some very modest sums transferred from advertising and promotion to improving the design, be it the quality and reliability or any other aspect, would be amply repaid. This point of balancing the promotion of the product with the design expenditure is not considered often enough by industry for the reasons I have stated, namely that design doesn't have the high priority accorded to it in Olivetti or IBM. The absurd situation is that the more second-rate a product is, the less competitive it is, the more one has to spend on advertising in order to sell it. Pure Alice in Wonderland.

The current school of thought that puts a great emphasis on engineering and the commercial aspects of design will hate me for saying this, but I feel that, as always, we have overreacted. Once again we are back to Newton's third law of motion which states — every schoolchild knows — that to every action there is an equal and opposite reaction. In the past few years we have made great efforts, quite rightly, to get away from the concept of design as a cosmetic exercise. In the process of doing this we are in danger of forgetting that in order to sell, a product has to have a pleasurable element in it, whether we admit this consciously or subconsciously. This is almost as if we regarded the two aspects, namely the function and reliability and, let's call it, the sexiness of the artefact, as being mutually exclusive. Why should they be? A lot of foreign manufacturers have succeeded precisely because they have combined the two factors of function and what I might call the 'feel' of the object.

In fact, one of the bad habits that we would do well to get rid of is our national sport of pigeonholing. The design world produces some of the best contributors to the sport. We not only talk about engineers in one pigeonhole and stylists in another, but broad education versus specialisms, technicians versus Nobel Prize candidates, beauty versus function, and so on. Life is not like that and what we need is an intelligent mixture according to the requirement of society and the market.

THE SIGNIFICANCE OF ERGONOMICS

Ergonomics has always played a vital role in the design philosophy of Olivetti. In fact, we recently produced two books on the ergonomics of computer terminals which Professor Grandjean of the Swiss Federal Institute of Technology called 'an excellent and highly objective study of present ergonomic knowledge, related to visual display'. Not only do we see ergonomics in social and human terms — that is, the responsibility of a company to improve the working environments that relate to its products, but as a clear contributor to the bottom line. The examples are legion both within Olivetti and outside it. To quote just one example, two or three years ago building societies in the UK had the problem of accommodating the devices relating to the new real-time networks within a one-metre wide front counter. The size of each element (printer, video, keyboard) and the working relationship between them became vital considerations. While technology and function-alism were obviously the primary considerations there is no doubt that such items as the slim keyboard and the horizontally fed pass-book printer designed by the English designer George Sowden, working in our Sottsass studio in Milan, plus all the ergonomics studies carried out to solve the problem, had a clinching effect on orders that ranged from 2 to 20 million pounds. Our share of the UK building society market shot up from zero to 40 per cent in 18 months. And in the case of our office desk designed by Peter Bosson, another Englishman, and George Sowden 50 per cent of the large orders from Barclays Bank were deemed to be due to its ergonomic considerations.

LONG-TERM DESIGN RESEARCH

Long-term *design* research not related to any project, is yet another commitment that Olivetti has had over many years. In a sense it is part of the ergonomic thinking. For example, research into colours and their effect on the mind, on readability, and the effect on the eyes and on environments. George Sowden is presently working on long-term problems relating to keyboards of all kinds — word processors, computers, or anything else.

INNOVATION

'The art of life lies in a constant readjustment to our surroundings'
        (Kakuzo Okakura — poster by Alan Fletcher for IBM)

A vital aspect of our long-standing practices relates to the philo-sophy of a continuous innovation process. A company will not survive unless there is an unquenchable thirst for innovation. Perhaps one of the greatest deficiencies in our design totality is that this thirst for innovation is absent in some companies in the UK and the continuous redesign of a product does not come naturally to many. As always there are plenty of examples to prove the opposite but the fact of life is that for years imports have gone up and exports have, at best, stayed still in many industries. Part of the problem must surely be lack of innovation.

There is a popular misconception that innovation means some technical quantum jump. Not at all. As noted in that admirable booklet, *Design & Technology* by Dr Rothwell and Dr Schaft: 'By far the majority of patents relate to small design modifications.' You can't rely on a hovercraft or a jet engine being invented every day.

Innovation has an infinite number of faces. For example, the high-speed train in the 1970s was an interesting aspect of innovation that paid off handsomely. The number of passengers carried shot up by 25 per cent partly due to the greater speed but very much due to the attraction of the design and the comfort of the interior. I myself changed from flying to Intercity the moment the train was launched.

In the computer industry, competition is so high and obsolescence so rapid that constant innovation and redesigning is part of our daily life. We are certainly not short of innovation in our own company, but time prevents me from giving you more than two or three examples. In the 1950s when Nizzoli designed the first streamlined typewriter, the Lexikon, which made previous typewriters seem a generation older, he proved that a quantum jump in design sometimes pay off. The typewriter became the world's best seller for many years. Some twenty years ago, when we designed the world's first desktop programmable computer, the P101, its distinctive and striking design certainly complemented the totally new technology, and again it became an absolute top seller, and the forerunner of today's microcomputers. The world's first electronic typewriter designed by Bellini also set a new trend, copied worldwide. A dust-proof membrane for a calculator is yet another outstanding example of success.

We're always told that the Japanese are the great innovators. No, they are great and competent redesigners. I happen to believe that their incredible success comes from doing everything a little better, rather than from great innovation.

It is not just industry that can innovate. The Department of Education & Science White Paper on higher education is not white, and it is not like any other White Paper that I have seen before, most of which are, to me, just substitutes for Mogadon. It is readable. It is design orientated. And it is the first of its kind. It reflects a change of attitude and a consciousness of the need for design in every aspect of life.

To end this focus on innovation, let me quote the wise words of John Bloxcidge, formerly Managing Director of Imperial Tobacco, who said: 'Innovation leads us businessmen to the world of design and to those vital creative juices we do not possess. It galvanises management, inspires the workforce, enthuses the retailers and excites the consumers.'

HIGH STATUS OF DESIGNERS

The final item on my list of long-standing commitments in our company is the high status accorded to Olivetti consultant designers. I have separated this subject under four headings:

a) Outside involvement: importance of spending half their time outside Olivetti
b) Wide background: broad cultural background and world renown
c) Long-standing relationship: long-standing relationship with the company
d) Early involvement: involvement at a very early stage of the design process, allowing briefs to evolve.

Importance of Outside Consultancies

The designers in Olivetti are not employed by us but act as outside consultants positively encouraged to spend half their time in closely linked industries which are not competitive but complementary. For example, Bellini is very actively involved with Yamaha in electronics, but not on our side of the fence.

You can see the mutual advantage of this in the similarity of a Yamaha music control device and one of our Olivetti calculators.

One of the main reasons for this policy is that the designer can never become stale but, on the contrary, can bring into the company inputs from different countries and from different industries which are extremely valuable in keeping design fresh and to the forefront. This is not to be confused as a kind of industrial espionage; it should be seen as an understanding of the culture, if I can use the word, of a particular industry, and its approach in different parts of the world. The designer has, or certainly should have, a richer understanding of the total commercial scene as a collection of designed objects, than anyone else. As Kenneth Grange, one of the best-known industrial designers in the UK says: 'The designer knows what the streets look like, what the pavements look like, what the cars look like, what the fashion looks like, and the way the trends are shaping.' His mind is trained to see this and he can bring this knowledge into the discussion at the strategic moment. This 'panoramic' understanding of industry, which many good design consultants possess, is probably one of the least-understood aspects of design. It is a straightforward case of Catch 22. An industrialist can only understand the value of the designer's global knowledge if he has had discussions with the Kenneth Granges, the David Carters, the Bellinis, the Rodney Fitchs of the world, but, to have such a discussion requires an understanding of the need for it in the first place.

Cultural Background

Our designers have in common a very deep understanding of society's needs, coupled with a humanistic approach and a clear understanding of marketing, business management and allied subjects. I don't believe that in today's society, a good industrial designer can operate without a clear understanding of these disciplines. Perhaps, above all, good designers have to have an instinctive problem-solving approach to life. However, life today is much too complex for the designer — who is *not* some kind of God — to be an expert in every field. What he needs is

47

the ability to co-ordinate a number of skills, to understand the implications of his actions for society: to understand the commercial implications, the manufacturing implications, and the financial implications. To do this he has to transcend the traditional specialism which we associated with designers in the past. It would be nice to think that a modern Leonardo was available but I am afraid that society has changed too much for that ever to happen again. The nearest we shall get to that is to find designers, design managers, consultants — call them what you like — who have a very sound cultural background combined with a thorough understanding of industry and commerce. But to find men of such calibre the industrialist has to revalue his views of designers totally.

At the moment the designer is not listened to with the sort of reverence accorded, for example, to a solicitor with whom you would be unlikely to dispute a point of law. We at Olivetti start by accepting and then discussing afterwards — the points put forward by such eminent designers as Bellini or Sottsass. They are the, so to speak, design solicitors with great experience, seniority and authority behind what they say. Most companies do *not* start by accepting what the designer says. The other side of the same coin, of course, is that designers must be able to come up with clear, intelligent proposals which take into account *all* aspects of a company's problems. The proof of the importance of this wide cultural background is perhaps evidenced by the incredible success of Italian design throughout the world, which I mentioned earlier. One undoubted contributing factor is that most of the top 20 designers are in fact architects. The significance of this is that they have a much wider background and understanding of industrial society and its problems.

Long-Standing Relationship

A word about the long-standing involvement with our designers, my third point. Again this is a policy that has evolved over many years. The relationship is with the specific designer, an individual, a very special human being, whom we've learned to like and respect. It is a kind of contract that dies, so to speak, with the person. We have, over 70 years, had three such relationships. First was Nizzoli, then Sottsass and finally Bellini. It is a very strong, very unusual relationship which ensures that these three great names in the world of design understood our company at least as well as we understand it ourselves.

Early Involvement with Design Process

The involvement of our design consultants at the strategic level is fundamental to our thinking. The designer's input will come from many contacts inside and outside the company, with universities, customers and clients from other fields. I believe I am right in saying that this early involvement is accepted as fundamental in those companies where design plays an important if not a vital role. A good designer should be able to identify not only the solutions but the *problems* of a company from his wide knowledge *and* be able to point a clear finger to the future.

DESIGN AND THE FUTURE

It's a sobering thought that perhaps 50 per cent of the artefacts we shall use in the year 2000 have not yet been thought of — let alone designed.

I believe that many designers will need to adjust to a changing society where — as we all know — leisure will play a very prominent part. I agree with John Bloxcidge, formerly of the Imperial Group, that with it will go an increased demand for quality and reliability, a return to craftsmanship, an inevitable interest in health — be it through sport, through home gymnasiums or whatever is the successor to aerobics, Cambridge diets and the rest. Designers will perhaps need to know a great deal more about designing software hand-in-hand with the software experts to ensure that the ever-increasing demands for evermore user-friendly computerised systems in the home, on the road and in the office, are satisfactorily met. Another phenomenon that is gathering momentum and which might have an impact on designers is so called tele-working — not the old-fashioned cottage industry, but serious and regular corporate employment at home, based on ever-more sophisticated technology. Not only will designers be required at the computer end of design but to work on the best deployment of home space.

EDUCATION

All this means a thorough look at our design education. Kenneth Baker started well by calling a brainstorming meeting on the subject at the Royal College of Art, and none too soon, for, in 1867, Lionel Playfair, of Great Exhibition fame, wrote to *The Times* deploring the failure of our design and technology education and, in 1916, Lethaby of the Central School complained that our education lacked hands-on experience and that it was not directed to action.

In fact, as Chairman of the Design Board of the Business & Technician Education Council (BTEC) and design member of the Council for National Academic Awards (CNAA), I would be failing in my educational duty if I did not make at least a passing reference to the subject of education in the context of this design conference.

In the litany of problems attributed to the UK design world, that are heard daily and *ad nauseum* in the various design cathedrals, we hear that our designers have no difficulty in finding jobs abroad while they are totally rejected by the design-illiterate British employers. First, a lot of this is grossly exaggerated. BTEC recently carried out a survey and found that 74 per cent of Higher National Diploma (HND) students taking BTEC courses found jobs in the UK within a year, 8 per cent continued full studies and 14 per cent were not traceable. BTEC courses turn out 20,000 qualified design students a year, all of whom have had work experience and all of whom have attended courses which have included technology, business, management and communications.

However, there is no doubt that our designers are, or will be, in demand abroad. How should industry and education, jointly or separately, react? We could take a practical stance and say: 'Let them go abroad to complete their training at someone else's expense and after two or three years we will make them offers that they can't refuse.' As the Principal of Berkshire College once said: 'Students can change the world but they must know what the world is before they can change it' — so let them explore. However, my feeling is that once they have flown the UK nest you are not likely to see them again or, at best, you have to compete with other countries, including the States, to get them back. Therefore, I would act NOW. That means scouring the better design education establishments and also contacting BTEC or the CNAA for advice which they will be very happy to give. The important point is to pick your students now. It's likely to be more fruitful than so many of the other investments that we take for granted, whether budding accountants, mini marketeers and apprentices of all kinds. As that giant of the fashion industry, Jean Muir, puts it: 'Students are more in touch with our society than you are. They are the *now* of the world.'

We should not forget that students — during their courses — become very familiar with the use of materials and can often indulge in experimentation which would be prohibitive in an industrial environment. The results of such experimentation can prove a very valuable input to industry.

Many years ago, when I was Chairman of the Governors of the Central School of Art & Design, industry regarded design students as untidy, long-haired twits. They just did not relate to them or understand them, and vice versa. Things are now very different. Students are really quite normal people: no horns, no green skins, not even long hair.

In fact, the design training with its emphasis on problem solving could admirably fit people for future management posts not necessarily connected with the design field. This is an aspect that has been totally ignored by industry and it is again a by-product of an outdated attitude to design.

One aspect of design that has, fortunately, been recognised by industry and by education is the absolute need for multidisciplinary teamwork on whatever the project or product

51

is. As a result there are some very interesting experiments currently being undertaken by colleges within the CNAA remit, where design students take courses in all aspects of business and management. Conversely, the London Business School under Peter Gorb has for some years conducted what are known as design electives whereby business and management postgraduates are given an introduction to, and a perspective, an appreciation, of the design world. We ourselves have, on a number of occasions, taken on such students and they invariably come up with some extremely useful input. To give you just one example, two years ago the project we set them was a major exhibition of Olivetti's standing in the UK and they came up with the idea for a logo and a title for the exhibition which we adopted immediately.

Work experience for design students is absolutely vital and industry will be helping itself by providing the opportunity. On this subject I strongly recommend a booklet published by BTEC in conjunction with the Department of Industry called *Design Experience*. It gives some very useful, practical, down-to-earth hints on the best way to handle work experience for design students in industry and we shouldn't forget that if we in industry want more highly experienced graduates we must give all the help we can to the educational system.

Apart from the institutions undertaking pilot schemes, the teaching of business, of markets and of management is not as universal as it should be. The fault here could be in the fact that the teachers themselves do not have sufficient contact with industry and if they have been brought up in academia over many years it is unlikely that they would be able to convey the importance of these disciplines to their students. One of my main beefs, however, is that elementary aspects of design, of visual appreciation, of spatial relationships, of colours, of drawing, and so on, should be subjects which are as natural in primary schools as the English language. At the moment the emphasis seems to depend entirely on the inclination of individual teachers. Personally, I've always regretted not having been taught to draw. As I've said before the only thing I shall ever draw is my old-age pension.

I said at the beginning that this conference would be judged in terms of any change that it stimulates. It might be helpful, therefore, if we stated what sort of activities we would like to see highlighted. The suggestions below are prompted by the belief that the fault is *not* so much in the quality of the designers, *not* so much in our design teaching, *not* so much in the quality of the product. As Shakespeare said: 'The fault, Dear Brutus, is *not in our (design) stars but* in ourselves, that we are underlings', and must change our attitudes.

My selection — which is simply common sense revisited — is under four headings:

EDUCATION	industry should forge closer links with design establishments, and vice versa.
RESOURCES	re-examine your allocation of resources to ensure sufficient funds for product development.
ENVIRONMENT	co-ordinate all visual aspects.
COMMUNICATIONS	ask yourself: is your management style conducive to team work and innovation?

Most of the suggestions have been tried at Olivetti where good design has certainly helped towards our current profit which is in excess of $1 million a day, but this is because design thrives where management is efficient. It can't reverse bad management. It is not a panacea for all management ills and we should not pretend that it is.

Finally, let me take a leaf from the marvellous French philosopher and theologian Pascal, who made the point that you have nothing to lose and everything to gain by believing in God, because if you're right and God exists you're the winner, and if you're wrong and God doesn't exist then you've lost nothing. My exhortation, therefore, is: try all these experiments with design — you have nothing to lose. If you do so, as the Bible says, the rest will be added to you.

Identity — The Corporation's Hidden Resource

Wally Olins

Wally Olins may not have invented corporate identity design, but no-one has done more to establish it as a key resource in the field of strategic business planning. The consultancy Wolff Olins, of which he is Chairman, is the leading one of its kind in the UK, and has an international reputation.

His book The Corporate Personality *and his various other publications have become the starting point for many studies in the field.*

In this paper he makes the case that corporate identity is best expressed through design, and outlines three identity models which relate to corporate organisations. He suggests that identity is far more than a corporate marketing tool; rather, the visible expression of a corporate purpose, often complex and always at the heart of what the business is about. He argues the need to manage this powerful tool in the same way that finance, personnel and other key management functions are managed.

Identity is a profound, simple and basic manifestation of the human condition. We all, as individuals, want to belong. What is more, we all want to be seen to belong. In every country in the world, human beings demonstrate their affiliations visually. Words like *laid back, yuppie, redneck, white collar, blue collar*, or Catalan, Basque or Corsican all demonstrate and underline this.

People live and sometimes they die for their identity. Look at the Palestinians, the Israelis, the various factions in Ulster and elsewhere. The outward and visible manifestations of belonging are immediately recognisable, both to other people who belong to the group and to outsiders. People deliberately drop visual hints about who they are and what their affiliations are. What they look like demonstrates their beliefs. It's their style.

What is interesting and significant is that these signs are more or less natural. What emerges on the outside is not so different from the inside. Equally important is the fact that identity emerges primarily, though not exclusively, through design.

The thing about many manifestations of identity is that they do emerge more or less naturally. Just as groups of people emulate each other, so do organisations.

THE EXPLICIT MANAGEMENT OF PERCEPTIONS

There are at least three points to consider.

1. That every organisation has an identity; usually the identity emerges naturally in a rather haphazard, unmapped way; that often organisations doing the same kind of things share the same kind of identity.
2. That identity emerges primarily through what you see: it is mainly visual. Design is the filter through which identity emerges.
3. That design does not involve a few, large things, but also a multiplicity of smaller things. It manifests itself in a holistic way, taking into account everything from the very large to the almost insignificant.

What we call corporate identity is the process of explicit management of some or all of the ways by which the organisation is perceived.

In business organisations — more or less any business organisation — identity emerges through three areas of design:

— products or services, ie what you make or sell
— environments, ie where you make or sell it
— communications, ie how you present what you do, and how you do it

Co-ordinated design is the key by which these areas can work together.

55

Identity also emerges through one area that you can't see — although it's just as palpable — and that is behaviour. In small companies run by one person, the identity is an expression of the personality of the founder, his obsessions, dreams, ambitions. In larger companies, things are different. The relative significance of each of these manifestations of identity will vary according to the nature of the organisation.

PRODUCT-BASED IDENTITIES

For example, in a product-based company, say an automobile company, the product is the most significant way by which the company's identity emerges. Here the product designer is responsible not just for the product but very largely for the company's identity. It is primarily the way the car looks and feels, how the doors open and shut, how big it is, what kind of engine it has, how it performs, what it costs etc that makes people feel the way they do about it. To paraphrase an ancient McLuhanism, the product is the message, environments and literature affect the issue peripherally but it is primarily the product that dominates — that conveys the identity idea.

ENVIRONMENT-BASED IDENTITIES

There are many situations in which an identity is not product- but environment-led, in which case environmental design will lead the identity process. In retailing — in leisure, hotels and theme parks, for example — it is the environment that dominates the identity mix. Here the environmental designer, the architect, the space planner and the interior designer carry the main burden of projecting the company's identity. And environments can be very different from each other. Holiday Inn, for instance, offers something different from Italy's Ciga group.

In retailing it's certainly the case that there isn't much that you can get at Bloomingdales or at Harrods that you can't get anywhere else. It is the experience of shopping at Bloomingdales or Harrods — the environmental experience of these stores that makes them special places to visit. It isn't that product and communication are unimportant. They are not. They are simply *less* important in the identity hierarchy than the place itself.

ADVERTISING AND CONSUMER PRODUCTS

In many service organisations there is a peculiar mixture of environment, product and service that makes the mix work — or not. However, there is also a vast range of products and services which, in identity terms, are communication-led. Almost all consumer products, for example, have little character of their own, no strong personality. A personality is bestowed on them by the way in which they are packaged and advertised ie promoted. They are given life through advertising. Traditionally advertising is so powerfully and overtly associated with identity (or, more precisely, with image) that many people erroneously believe that advertising makes identity. This is a dangerous idea. First, because it devalues the real power of product, environment and behaviour in the identity mix and second, because it inhibits real and genuine co-operation between all those people within an organisation, product designers, graphic designers, architects, management development people and communications people who are collectively responsible for identity. Organisations that fail to see their own special mix clearly usually put identity under the communications umbrella — frequently with lamentable results.

In a product-led company, product design should lead the identity mix. In many service companies the identity should be environmentally led, but in others the identity is most clearly conveyed through behaviour. When, as is often the case in services businesses, the most junior echelons of the business have the most frequent contact with the outside world (eg the police and airlines), their behaviour powerfully affects the way the organisation is perceived.

So organisations, like people, indicate clearly what they are like, what they think of themselves, what their standards are by the way they present themselves — by their visual and behavioural styles. But identity is also used to convey a complementary and equally significant set of messages relating to corporate structure.

IDENTITY AND CORPORATE STRUCTURES

In the past, most companies were simple, monolithic structures. They used only one name and one identity. Most little companies are like that today, so are a few very big ones — including IBM. In fact, in the first companies which consciously used identity programmes, the railways of 19th-century industrialising Britain, identity programmes were developed as a homogenising tool to hold together organisations that were geographically disparate. Companies using a monolithic identity usually operate in a narrow band of activity, eg the oil industry, airlines, computers.

Monolithic identities are always used by companies that have grown organically. But the majority of companies do not grow that way today: most grow by acquisition. They buy competitors, customers, suppliers; they expand vertically and horizontally. Each of these acquired organisations has its own name, reputation, tradition and culture. Each has its own network of audiences, each its own goodwill. The company that makes the acquisitions usually ends up by keeping some, if not all, of the names of the companies which it has acquired — but then it has to deal with the complexities which this situation inevitably creates.

The intention of an endorsed identity is to show how organisations forming a group can retain their independent identities and at the same time be part of the group as a whole and share the values of a group. Companies that seek to create a corporate identity involving a group of subsidiary organisations with complementary but sometimes competitive backgrounds have a difficult task.

On the one hand, certainly at corporate level and for corporate audiences (shareholders, investment analysts, recruits at various levels) organisations want to create the idea of a single yet multifaceted organisation which has a sense of purpose. On the other, they want to allow the identities of the numerous companies and brands they have acquired to continue to flourish in order to retain goodwill in the marketplace — particularly, of course, for their customers. This requires a balancing act. These aims, in a sense conflicting, can only be achieved simultaneously if the greatest sensitivity is used.

Most commercial companies try to achieve this balance. Some do it well (eg United Technologies); most do it badly. Curiously, the one organisation that does it superbly is the Army. The complex military hierarchy with its matrix of corps, divisions, brigades on the one hand, and its various fighting and service arms on the other, is a model of an endorsed identity at work. If any consultant attempted to introduce such a concept into a business organisation, he would be told that the whole thing was much too complex to be practicable.

BRANDED STRUCTURE

The third kind of identity is the one in which the company operates through a series of brands which are apparently unrelated either to each other or to the organisation as a whole. Companies that operate in this way are often in the food and drink or other fast-moving consumer goods business. These companies at corporate level reach out to all audiences of the monolithic or endorsed company, but they don't present any kind of corporate face to the consumer. As far as the final customer is concerned, the corporation doesn't exist; what the customer sees is only the brand. Sometimes this policy goes to such extreme lengths that two competing companies find themselves owning the same brand in different countries. Persil, for example, is owned by Henkel in most countries but in Britain and France by Unilever.

The reason companies pursue this branded policy is that

brands are thought to have a life cyle of their own, quite distinct from the company's. The system allows competitive brands from the same company to appear on the same supermarket shelves: some brands, it is felt, should present specific identities of their own, appropriate both to the nature of the product and the consumer for whom they are intended, in which the symbolism is simple, even naive. Certainly, these identities are often regarded as inappropriate for a large, sophisticated organisation. Brut is for men, Poison for women, Bonio for dogs.

Interestingly, Japanese companies (a theme to which I will return later) are for the most part inclined to be monolithic. Mitsubishi has no difficulty in operating under the same name in the world of technology (aircraft), automobiles, consumer goods (tinned salmon) and banking. Yamaha makes motor cycles and pianos, but IBM probably wouldn't move into carpet slippers.

It is often mistakenly assumed that identity is some kind of marketing tool — that its prime purpose is to project the idea of the organisation and its products to its customers. And this means that identity is the province of the corporate marketing men. To think this is to misunderstand — to under-estimate — its power and its purpose. In fact, every organisation has a wide variety of audiences. And it isn't the case, at least in identity terms, that the customer is necessarily the most significant, although ultimately he may be the most important.

AUDIENCES

In the first place, from an identity point of view, the organisation has to deal with itself. Its own people have to know what it is, what it does and how it does it. If the organisation is to articulate an idea of itself effectively, its own staff must comprehend it because they will be the prime channels by which such an idea is communicated. The organisation has many internal audiences. It has internal audiences at different levels, in different places doing different things. All of these are prime targets. It also has what might be called quasi-internal audiences: people who own its stock, former employees and their families etc.

The external audiences are the people with whom in one way or another the organisation does its business. Some of these are close and have a special relationship with it eg direct customers, dealers and end users. Others are equally close but have a different relationship with it eg competitors, suppliers, the local community, trade unions.

Finally, some of the organisation's audiences are not so close. These are often called opinion formers: the legislators, journalists, investment analysts, educational institutions, trade and industry associations.

All of these audiences are in some senses separate from one another, and particularly, each has a somewhat different relationship with the organisation. The organisation will want to present a slightly different view of itself to its customers, for example, from the one which it will present to the local community. On the other hand, however, all of the audiences are also overlapping. Some customers may live in the local area. Others may be pensioners. Still more may be stockholders or parents of children who are thinking of coming into the company. Customers will be married to stockholders, and so on.

It is unrealistic to put all audiences into separate compartments and assume they have nothing to do with one another. It is therefore unrealistic to attempt to convey different, even contradictory messages to different groups of people. Each of the different audiences of an organisation will form a view of it based on the totality of the impressions that it makes upon them. People will inevitably form their ideas about an organisation from more than one source: from both advertising and editorial in the media; from personal experience and that of other people; from rumour and gossip. Where these impressions are contradictory the overall impression will be negative and confusing. This is why an organisation needs to plan its identity programme.

The fundamental idea behind a corporate identity programme is that everything the company does, everything it owns, everything it produces should project a clear idea of what the company is and what its aims are. When an organisation has failed to think through what it is really about, how it is really different — it will inevitably show.

IDENTITY OF THE CORPORATE WORLD

Organisations, like people, have rather different personalities — they actually are different from one another. It is both absurd and counter-productive, therefore, that simply through neglect and ignorance they should look the same. Similarly, organisations, like people, are often dominated by a single, simple idea, which colours their attitudes towards, say, marketing, profitability or technology. But organisations are also confused by the need, as they see it, to react differently to different audiences; to say different things to different people, and above all to emulate one another. In doing this, they often fail to present a comprehensible face to all of their audiences, a face which each audience can recognise as being part of a coherent whole. Organisations for the most part act as though each audience with which they deal has no relationship with any other. If each manifestation of the organisation is separate and different, collectively they will make no sense.

Let's look at all this in more detail to see what organisations do with their identities, why they do it and to what effect.

Conspicuous Display of Wealth and Power

The overt values of western business organisations emerge through their buildings, their products and their communications, through what you can see — through design. The messages that emerge are often conflicting and contradictory. At one level, corporate environments, especially perhaps corporate head offices, are frequently intended to be conspicuous displays of wealth and power. They are designed to look smooth and seamless. They are created apparently to project an idea of an omniscient, omnipotent company run by rational, benevolent, cool supermen, who, in their corporate wisdom, plan wisely in the interests of the greater good of mankind.

The world of the corporate head office is not that far away from the world of corporate advertising and of annual reports. Here, too, groups of wise folk sit about earnestly engaged in activities apparently intended for the common good.

Meaningless Mission Statements

A series of banal, trite phrases, one indistinguishable from the other, lacking any kind of credibility, usually characterises this area of corporate-speak. The words that are used in corporate reports are not very different from the impact made by the physical presence of the corporate head office. All this is sometimes encapsulated in the form of the mission statement. Sometimes the statement is a sensible reasoned summary of a corporate view: 'We want to be the best, this means we can't be the most profitable or the largest', or even 'We want to be the most profitable, this means we may have to accept the quality implications that this aim implies', although I have to confess that I've never heard a mission statement expressed that simply. Mostly, the mission statement emerges after all the corporate mind bashing as a mish-mash of contradictory, half-baked, compromising platitudes, which are quite properly ignored by those for whom it is intended.

The move from the world of corporate-speak to product-speak is abrupt and jarring. At the level of the marketplace, in these very same apparently high minded and lofty institutions, a kind of corporate Ramboism takes over. At the sales level, the level of trade journals, company briefing meetings, sales conferences, dealer weekends etc, corporate-speak turns into macho-speak. What matters here, often the only thing that matters, is profit and sales now.

The other day I heard a man at a sales conference say 'I was put on this earth by God to make a profit for the XYZ company.' They call that motivation. Through an unspoken conspiracy, everything said or implied at the corporate level is, by implication at least, rejected as sissy, as unrealistic. What rules is the magic bottom line. Bottom line is the euphemism for male conquest. Here the imagery is crude and military, or sexual.

Second to profit, and only just, is size; what is called in the unlovely jargon of the day, market share.

In all this cacophony, real values, genuine characteristics, quirks of personality, and strengths often get lost, distorted or derided.

Scrooge in the Purchasing Department

There are lots of other messages that go out from the company which overlap, conflict and confuse. For example, purchasing departments often speak a language unrecognisably different from marketing and sales. Here the world is very often mean spirited and cheeseparing, quite different from what the organisation claims in its corporate material. Economical is mis-interpreted to mean miserly. Brownie points are awarded not for intelligent purchasing but for Scroogism.

Silent War Inside the Company

Not surprisingly, all this confusion going on outside the company is reflected by equal confusion within. What looks like a large, undifferentiated lump from the outside, turns out to be a pullulating, seething mass of ill-co-ordinated, secretive, competitive gangs arranged roughly into power bases with names like R&D, personnel, marketing, and sales. These gangs compete fiercely with one another for power and prestige, for budgets, for the president's patronage, for more power. Internally the company is in a state of perpetual war.

But the problem doesn't end there, it actually gets worse. Any individual corporate strengths and character that may linger are destroyed by misplaced marketing enthusiasm. Virtually every self-respecting modern-minded company claims to be marketing minded. This means in simple terms that each company competing in a specific field will try to find out what the consumer wants and then make it.

CORPORATE IDENTITY AND THE CONSUMER

In order to find out what the consumer does want, companies will use similar techniques. They will ask the same consumers the same questions and therefore get the same answers. This results in them producing products and/or services that are all the same, more or less regardless of what their real strength is.

So, despite the fact that each company will claim that it is unique, different, special and so on — in fact, unless it is very careful, it is going to end up manufacturing and marketing more or less identical products to those of its competitors, especially the market leaders. In other words, marketing in the present debased form in which it is currently most frequently practised, far from making companies different from each other and therefore giving the consumers more choice, is actually making them *more* like one another.

Some companies, recognising the mess that all this gets them into, try to use communication techniques in order to re-introduce a phoney differentiation between their product and those of their competitors when the real differences have been eliminated by marketing. People can always tell true from false, so that endeavour only induces more cynicism among all of the audiences that it is intended to persuade.

If you put all these things together, what is the result? Companies saying different things to different external audiences, different things to different internal audiences, claiming unique characteristics and ending up producing more or less the same stuff as the next one. In other words, companies who haven't the faintest idea what they really are.

WHY DON'T MORE COMPANIES COLLAPSE!

As individuals we all know that we cannot present totally different and artificial pictures of ourselves to different groups of people. We all know too that we have to come to terms with our own reality, our own personalities, our strengths and weaknesses. We also know that where there is too large a gap between what we think about ourselves and what we say to other people — we go crazy, we become neurotic. And yet this is the condition in which many companies in the West permanently exist. In psychiatric terms they are schizoid. No wonder many companies are in such disarray. No wonder the people in them are so often frustrated and unhappy. What amazes me is that more companies don't go mad — and collapse. Some do, of course, collapse, from time to time. Gulf is perhaps one of the most interesting recent examples.

Gulf was one of the world's largest corporations. It looked and acted like every other major oil company. It conducted its geo-political discussions with the Marxist government in Angola. It explored for oil in some of the most remote and most turbulent quarters of the earth. Its service stations dominated the southern states of the US; they were part of the scene in the Old South. Its aristocratic Pennsylvanian home seemed stable and everlasting. And then T Boone Pickens came along, and the whole thing fell down.

Gulf had for so long said so much to so many people that it no longer believed in; it had for so long shuffled along with all the other oil majors, mindlessly following them — going into refining, coming out of refining, going into Europe, coming out of Europe — that it no longer had any mind of its own. It was just a huge mass of mindless conflict. It suffered a crisis of will. It didn't know what it was: it no longer believed in itself.

Gulf is only one example. There have been many others. In Britain we have, unhappily, far too many but the US has also had its fair share. Of course we know that there are plenty of major western corporations that know what they are good at and do it: Boeing, Pepsi and Disney, for instance. We even have a few of our own in Europe: French Railways, Jaguar, ICI, Siemens, but on neither side of the Atlantic can we claim a happy record.

IN JAPAN THEY DO THINGS DIFFERENTLY (OF COURSE)

It is not, I believe, an accident that, while many large western companies have identities which are confused and contradictory, in which the outside and the inside have nothing to do with each other, and in which employees and customers receive totally different messages, the Japanese appear to order things differently, at least in some companies, in some respects.

It is, of course, a cliché to say that Japanese management systems are becoming the admired model — quality circles, just-in-time sourcing, and all that sort of thing. Nevertheless, increasingly western managers are looking at the way the Japanese manage themselves.

In identity terms, too, the Japanese are worth looking at. The core idea in the western company is competitiveness. The core idea in the Japanese company is harmony. This is, of course, a simplification but not too far off the mark. Enormous effort goes into creating a spirit of co-operation between the various individuals and departments inside the Japanese company and between the company and its suppliers, its dealers and its customers. The better Japanese companies have a cohesiveness of behaviour that leads to the development of powerful loyalties and an immensely powerful and stable identity, which is clearly understood both internally and externally. Relationships are built to last. The company is predictable.

The identity of many Japanese companies is so powerful not only to the employee but also to the consumer that the place of the brand in Japanese society is much less significant than it is in the West. Of course some companies run brands — like Matsushita — but many more don't, even many of those in the consumer area.

Mitsubishi — the Name on Everything

Because Mitsubishi is a name that commands respect, it can put its name with equal credibility on canned food, aircraft, a bank

67

and motor cars. The identity of Mitsubishi is large enough and permanent enough to embrace all these products and services without causing any dissonance. Mitsubishi's appreciation of quality and integrity transcends products. It is equally applicable in any area of activity which the corporation chooses to enter.

How many western companies have reputations so secure or, perhaps more important, *feel* they have reputations so secure, that if they enter a field entirely different from their traditional one they can keep using their existing name? Daimler Benz, Mercedes, a company with a reputation for quality that is stupefying, has recently bought AEG, Dornier and MTU — all companies not so far from Mercedes' traditional areas of activity. AEG is in electronics and white goods, Dornier in aerospace and MTU in engines. I wonder what Mercedes will do with their acquisitions. If they were Japanese, there wouldn't be much doubt. The whole thing would become Mercedes. The identity of the acquiring company would be imposed, because the standards which the name represents would inevitably become those which the new, enlarged corporation would seek to promote both inside the organisation and outside it.

The real point is that in the best Japanese companies the identity is not a meaningless and bombastic farrago of words and symbols, not a mindless aping of the norm in the industry in which individuality has been destroyed, but something individual, real, powerful and recognisable — recognisable both to outsiders: customers, suppliers, stockholders, the local community, potential recruits, and to insiders: employees at all levels, in all departments. When identity is carefully nurtured it becomes a priceless corporate resource. Some, though by no means all, Japanese companies have remembered what so many western companies have forgotten, which is that you must find out what you really are, and be true to it, and that you cannot present an effective and powerful face to the outside world unless it is a manifestation of what you feel yourself actually to be.

THE IDENTITY OF NATIONALISM

Curiously enough, at a national level, this is perfectly understood in the West. National identities have been developed, in some cases virtually invented, not merely to tell outsiders what people stand for, but, equally significant, to give a sense of cohesion and pride to the aspiring nation-state. Nineteenth-century European liberal-nationalism is a series of textbook cases in the development of identity. First in France with the Revolution, followed by Napoleon, and later in Italy, Germany and all the nations of Eastern Europe, language, national flags, national costume, architecture, food, literature, music (product, environment and communication) were all contrived both to raise internal consciousness and to let the outside world know that a new, aspiring national was knocking on the door. Very often the people involved in creating, developing and projecting the identity knew exactly what they were doing. In this sense, in what became Czechoslovakia after 1918, Dvorak, Smetana and Masaryk were all consciously working towards the same end. It was all carefully orchestrated. *The Good Soldier Swejh*, that marvellously funny book by Hasek is, in effect, a 600-page celebration of the Czech national identity.

THE SHORT-TERM VIEW

There are a number of reasons why identity has failed to be used to the extent that it ought to be in western corporations, to the extent that it has traditionally been used in nascent western liberal-national countries and is currently used in Japanese companies. One of them is that inevitably identity is about longer term goals and, unhappily, too many western companies, dominated by Wall Street and the City of London, have a very short-term tactical outlook. Another reason is that there is no clear place for identity in the western corporate infrastructure.

With the urgent, immediate thrust towards profit now, me-too marketing and product development, overlaid by standard corporate rhubarb-speak, the real identity issues have been squeezed out of current management thinking.

There is an overwhelming need for identity to be introduced as a significant overt corporate resource into major western companies. It isn't the newer, smaller, more rapidly growing companies that need it — an early stage of growth identity is always an intrinsic part of the management mix. Look at Apple in its early days or Xerox — it's when these kinds of companies get big and lose their sense of purpose that their troubles begin.

IDENTITY'S PLACE IN THE CORPORATE HIERARCHY

A place for identity and identity management must be found within the corporate hierarchy. There is a natural place for it. A clear, straightforward place, right at the centre, where the company manages its affairs.

Most large companies today are trying to do three things:

— diversify
— decentralise
— internationalise

To do this effectively means setting up separate cost and profit centres around the world. Managers in distant countries working in recently acquired companies in technologies unfamiliar to the main company want to be left alone to get on with it. And often they are. They claim, quite reasonably, that if they are given the profit responsibility they should also be given the means to achieve it.

IDENTITY, A CORPORATE RESOURCE

But, inevitably, this attitude creates very powerful centrifugal forces. If you leave them alone, they will simply tear the company to pieces. In order effectively to control a diverse, international, decentralised company it is essential for a central management to create a countervailing set of co-ordinating forces. In a sense, this is another version of the old battle between centralisation and decentralisation. The centralising resources that a management at the centre normally retains in order effectively to continue to control the business are:

— finance
— investment
— R&D
— management development
— product quality
— technology

And at the centre is exactly where the identity resource ought to go.

Identity is an input into both strategy and structure. Curiously it is also an output of them as well. When personality, strategy, structure and identity work together harmoniously, the corporation is able clearly to indicate where it is going.

Identity is a central management resource. And it is essential that the identity resource is overtly recognised and managed from the centre like all the other central resources.

MANAGING IDENTITY

All this means co-ordinating in some way the areas in which identity of the corporation manifests itself — the visible ones eg product, environment and communication, and the less palpable ones, like behaviour. The precise point from which identity is managed will depend upon where the company's priorities lie. In a company which is dominated by product, identity management will have a strong bias towards product design. In a service company, such as an airline or a car rental business, it will largely be involved with behaviour and training. It will take different forms in different companies — it may even have different names: identity management, design management, communications management — but its essential task remains the same. It will be to manage the company's

71

identity across every single thing it does in order to project a clear, coherent idea.

The first step is for this overt recognition of identity as a corporate resource to take place, and for corporations to recognise that identity must be managed. When there is such recognition, when appropriate board appointments have been made, the need arises to set up systems to manage identity.

THE MODEL — FINANCIAL MANAGEMENT

In order to manage identity effectively as a corporate resource we need to look for a model. Curiously, financial management is an instructive model for our purpose.

Every management team is aware of the significance of finance as a management resource and in most organisations financial reporting systems are standardised and every department accepts the need for financial management. In identity management it is also the case that every last little thing is affected, and every department involved. What is more, in every corporation there is a financial vice president or a board member formally responsible for the management of financial matters. A very similar system should be set up so far as identity is concerned, with a board member and an appropriate structure.

Naturally, setting up such a system will inevitably invite problems — problems of overlap between various departments, problems of status and problems of interpretation. It is not easy. The identity of the corporation, what it stands for, what its strengths are, and how it can project these clearly in everything it does so that what emerges both for inside and outside audiences is coherent and credible will, in most companies, need to be rediscovered. The present situation in which most companies seem to think corporate identity is something to do with a quick fix from a design consultancy company, resulting in a new jazzy name, purple stripes and yellow spots on the corporate notepaper and trucks, is very far from what I have in mind.

Reviewing an identity is a profound and complex process. It does need outside consultancy help, both in analysis and creation. It is often very uncomfortable, even agonising. It may mean discarding treasured myths, it may mean being forced to face an unpleasant reality. The consultant can assist. He can help the company to rediscover truths about itself and re-present them. But if corporate identity is to work, it cannot be carried out half heartedly or superficially. Nor is it a task which in the end can be wholly delegated to outsiders.

Identity is the corporate purpose made visible and for this the organisation itself must take responsibility.

Current Business Trends and Corporate Identity at 3M

Donn Osmon

Donn Osmon is Vice President of Corporate Affairs at 3M, the American company with 50,000 products which is best known for its ranges of industrial and consumer tapes which dominate world markets and, more recently, for the ubiquitous yellow Post-it notes. This first paper by Donn Osmon describes his responsibilities for design within 3M and how design contributes to corporate strategy through its influence on issues such as quality control and product determination in international markets. He also presents a case study on product innovation in the last section of the book.

The subject of this paper is current business trends and corporate identity — two subjects which, from the point of view of 3M, go hand in hand.

My presentation will take the form of remarks on how corporate identity ties in with a business strategy, and give examples of how it does so at the 3M company. I will use 3M as a base from which to examine the opportunities available today and to show that businesses have to use aggressively corporate identity and design to enhance revenues and profits.

Let me begin by developing the situation as it exists. We will explore three areas. In particular

1. What is 3M?
2. What are the trends that affect our business?
3. What can we do with our corporate identity programme to communicate and harmonise our business objectives?

3M is basically a company that manufactures coated products. Today we have approximately 50,000 individual products — give or take a thousand. We have wholly owned facilities in 51 countries. We trade with 130 countries. Our products are both consumer and industrial. I am sure you can imagine the number of languages we work with and the problems they cause us.

We consider ourselves to be technology and new product driven. One of the goals of the company is to derive 25 per cent of our business each year from products or services that are less than five years old. That may sound like an ambitious target but, in fact, we do attain this average each year and did so again in 1984.

Our primary trademarks are the Scotch brand name and the 3M brand name. However, we do have about two hundred other trademarks in the US and several hundred elsewhere.

Our business plan is to grow in sales and profits at about 10 per cent a year. We have approximately 40 per cent of our business outside of the US and in the long run this percentage should grow.

We operate over one hundred subsidiaries around the world. We place great value on individual freedom for employees, and for divisions, departments and other business groupings. Yet we understand that a policy of strong central control in some areas such as finance, personnel and indeed corporate identity are mandatory. I will comment more on this area later.

The central point of this description of 3M is to point out to you the key features of our corporate identity strategy and programme, which must be a living, dynamic concept that can at the same time accommodate frequent change in our product line and yet communicate our company's permanent values of quality and service.

At 3M we have realised that we must be aware of and respond to social and market driven forces if we are to achieve our goals. Some of the major trends that have affected us in our planning for the last half of this century are:

1. Globalisation or non-globalisation of markets
2. Quality

3. Cost effectiveness of marketing operations
4. The changing market and distribution patterns
5. Public policy.

I will address each of these trends individually.

GLOBALISATION OR NON-GLOBALISATION

Professor Theodore Levitt, of the Harvard Business School, has been advocating recently that for businesses to succeed they must look at world-wide markets. He calls this the 'globalisation of markets', and indeed makes a sound argument for a single, global marketing strategy based on standardised products — or for selling the same thing in the same way everywhere. His argument is particularly convincing if we look at consumer goods — Coca Cola, for example, or British and American brands of cigarettes.

However, at 3M, we do not believe that global marketing fits every business or every product. I can give you several examples of this.

Coated abrasives, or sandpapers, for example, have totally different standards and technical requirements applying in Europe and in the US. These differences are not just customer choices, but are incorporated into national and industrial codes. We cannot export US products to Europe — or the reverse. The common thread of our world-wide abrasive business is not common product, but common manufacturing technology and corporate identity. The fact is that the only global aspect of our abrasive business that the customer sees is our global corporate identity.

In the Philippines we sell 'Scotch-Brite'. You might know this as a scouring pad used in the kitchen. But one of our largest markets in the Philippines is for these pads, cut to the size of a foot so that women can clean and polish the floors by moving their feet across the tiles using these foot pads as abrasive cleaning materials. This product innovation replaced the coconut shells that were used previously. I question whether the product has global appeal, or indeed whether we would want to spend the money to introduce such a product world-wide. Yet this non-global product is very important to our Philippine company.

In the US and Europe we supply tape for fastening disposable diapers to many of the diaper manufacturers. We would like this to be a global product. However, in Brazil disposable diapers are far too expensive for the market. We therefore sell a masking tape under the brand name of 'Baby Fix', which tapes cloth diapers together as a replacement for safety pins. Brazil is one of three countries where this product is used. Again, this is a product which is very important for our Brazilian company but which has no appeal in the US or Europe.

It is another example of local markets dictating local product development for local needs. It demonstrates that globalisation is not yet and may never be a universally applicable concept. Globalisation is indeed a trend but not yet a tidal wave. The standardisation of products and services does not fit a global company as the *only* marketing or product development strategy. We believe that any effective corporate identity programme must be designed to accommodate these real facts of life.

QUALITY

A second major trend is quality. This is an often heard, and in many respects a much misunderstood, word. We define quality at 3M as products that meet the customer's requirement. To be a little more blunt, we want every consumer of our products to believe that he or she has received exactly what was paid for. This driving force permeates our basic business strategy throughout the entire company. It also presents us with the single greatest opportunity for efficiency in all of our operations, from development through manufacturing and marketing. Our experience shows that as we drive quality up we also drive unit costs down.

Let me repeat that premise — as our quality goes up our unit cost goes down. Also this does not only apply to manufacturing. This same phenomenon exists in every aspect of our business. It is as real in our marketing operations as it is in administration. The impact of this practice can have profound effect on any business and all professions. If quality replaces price as the key element in the decision-making process, the freedom to innovate and create takes a quantum leap forward. The objective of selling quality permeates our marketing efforts.

Certainly the identity of our products in their packages and presentations is the key to having consumers select our products. The impression that we make and the quality we convey is intricately bound to good design in our packaging area. We understand this, and believe me, it is something we work with constantly.

COST-EFFECTIVE MARKETING

The third major driving force in keeping a company like ours competitive and profitable is the ability to have cost-effective marketing. If you think back to the thousands of products that we sell, and our objective of having 25 per cent of our annual business come from new products that are less than five years old, you can begin to appreciate the value we attach to a workable global identification programme at 3M. We must have a simple global system which gives us the ability to introduce many products quickly and successfully under a consistent Scotch brand or 3M brand image. Without the identification of these new products in a positive and forceful manner, our ability to introduce hundreds of new products each year would be more limited and certainly more costly.

Our belief is that our best opportunity to sell new products comes from our established customer base. The need therefore is to link through identification our company, our satisfied customer and our new products. Let me give two examples of how this works.

Post-It

A few years ago we invented an adhesive that didn't stick very well. We didn't know what to do with it. Someone suggested a note pad that stuck but which was removable. We tried advertising it. But we couldn't get the story across. We tried purchasing agents. Eyes rolled at the idea of trying to get people to replace their purchases of 15 cent pads with $1 ones because they didn't stick. Blood pressures went up. The salesman were shown the door. Morale was rock bottom.

We had a rethink. We considered what our assets were. We knew that we had a useful product. We had a good image and our large base of Scotch tape. We had our existing customer base. We had a good name with distributors. The answer lay with sampling. The rest is history.

Without our identity we could not have moved this product.

Floppy Discs

There are over forty brands of discs available on the market. The customer has little knowledge about his/her purchase. He buys on price or name recognition. The linkage in this case with both the customer and the distributor is the company name and our identity.

Image makes the first sale; quality holds it.

CHANGING MARKETPLACE

A fourth major trend affecting our plans has been the changing marketplace. Two facts are now evident. First, historically we believed that 80 per cent of our sales were to 20 per cent of our customers. We now believe that this formula is approaching 90 per cent of our sales to 10 per cent of our customers. The impact of this shift is obvious — as we sell more and more to fewer and fewer our personal contact with industrial customers is decreasing. It is obvious that more non-personal, non-verbal communications will now need to carry the message.

79

This point can be more clearly understood if we look at computer-to-computer ordering, which is rapidly accelerating, and many of our major customers are now approaching a non-paper relationship with us.

Perhaps the results of a recent survey of purchasing agents best demonstrates the changes taking place in terms of how customers and suppliers currently and will, in the future, relate to each other. The survey showed that purchasing agents expect to see fewer salesmen and women and to see them less frequently in the future. The traditional relationship will be replaced by computer-to-computer ordering and electronic communications between inside sales people. These changes once again point to the need for companies to think through the methods of communications that will replace the face-to-face contact which we have been using.

GOVERNMENT POLICY

The fifth major factor affecting our business is the impact of public policy or government policy. Its effects on our ability to run our business range from environmental, regulatory, consumer regulations, tax policies, to import regulations. It is important that the company is perceived as important, worthwhile, a part of the high-tech era and a provider of quality products especially when government regulators look at our proposals. The image of the company and its products as a socially responsible organisation is best conveyed by our customers being satisfied with performance, quality and price. It is also important to remember that government employees are also private consumers, and so they meet our business in their private lives as well as in their business or professional roles.

In short, the impression that we make on people through our products and their quality is unquestionably important when we are attempting to work with or promote change in public policy.

The point I wish to leave with you is that image — or if you prefer reputation — in the private sector is quickly translated into public policy. In effect, while form cannot replace substance, neither can we depend on substance alone.

At this stage, let me summarise what it is we are attempting to do with corporate identity. First, we want our identity to convey our values. Second, we want synergy through all of our products and services. And, third, we want our divisions and subsidiaries to have maximum flexibility using our corporate identity principles, although we insist that they meet certain basic standards of the type that I have mentioned. To achieve this within 3M we have a department which acts as adviser, counsellor, innovator, auditor, policeman and judge on matters of corporate design. While we strive for maximum flexibility and creativity, we also centrally administer our guidelines. In short, due to the importance that we attach to corporate identity, we run it as an authoritarian force within the company. If appropriately and aggressively used, we believe corporate identity has a key role in enhancing our short- and long-term sales and profits.

PART 2
Design, the Product and Product Innovation

The Importance of Design

Sir William Barlow

Sir William Barlow F.Eng is Chairman of the Engineering Council, and also Chairman of BICC, a major UK company in the fore-front of information technology, power and construction. He was also the Design Council's Chairman from 1980 to 1986 and is a passionate advocate of the close links that need to be established between design and engineering.

The paper reproduced here, on which he based his seminar discussion, was originally published in the Proceedings *of the* Institution of Electrical Engineers in May 1983. *In it he describes the range and relationships of the design activities and how they each contribute to the product innovation process, deals with issues of time, cost, and product performance, and concludes with some successful design cases about new products.*

In this paper I aim to do three things:

1. I make a few general observations on the broad nature of product design, its relationship with associated disciplines and the profiles of competence that are required by designers today.
2. Interwoven with this I give a few thoughts on that cornerstone of successful products, the design brief.
3. I give a few 'good news' stories (or to put it more accurately, stories that ultimately turned out to be good news) and draw certain conclusions from them.

The first of my general observations concerns the relationship between research and design. I feel it is necessary to draw a distinction between these two quite different activities as it is still common practice to refer loosely to 'R&D'. The fundamental point about research is that its object is to create knowledge. This knowledge may be important for the creation of new products and may involve creating research hardware. For example, the Flying Bedstead was produced almost thirty years ago to study the problems associated with vertical take-off and hovering flight. This device was never intended to be a marketable product but yielded much information that was well used subsequently. Creating the highly successful Harrier aircraft was an exercise in design and was a good exploitation of the research data gained previously. And this makes the point: the function of design is to create new products, not just new knowledge.

A new design may have to undergo a lengthy period of testing, evaluation and improvement before it has fully matured into a dependable and (with any luck) profitable product. Such a process was certainly required for the Harrier and is often referred to as 'development'.

But the term 'design' requires further explanation. In some circles 'design' is regarded (quite properly) as an art-based activity with an emphasis upon the visual aspects of product design. Elsewhere, design is regarded as an engineering-based activity concerned perhaps with the correct application of sophisticated components to complex systems, for example, incorporating a microprocessor into an electronic control system. It is, therefore, reasonable to ask whether there is any common ground between these different areas of expertise and to consider to what extent a practitioner in one field should appreciate the skills that obtain in the other.

Take, for example, the range of very beautiful wall tiles produced by Sally Anderson. Sally Anderson is primarily an artist, and the most striking feature of her product is its aesthetic quality, but to assume that Sally Anderson requires no technological expertise would be a mistake. The selection of the pigments and the glazes can be a tricky business, and the subsequent firing of the tiles requires precise control of temperature and time. Packaging the tiles to reduce breakage in transit in a further headache.

The Pegasus vectored thrust turbo fan that powers the Harrier aircraft is a very different type of product. Unquestionably the work of engineering designers, it involves some of the best application of technology to be found anywhere, for example in the design of the air-cooled turbine blades and the optimising of the fan for maximum mass flow. The thrust development of the engine has more than doubled during two decades of continued improvement. It seems that the Rolls-Royce designers are still far from finished and the introduction of plenum chamber burning and other factors will improve the thrust still further. One fascinating point is that the Rolls-Royce designers have not spurned simple solutions when they seem to be appropriate. For example, the rotating thrust nozzles are driven by a simple sprocket and chain, just like a bicycle. Visually, the Pegasus is an impressive artefact, but it was not designed for its visual qualities, and in fact it is intended to be buried inside the aircraft structure, hidden from view. Does this mean that the art-trained designer had no role to play in creating this product? Of course not! In addition to the various items of graphics that have to be included on the engine itself, the engine as a product must be accompanied by a considerable amount of literature, some technical (for example, maintenance manuals) and some promotional (sales leaflets and advertising), but all requiring layout and illustration. And, of course, there is the famous Rolls-Royce logo itself!

For historical reasons the art-based designer is known as 'an industrial designer'. Figure 1 illustrates in a simple way how products can require a varying mix of design skills. At one extreme a textile is (let us suppose) 100 per cent within the domain of industrial design. This may be something of an over-simplification due to the technological aspects of the textile (for example, fire retardancy or wear resistance), and the available production facilities may well set some constraints upon the details of the visual design. But the industrial designer (or textile designer) is unlikely to require significant help from a technologist and would certainly consider the design of the textile in question to be uniquely his or her responsibility.

At the other end of the spectrum an electromagnetic solenoid would in all probability be the work of an engineering designer specialising in the field of electromechanical devices. Some small degree of assistance might be required from other experts, but again the engineering designer would certainly

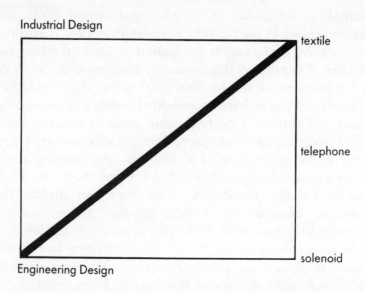

Industrial Design

textile

telephone

solenoid

Engineering Design

Figure 1 *How products require a mix of design skills*

consider that the design of this product was within his own pre-rogative. At the 50–50 point I have chosen a telephone as an example because this seems to me to be a product that requires roughly equal inputs from the industrial designer and the engineering designer; one to ensure that the internal electronics and other components function properly, and the other to ensure that the visual and ergonomic aspects of the product are satisfactory.

Figure 2 goes one stage further and shows the approximate industrial design and engineering design costs associated with a wide range of products. At one extreme a simple textile or wallpaper design can be purchased for quite a small sum, while at the other extreme the total cost of the Concorde research design and development programme was of the order of £1 billion. Intermediate products include a computer, a motor vehicle and a warship. There is a rough relationship between the two cost elements, and I would not suggest that a straight line should be drawn between this plum pudding of points nor that anyone should attempt to define the parameters of such a line. But I do think that the existence of a rough relationship

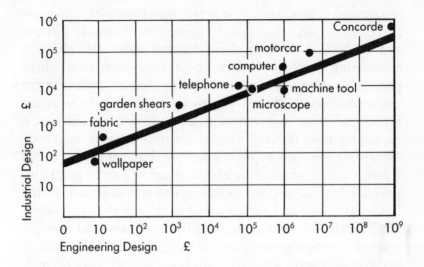

Figure 2 *Spectrum of costs, etc*

between these two cost factors should be noted and, for example, if anyone is involved in an engineering design project costing, say, half a million, then it is likely that a significant sum should be allocated for the associated industrial design work, say perhaps £10–20 thousand.

So far I have discussed only engineering design and industrial design, but of course this is an oversimplification, and the spectrum of design disciplines has to be explored in rather more detail (see Fig. 3). It is sometimes helpful to think of the range of design disciplines as a spectrum ranging from purely aesthetic work through ergonomic and human factors to forms, structures and then the elements of mechanical engineering, including drive systems, mechanisms and machines, this merging into the field of electromechanics with motors and relays and thence into the field of electronics and advanced systems on the extreme right. In Figure 3 rough ability profiles are shown in relation to this spectrum for the industrial designer, the mechanical designer and the electrical designer. These profiles have not been drawn casually and note, for example, the sharp cut-off of the electrical designer as soon as the spectrum changes from electrical engineering into the field of mechanical engineering. It is a fact that most electrical engineers believe that mechanical engineering is usually obvious and as such is beneath their interest. After all, electrical engineering is difficult because one can only infer what is happening by using instruments of various kinds, some of them very sophisticated. But in mechanical engineering the situation is quite different, as anyone with a pair of eyes can see what is happening in an instant, or so the electrical engineer supposes. Conversely, the mechanical engineering designer has in general a deep mistrust of anything electrical and will often go to considerable lengths to avoid including in his product any of that unfamiliar, frail and even somewhat sinister electronic logic. Much better to have something really dependable (for example a pair of cams or a gearbox), and if things become difficult there is always pneumatic logic to fall back on. The net result of this is that electrical engineering designers and mechanical engineering designers are usually friendly enough with each other but show a disinclination to operate beyond the bounds of their own specialisms. The resulting design sins are usually sins of omission caused by lack of communication or willingness to select the best design solution on its merits.

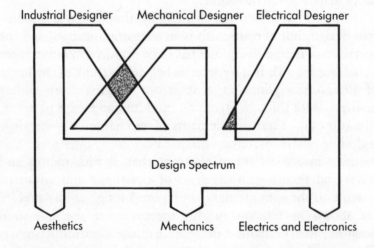

Figure 3 *The design spectrum*

Consider locomotives. An interesting example was when large diesel locomotives were being conceived. Mechanical designers hankered after a mechanical solution, and one was the Fell locomotive which drove the wheels through gearboxes. It was mechanically very complicated and expensive to maintain and proved to be unreliable. Another solution was the diesel hydraulic locomotive. Quite a number of these were built by British Railways and served on the Great Western section for many years. They proved very expensive to maintain, although they gave an excellent performance. It was said they had more electrical control and protective devices than had diesel electric locomotives. The best solution was diesel electric such as the English Electric type 4 or top-class 56 locomotive. On these a conventional diesel engine drives a diesel generator which trans-mits power to DC series motors. The Deltic locomotive is also diesel. When they were put in service at 3000 horse power, they were the most powerful diesel locomotives in the world. The engine design had three crankshafts linked by a complex gear train, but, despite this complexity, they gave many years of good service and have only recently been withdrawn.

Moving to the left along the design spectrum shown in Figure 3 we encounter a different situation. The industrial designer is typically reluctant to regard himself as a mere stylist or aesthetician and often claims expertise in the field of forms and structures, sometimes with good reason. But this is the legitimate terrain of the mechanical designer, who incidentally often feels that he too has an eye for the appearance of a product and certainly can speak with authority on matters relating to the product–human interface. The tails of the two profiles cross over and overlap, and this is a source of continuing conflict, each practitioner believing that his authority is being usurped by the other.

But how does the electrical engineering designer get along with the industrial designer? For, after all, if they are to sell well, electrical products must also look good and be fit for their purpose. Things are usually a little easier in this context owing largely to the fact that neither in general has a clear under-standing of what the other is talking about. To the industrial

designer a 'half adder' or 'shift register' might as well be classical Greek and communication becomes even worse when the
electronics expert expresses himself almost entirely in acronyms,
which is usually the case. But what is the electronics expert to
make of terms like 'colophon', 'sans serif' or 'fenestration'?
Practically nothing! It is like imagining a conversation between
Old Mother Riley and the men from Mars.

But there is one more point about this design spectrum,
and note it is so far only a spectrum of design technologies,
making no reference to the other skills and attributes required
by the designer. The point is that the design spectrum is so
broad and so complex that it is beyond the grasp of any one
person to possess a professional competence throughout its
entire extent. How about Brunel, or Stephenson or any of the
great universal designers of the past? Yes, but these were excep-
tional men, and in any case the breadth and complexity of the
design spectrum has expanded very considerably since their day.
Is it likely that Brunel could have mastered the whole of electrical and systems engineering as well as the more modern
aspects of his own field? The hard fact is that design is a profession for specialists, each of whom must be professionally competent in a particular increment of the spectrum. Another
equally hard fact is that most products require inputs from
many, if not all, parts of the design spectrum. The number of
products that can now be designed wholly by one individual is
comparatively small, the corollary of this being that most products must now be designed by a team.

The required ability profile of a typical designer with
respect to the spectrum of design technologies contains two
essential elements: one specialist and the other generalist. If
these two factors are not present, any hope of setting up a well
co-ordinated and successful design team must be in doubt.

In my experience designers, particularly young designers,
are seldom grossly deficient in the area of specialism, but many
are grossly deficient in the area of generalism; a criticism that
might be noted by those who are considering the education and
formation of our future engineers and designers.

It is often assumed that knowledge of the appropriate

technology is all that the designer requires, but this is emphatically not so. Of course it is very important that the product being created should function properly, but, although this is necessary, it is far from sufficient if the product is to be a success. There is, for example, the critical question of costs, and this means that the designer must have some appreciation of production processes and what costs what. The crucial factor of quantity must be taken into account by the designer (although it is all too often ignored) and the designer must be aware of the various design constraints that will be imposed by the production methods demanded by various quantity requirements. For example, in small quantities a simple component might be a sandcasting, but larger quantities might indicate that an extrusion would be cheaper, provided of course that the cost of a suitable die can be amortised over the quantity in question. But does everyone realise that an extrusion must have a constant cross-section and that a component designed as a casting may be quite impossible to manufacture as an extrusion?

Similar observations can be made about quality assurance (how is the product to be tested?), reliability (does the designer know about the penalty clause in the contract on reliability?), maintainability (does the word appear in the design brief at all?) and safety (did anyone think of conducting a standards search before it was too late?).

These are all areas of necessary design competence, each I suspect with a separate, perhaps small, identifiable body of knowledge leading to an associated set of core material that should be obligatory for all designers in every field.

I now turn to the original specification (as it is commonly referred to by engineering designers) or design brief (a term used widely elsewhere).

This subject was addressed by Sir Kenneth Corfield in his Report 'Product design'. He took the view of top management and compiled a list of questions which have to be answered satisfactorily before design and development proceeds. These questions were:

a) For what market is the product intended?

b) Has the relationship between eventual price and revenue been properly assessed given the total costs of design and production?
c) Can the design be manufactured economically?
d) Does the design incorporate up-to-date technology?
e) Are the materials and components available?
f) Has the relationship between reliability and maintainability been fully investigated?
g) Have the critical phases of development been identified?
h) Are the planned delivery dates achievable?

These questions are all of the utmost importance and are relevant to the content of the design brief, but I shall extend the argument and examine the content and structure of the design brief in some detail.

The requirements upon the designer can be considered under three main headings: time, performance and cost. It is obvious that each of these is of fundamental importance and inadequate achievement under any one heading may cause the product to fail. Yet it is surprising how often the design brief omits any mention of either time-scale or costs (and sometimes both), concentrating solely upon the performance requirements.

Let us look at some things that may be specified to the designer under these three headings.

TIME

a) *Project completion on date and intermediate milestones* (To give examples: completion of concept, drawings, prototypes or evaluation).

b) *Proposed date for launch or commissioning:* Failure to do this may mean that penalty clauses are invoked or market opportunities lost.

c) *Sales span and overall life:* The designer should be given some idea of how long it is intended that the product should be available for sale and for how long it is intended that the product should last, given appropriate product support.

There is nothing mysterious about this information, and all the data will be known to various members of company staff. Is there any sound reason why the designer should not be put in the picture?

Figure 4 illustrates the relevance of time-scale by showing the cash-flow relationship with time for a typical new product venture. Investment in the new product commences with research, design and development phases and the cash flow negative. It sinks still further as investment in tooling, piece parts and production is included. With early and profitable sales the gradient of the cash-flow graph turns positive and after considerable sales the investment is recovered. Further sales yield a net profit, and finally in this example the cash-flow gradient again turns negative as the final sales turn out to be unprofitable, perhaps due to increased market competition and the product is discontinued.

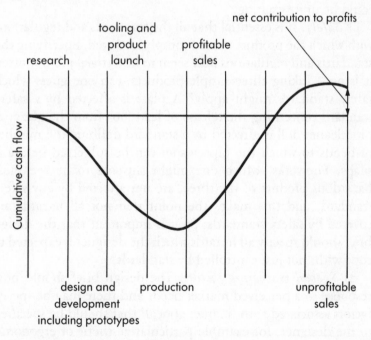

Figure 4 *Product cash flow graph*

PERFORMANCE

a) *Static requirements:* These include weight, size etc and seldom present undue difficulty.

b) *Dynamic requirements:* All products must 'work' in one way or another. A rising chair is a good example of a product that has to function satisfactorily throughout a range of varying requirements. The cushion is hinged to the chair at its leading edge and a large spring causes the cushion to move sharply upwards and forwards about this hinge when the knobbed lever at the side of the chair is released. Old people sometimes have difficulty in standing up from an easy chair and the spring assistance provided in this product is designed to overcome this problem. But the spring must be matched to the user! With a soft spring and a heavy granny the product is not worth much, but with a good strong spring and a flyweight granny the results could be quite exciting.

c) *Safety:* It is essential that all the standards and regulations with which the product should comply are listed. Specifying the standards and regulations may seem to be a trivial job but often it is not. Taking three simple products, can one guess which safety standards might apply? A plate is affected by a safety standard concerning the release of lead ions from the glaze. A pipecleaner doll is affected by a standard defining the number of bends to which the pipecleaner can be subjected before it snaps. Fireworks, which one might suppose to be the most hazardous product of the three, are not affected by any safety standard, and this makes the point that not all hazards are covered by safety standards. So it is important that the design brief should specify all hazards which the designer is expected to cope with, not just controlled by standards.

d) *Special marketing factors:* The design brief should be a response to a perceived market need, and there may be special factors associated with 'market appeal' that should be specified to the designer, for example particular aesthetic or ergonomic considerations. In some contexts these factors may be very important indeed and, in many cases, the buying decision may be determined by the visual quality of the product to a far greater degree than the purchaser would ever admit; for example, the Range Rover is sold on a durability ticket and is designed to appear tough, rugged and reliable. But this sort of thing is best left to the expert and if overdone can lead to results that are ridiculous. A road roller with a top speed of, say, 5 mph might well have careful attention paid to its visual and ergonomic qualities. But it is surely absurd for such a product to be designed to reduce its drag coefficient to the lowest possible figure with streamlined and raked windscreen and cab. A further point in this section is that the countries and types of purchaser for which the product is intended should also be listed as 'special marketing factors'. Particular markets have particular requirements, some of them mandatory, and it is helpful to the designer to know of these requirements at an early stage. Successive modifications at a late stage (when no doubt the product has been fully noted) to meet different marketing requirements can be an expensive and frustrating business.

COSTS

a) *Project costs:* Design itself costs money and the designer should know how much the design project is expected to cost, not least so that he can monitor his own expenditure against achievement.

b) *Manufacturing costs:* It is essential that a target manufacturing/selling cost for the product should be specified and that this should be related to the predicted rate of production or overall quantity. For example, the original McArthur Microscope which was a novel and original design, was intended for small-quantity production. Many of the components had to be machined from solid and the product was expensive. At a later stage the Open University announced a requirement of some 10,000 per annum, and this made the whole project look quite different. Substantial investment in tooling enabled most of the components to be moulded from plastics and the ultimate cost of the microscope came down to the order of £10.

The designer must know whether there are any limitations in the available manufacturing facilities and he must be aware of any company policies on subcontracting. For example, the highly successful Sinclair ZX81 is designed to be manufactured entirely by subcontract, with components being purchased from those who are best able to supply them. In this case the product designers had few constraints and were able to shop quite literally around the world.

The designer may have to work to a tooling budget and observe requirements for rationalising components. The point about rationalising components is important. Substantial funds may be tied up in stocks and work in progress and, if the variety of components can be reduced, substantial savings can result. A large variety of instrument displays can be installed in a Ford motor vehicle using just one instrument surround. Just think of the variety of components that do not have to be purchased and stocked resulting from this design!

c) *Cost of ownership:* Reliability requirements, maintenance requirements and the requirements of overall life should be made clear to the designer and should be specified precisely and numerately. For example, inserting a vague phrase into the design brief 'product must be easy to maintain' is almost useless. How easy to maintain? And, if it exists, what are the terms of the maintenance contract?

I conclude with some 'good news' stories, some taken from Thorn EMI and others taken from widely different fields. In the early 1970s it became clear that there were excellent market prospects for a sophisticated, versatile and efficient louvre system, particularly if the price were competitive. In the universal louvre system that was developed, the most interesting feature was the efficiency of the louvre in permitting ventilation while excluding rain; a beautiful straight edge was also achieved, indicative of the precision and quality control exercised by the manufacturer. There was a surprisingly wide demand for such a louvre. The louvre won design awards in 1975, 1979 and 1981 in the UK, Australia and West Germany, respectively, and a very substantial increase in turnover has been gained over the period. The manufacturers say that they correlate their success directly to these awards.

My next example comes from a quite different area, namely the manufacture of false teeth. Consider the problem of designing and manufacturing such a product. It is not easy and there are several factors to be taken into account. The load that can be supported by such a prosthesis is only some 20 per cent of the force that can be born by a genuine tooth, and this can have serious consequences upon the masticating ability of the false teeth unless the cusps are designed very carefully for optimum food grinding performance. Computer-aided design techniques were used to optimise tooth profile from this point of view, and with considerable success.

The cost of these teeth is amazingly low, a little more than £5 per hundred or 5p each. It is, perhaps, not surprising that the company that made the development is now the largest manufacturer of false teeth within the EEC and exports 70 per cent of its output.

My next good news comes from Thorn EMI, although it had a somewhat uncertain beginning. There has been substantial interest in automatic fare-collection systems for at least a decade. As well as saving labour costs, a device that reads magnetically encoded railway tickets automatically to permit entry or exit from the platform is an effective deterrent against fraud.

Comprehensive systems have been installed already by both the French and the Americans and serve as convincing demonstrations to potential customers. Where have we got to in Britain? A design brief was produced by British Rail for such a system ten years ago. I cannot accuse this design brief of being inadequate: it ran to four volumes, each of more than 20,000 words. But there was a snag. London Transport was also investigating automatic fare-collection systems and had its own ideas which were not identical with those of British Rail. As many commuters take the interchangeability of tickets on British Rail and London Transport for granted, having two completely independent systems was a worry, and still is. There the matter rests and a substantial investment lies unused while export opportunities slip by. The prototypes have functioned satisfactorily in the laboratory for five years but have never been used for real passengers.

So where is the 'good news'? I am glad to report that the expertise and experience gained are now being put to good use. British Rail are in considerable need of a machine that can be used by the booking clerk to issue tickets to all destinations accurately and efficiently. The general-purpose ticket issuing system is a very compact and versatile product that provides a solution to this long-felt want. It incorporates three micro-processors and a matrix dot printer. The keyboard is operated by the booking clerk and in most instances only three buttons need to be pressed to produce the required ticket, the two banks of buttons on the extreme left being allocated individually for the tickets that are most frequently requested. More unusual requests require the clerk to type in the first three letters of the name of the destination, whence the machine grasps precisely what is wanted and displays the destination in full to the clerk for confirmation.

It is still early days for this product but Thorn EMI are confident that sales will be excellent, particularly in view of a very attractive price. The industrial designer's original concept of this machine differs somewhat from the final version. The changes, which may or may not be felt to add to the aesthetic quality of the design, were introduced all at the specific request of the customer. Is the customer always right? There must be occasions, particularly when the customer is in such a powerful position, when the truth of this old adage is open to some doubt.

My final 'good news' story concerns a product known as a streamer which is used by the data-processing industry. A modern computer has the capacity to store and manipulate vast quantities of data, and, although modern machines are very reliable, it is prudent, at intervals, for users to make a record of all the data retained in the computer so that, if the worst were to happen, all the information would not be lost. The use of non-interchangeable Winchester disc drives requires periodic 'back-up'. Equally, for example, the consequences of a fire in the data-processing facility of a major clearing bank or insurance

company could be absolutely disastrous to the business concerned unless a comparatively recent record of the data had
been taken, which would, of course, permit the situation to be
recovered.

It is obvious that with current technology magnetic tape is
one of the best means for creating regular data archives of this
type; the information is permanent (not destroyed by mains
failure), and tape is cheap, and also reasonably compact for
storage purposes. The tape drive that is needed for this application is known as a 'streamer' and has certain similarities to the
tape drives used with previous generations of mainframe and
mini computers. For example, the streamer uses half-inch track
magnetic tape and records the data in one of the standard IBM
formats, typically 1600 bits/in. But there is an important difference, which is that the streamer can record and replay data in
'streaming mode', without starting and stopping between con-
secutive data records. By comparison, a conventional tape drive
must be able to stop very precisely within the customary half-
inch or so gap between blocks of data, and this requirement
imposes severe demands upon the design of the drive itself.
The streamer has no such requirement and can therefore be
considerably simpler, cheaper and smaller.

The streamer is now a recognised item of OEM equipment
in the data-processing market, and this particular slice of the
market is contested keenly by some five international manufacturers, Thorn EMI being the only European contestant.

A very enthusiastic UK team has produced what promises
to be a world beater in this highly specialised and rapidly moving field. They have produced the world's smallest half-inch
(noncartridge) tape drive (occupying a volume equivalent to
two standard 8-inch floppy disc drives) at a cost that undercuts
the rest of the market by a considerable margin. Much of this is
due to the fact that the machine is microprocessor controlled to
provide the sophisticated speed control required for this application and to provide the most comprehensive set of self-
diagnostics for failure analysis possessed by any machine in this
field. The machine is autoloading, ingeniously using air from
the cooling fan to blow the half-inch tape from the inserted

spool to the take-up spool, the complex procedure for driving the spools during this process of course being controlled by the microprocessor. Any machine malfunction is 'fed-back' to the operator via the alpha-numerical display on the front panel, giving a ready diagnosis of the failure mode. The layout of the front panel this time survived intact from the original concept of the industrial designer.

Determination and meticulous attention to cost and detail have ensured that advanced design of data-processing equipment is not restricted to the west coast of the USA: in this particular area the running is being made at Wookey Hole in Somerset and the course looks good.

Are there any lessons to be learned from the four 'good news' stories? There are three common factors to which I should like to draw your attention:

a) In each case there has been a clear market need to be met. Streamers are an absolute necessity, as are ventilation and false teeth. In every case there was a clear demand for the product and none was an example of a solution looking for a problem.

b) A second common factor is that all the products have been well conceived with considerable attention to detail. A market need will not go begging for long and there is always competition. Almost always it is the best product that will get the most sales, and this is usually a question of ensuring that your product is a little bit better than the competition in many different ways.

c) Lastly, each of these products had to be created by a design team. Although each team may have had a leader, in no case could any one person claim entire responsibility for the product. The industrial designer had to co-operate with the team of electronic engineers in producing the streamer, and the ergonomist had to co-operate with the mechanical engineers in producing the pathfinder, and, most extreme of all, dental experts had to collaborate with experts in computer-aided design in producing the new range of false teeth.

ACKNOWLEDGEMENT

The author gratefully acknowledges the help received in the preparation of this paper from Mr Geoffrey Constable, Head of the Industrial Division, the Design Council, and Mr Henry Quick of Thorn EMI.

Design and Innovation at Novo

Mads Øvlisen

Mads Øvlisen is a Dane and the Managing Director of Novo Industries, an international manufacturing company in the fields of pharmaceuticals and enzymes. In a country in which industrial design has always been accorded a pre-eminent place Novo industries is regarded as a model for how design can be effectively used in every aspect of the company's activities.

In his paper he concentrates on the design contribution to product innovation and, in particular, how Novo Industries achieved world leadership in the development of insulin products. The more general contribution of a pervasive design philosophy to company success is also discussed.

Novo is a Danish-based, internationally operated manufacturing company. Our business falls into two distinct product categories: pharmaceuticals and enzymes, ie microbial catalysts for industrial use. Novo was founded in 1925, and today employs 4500 people, of whom 3500 work in Denmark.

Our company is research-based; 20 per cent of our staff work in the research division. The future of our company depends upon our ability to be innovative, or, speaking more clearly, our success depends upon our inventiveness. The power of invention is what started Novo, so let's look at our history through the eyes of product development.

SCIENCE AND INDUSTRY

In 1921, Banting and Best, at the University of Toronto, isolated insulin and demonstrated its use in the treatment of *diabetes mellitus*. In 1925, Harald and Thorvald Pedersen founded Novo and started to produce insulin. Insulin is manufactured by extracting the hormone from the pancreas glands of cattle and pigs. Thorvald Pedersen was a very good pharmacist, and his brother Harald was a mechanical genius. Together they succeeded in developing and manufacturing Insulin Novo, which was a better product, an insulin that stood far above the pills and solutions of other manufacturers. Insulin had been marketed as a pill of the *active* ingredient. But there were impurities inherent in the tablets, and the enzymes were degrading the insulin. Furthermore, it was difficult to shake up the mixture uniformly. The two brothers had now found out how to produce insulin as a clear solution that had uniform quality.

There was, however, still a lot of discomfort associated with the daily injections, so the brothers quickly developed new syringes that were sufficiently sterile.

Throughout the 1930s up towards 1940, the quality of Novo insulins had made it possible for the company to export its products to more than forty countries. Larger facilities were required; an old neighbouring dairy was bought and converted into a production plant. But the business grew at such a rate that a young architect by the name of Arne Jacobsen was asked to design a new building with more laboratory and production space; hence, a new building, of great character, went up.

In 1937 Novo acquired Hvidøre, a palatial residence, and turned it into a hospital for diabetic patients.

INSULIN PRODUCTION

But Novo was duly struck with problems in the insulin production in the Europe of the 1930s and 1940s: there was a shortage of raw materials, and there were restrictions on whom one could trade with.

The raw material problem was both one of declining supply, and of competing uses of the glands. Not only insulin, but certain enzymes, used in various medical preparations, were extracted from the glands: it was a question of insulin or enzymes.

To cope with this new dilemma, Novo invented a double-extraction process, whereby both the insulin and the enzyme trypsin were extracted without a loss of yield of either. This was commercially a very important step forward, and I believe we are still the only company in the world using this method. So, Novo got into the enzymes business, through products derived from animals sources.

Let us forget chronology, and have a look at the development of insulin preparations.

The next major development was in 1949; Novo invented the Lente Insulins, which were on the market in the early 1950s. The Lente Insulin was a *once-a-day* injection preparation, which minimised patient discomfort and pain, by developing an insulin with prolonged action. Novo achieved this goal; patients could manage with only one daily injection. The preparations were highly successful and accounted for almost one-third of the world's insulin consumption.

NOVO ARCHITECTURE

This development put more pressure on the physical facilities, and so a new laboratory and production building were installed. Arne Jacobsen continued to be our architect, and again proved to be successful and pioneering.

One of the company's needs was to build a new lunch room. At Novo we maintain the tradition of all employees sharing the same facilities, including lunch rooms. It is therefore necessary to create facilities in which blue-collar workers, researchers and sales people all feel at home. Some wear overalls, some white coats, and some shirts and ties. The furniture should be able to tolerate the wear and tear of such a group. It should also be practical furniture which can be piled up when the room is being used for other purposes, such as company parties.

The solution was a spacious room on the top floor of the building, with a high ceiling, and, that's right; the chairs! A modern classic was born. Arne Jacobsen and Novo had concurred that a new and better solution was necessary. So Arne

Jacobsen and Fritz Hansen got together and developed a very complex process, extending the known limitations of laminated wood, developing new tools and processes, and finally, namely, the famous *Ant*. One improvement to the chair came later, the four-legged version instead of the three-legged, but we are still very fond of our original *Ant*.

It was typical of Arne Jacobsen, as of his successors Dissing + Weitling, who took over where Arne Jacobsen left off, to work with the design of the *total* plant. Arne Jacobsen developed at this time new door handles, curtain textiles, and many other items for the plant, while still finding time to play with our logo and stationery layout.

INSULIN PRODUCT DEVELOPMENT

In the 1960s, British researchers explained the structure of insulin. The insulin molecule became known, and we at Novo were determined to utilize this new knowledge in our products. We wanted to make sure that patients did not inject contaminants which might cause long-term complications, but injected only pure insulin molecule. We were successful in this endeavour, and developed the Mono Component insulins. The concept proved to be correct. Several problems, especially short-term ones, disappeared.

The latest step in our insulin development story is the human insulation preparation. By means of advanced technology, we are now able to produce insulin which molecule by molecule is identical to the insulin man himself produces, or, in the case of diabetics, should produce. Human Mono Component insulins now set the standard, and have in fact become a theme at our conference stands.

Today, insulin has reached a very high standard, and there is general agreement that little will be gained in terms of patient benefit by the development of more sophisticated insulins. Patient compliance with therapeutic programmes, doctors' insight etc, must now be upgraded. Recent knowledge has shown us that the single most important aspect of treating a diabetic patient, with regard to longevity and quality of life, is to maintain a blood sugar level which is as close to normal as possible. Healthy people produce and utilise insulin as required by their intake of nutrition, their use of energy etc. The blood sugar levels vary, and insulin keeps them in line.

Now, that is *not* what happens if you get one large injection a day. So, our once-a-day preparations were fine since they reduced inconvenience, but now several daily injections are becoming the treatment of choice. This in itself presents a problem: implantable pumps which deliver minute doses of insulin as required have yet to be developed. It is problematic for the diabetic patient to carry around his syringe, his vial of insulin, his disinfectant, etc.

At Novo, we have developed a solution: The NovoPen®, and the Novo Penfill®.

THE PRODUCT TREE

The problems of the 1930s and early 1940s had emphasised the company's vulnerability as a one-product company. The brothers decided that we needed another leg, and decided to go into fermentation — a logical step for a company based in an agricultural country. In fermentation, micro-organisms grow in tanks and either produce or become useful substances, such as penicillins. Hence we decided to manufacture penicillin, and as our penicillin business grew, we required more space. Arne Jacobsen designed a new fermentation plant as an extension of the existing buildings. This building, like the two previous ones I have mentioned, received several awards. Jacobsen's attention to detail, as illustrated by the fire escape, a winding steel staircase housed in a glass cylinder, is but one reason for his success.

Novo was instrumental in developing a number of penicillin products, which perhaps seem trivial now, but were very innovative in their day. Hospital costs were, then as now, too high. The cleaning of syringes had become too costly. Novo developed the Novo jet syringe, disposable, reliable, and cheap to produce, for use with our penicillins. Making sure that the patients took their required penicillin tablets three times daily, Novo developed daily dosage forms with writing space provided.

ENZYMES

A little earlier, I mentioned the word enzyme. An enzyme is a catalyst, a protein which accelerates chemical or biochemical processes. No life can exist without enzymes. They break down the food we eat, and help build our bodies.

The ability to break down substances can be exploited in industrial processing, a fact that had been known for a long time but had not been usable. Having recognised the need, and using its manufacturing technology in fermentation, Novo now developed a series of microbial enzymes that could be produced in constant quantity and quality, at a regular price. The first major product to be developed was Alcalase®, to be used in detergents to break down protein stains. It was a difficult birth, but a commercial success.

New facilities were again required and subsequently built by Arne Jacobsen, in Copenhagen. Some neighbouring property was acquired, the old buildings demolished, and a new and beautiful plant was built. Again the architect and the company received a lot of recognition for this building.

A large piece of land was acquired in Kalundborg, some 100 km from Copenhagen. Arne Jacobsen now ventured into some modern materials; facades were made in Cor-ten steel. Functionally separated by a main street, many more buildings have sprung up. More enzymes were being developed, and so more laboratory space was needed, and it had to be closer to Copenhagen.

A site was chosen in Bagsværd, a suburb of Copenhagen, and a master plan was developed by Arne Jacobsen, working together with Novo's engineering and research staff. A current picture shows that we have maintained the original buildings and tried to respect the demands they put on recent expansion.

Novo was still in the process of expansion, and new

international companies were added. Arne Jacobsen, in his new clear Novo-style, designed a laboratory and production plant which were built in Mainz, Germany. I believe this building is my favourite. Another production house was built in Chartres, France.

THE SOURCE OF OUR ARCHITECTURE

Let us just pause here for a minute to sum up some of the factors influencing the way our buildings look:

— We are pharmaceutical and biochemical manufacturers with high demands on hygiene.
— We are research-based; a rational company dominated by people with technical and scientific educations.
— We sell products to chronically ill patients.
— We are in the public eye.
— We are a straightforward company.
— We like people to find their work place attractive and stimu- lating; hoping of course that this will stimulate creativity.

The sort of creativity I refer to is illustrated by the following example: Diabetes is a metabolic disorder; consequently the people at Novo know a lot about metabolism, the blood flow, and hormones. Utilising this knowledge led to the develop- ment of an oral contraceptive pill.

It is important that women take one, and only one, pill a day. For this purpose, Novo developed a very good packaging solution. This memo-pack carries the names of the days of the week. The dispenser will only move in one direction, thus ensuring compliance on the part of the user with the required dosage. In sequential therapy, the different hormones in pills are identified by the variously coloured packs used.

DIAGNOSTIC EQUIPMENT

Going back to my Product Tree, I will briefly mention our interest in diagnostic equipment. This again is closely connected with our insulin expertise. To develop these highly purified insulins, we had to be able to measure minute quantities of impurities. This was achieved through various immunological techniques which took us into both agents and equipment. The Lysotech is a fine example, designed by Dissing + Weitling. It is used to measure deep vein thrombosis. This equipment was awarded the ID Prize in 1981.

This brings me back to Hvidøre which, as you may remember, we purchased in 1937 and converted into a diabetic hospital. The building is a historic landmark, so adding the much needed new in-patient wing in compliance with building restrictions was difficult, but successfully accomplished by Dissing + Weitling.

DESIGN FOR THE FUTURE

A new granulation plant was recently completed for furthering the production of enzymes in detergents. The process occurs in a tower, as the enzymes are well-transmitted by means of gravity. The building runs with very little manpower and is highly productive and efficient.

Also recently completed was an extension for our Bagsværd research lab and administrative facilities, which again were designed by Dissing + Weitling. Its staircase is a good example of the integration of good structural design with an awareness of the kind of research that is conducted at Novo. It reminds you of the double helix. Another innovation that was introduced for the building was a special sign system to solve the problems of a quickly growing and flexible organisation.

Design and Product Innovation
on London Underground
Dr Tony Ridley

Dr Tony Ridley is Managing Director of London Underground and an international authority on urban transport systems. His paper refers to the heritage of design at London Transport — the outcome of the work of Frank Pick in the 1930s. He places emphasis on the management tasks of co-ordinating design and product innovation and describes the need to innovate not only in the design of trains and stations but in the entire 'package' of products and services that are offered to Underground travellers.

When my paper was in its early drafting stages colleagues, who know about design matters, suggested I had misunderstood the title. I was told that Product Innovation is only one element of the wide vista of areas that make up 'Corporate Identity' and not — as I suggested — one of the primary aims of my company. Well, we have resolved the dispute — we are both right. My definition, coincidentally, matches the expert's definition of the entire field of 'Corporate Identity'. As a transport operator, product innovation and the incorporation of design means the development of an entire package of service that London Underground Limited can offer to its customers. It is this process that I intend to discuss here.

A HERITAGE OF DESIGN AND PRODUCT INNOVATION

The concept of design and product innovation is not new to London's Underground. There are many examples; but, without doubt, the work carried out under the auspices of Frank Pick stands out. Examples of his role as a great sponsor of design include: 55 Broadway, which is the headquarters of London Transport; East Finchley Station, with its archer; and the Piccadilly Circus Station booking hall. However, there is one particular area I would like to use to illustrate my topic where this excellence in design is combined with the innovation of a new product.

This is the New Works Extensions of the 1930s and 1940s which represented a complete package of design and product innovation. The new customers using the Piccadilly, Northern and Central Line extensions were not only given a new service, but one which was combined with high quality design in graphics, stations and trains. This complete package was used to create a new identity for what was then the London Passenger Transport Board. Furthermore, design was used to focus the public's perception on the new service.

Frank Pick had the advantage of an Underground that had a firm place in the market and growing demand. As a result he was able to use design in the innovation of his product as a means of glorifying the public transport service.

THE LONDON UNDERGROUND IN 1987

In 1987 the Underground finds itself in need of the same philosophy incorporating design and product innovation. Changes in the business environment of the Underground have precipitated this need.

1. With the creation of London Underground Limited in 1985, as a wholly owned subsidiary of London Regional Transport the new company needed a new and separate corporate identity.
2. Since 1980 the Underground has undergone a change in management style, which not only makes the business more efficient, but makes the integration of design into the development of our product more easily controlled.
3. In the early 1980s we reached a low point in the level and

quality of service provided to our customers. After concentrated efforts a vastly more reliable service and an improving passenger environment has created an atmosphere of change and improvement.

The market is no longer captive for public transport. People have a real choice in both off-peak and peak periods between private and public transport. Further, the passenger's perception of what should be available has increased. Therefore in order to meet rising consumer expectation, and because of the need to make the Underground an appealing environment, design must be carefully incorporated into the development of our product.

These changes in our market environment have made the need for the management of design, product innovation and marketing far more pressing than in the days of Frank Pick. As a consequence, design has been identified as a way of making the Underground's product match the marketplace and as a means to help to attract passengers and so to benefit the business.

PACKAGING OF DESIGN

The Underground is in the early stages of re-orientation of its product. Traditionally the train service has been seen as the ultimate product. Now we realise that we must see the product as the *entire* experience that the passenger receives, from entering the system to leaving it.

To achieve this the Underground must brand all elements, from stationery to trains. We are fortunate that we are in possession of two very powerful tools in the form of the Underground roundel, and the New Johnston typeface. The corporate identity study demonstrated that we had taken a very disciplined approach to the use of our roundel and its application as a brand. An example of the care that has been taken to continue this is in our detailed 'signing study' to determine where misuse is occurring and how we might make improvements. Indeed, the study has recommended a more pure use of the roundel and a revised Johnston typeface. This format is to be tested in trials at Bow Road and Victoria.

CONTROL OF DESIGN INNOVATION

Until the early 1980s the control of design, and its integration of product innovation, lay with the architect or the design engineer. While these excellent professionals are able to apply their particular skills to their job, personal design bias may result and not necessarily fit in with the Underground's corporate ambitions. As part of an effort to gain greater control of projects, in all respects, the Underground has introduced a system of project management. One result has been the establishment of a 'client' for each job. In this the client maintains the overall interests of the business, while the project manager is responsible for completing a project on time and within budget. The client's role has allowed more control over design which has, in turn, given the scope for more interesting design briefs.

Importantly, the 'client role' in this has brought the control of design under much tighter discipline, while remaining subject to an overall review.

I like to compare the change we have managed to achieve, in terms of the control of design, with the process of buying a new house. By introducing project management, and determining a fixed role for the client, we have vastly improved our buying position. No longer do we purchase a mass-produced dwelling off the peg, where we are only able to choose the colour of the bathroom suite. Now we are able to brief the architect and designer fully and then review his work through its various development stages. This gives us a purpose-built home, which has not had its construction standards compromised, but matches our requirements fully.

The leadership and accountability of the client has enabled design to contribute significantly to the improvement of our product. This can be illustrated by a number of examples.

The implementation of our Station Modernisation Scheme is a visible sign of the upgrading of our product. Very carefully

115

three labels of design identity have been incorporated into each scheme:

1. The station identity, by providing a 'sense of place' through decorated panels.
2. The line identity, by dedicated plates that directly relate to the Underground map.
3. Company identity, by using the corporate branding mark.

This scheme allows good design and innovative thinking to take place on the station. It also takes account of two important corporate design considerations. These are:

a) the provision of information — through line identity, poster sites and the use of dot matrix train indicators;
b) the establishment of a firm corporate identity by means of a universal brand, namely the roundel and the New Johnston typeface.

From 1990 onwards London Underground is committed to a programme of rolling-stock renewals. This start date has given us the opportunity to consider, during a six-year gap in rolling-stock procurement, the design of one of the principal components of our product.

When the 1935 prototype stock was built its chief engineer said that everything was different on the new train, apart from the wheels and windows. The radical examination of engineering options on the 1986 prototype stock has even changed these. Additionally, there has also been a strong element of design experimentation. This was conceived, for the first time, by a firm of design consultants and is incorporated into three quite different prototypes. The Underground intends, through this process to:

— assist in the promotion of the corporate identity,
— develop new materials for colour and graphics, and
— incorporate new features to improve the passenger environment.

We have the opportunity not only to test these new features before we order production trains, but also to survey the reaction of our customers. As a consequence we hope this policy will acknowledge advances in technology, and act as a step change in the design of our product and its relationship to our customers' requirements. This policy of client involvement has been most important in all aspects of the development of new products, from our new ticketing system to our advertising material. It has meant that the corporate aims of the business have been well represented in every aspect of our activities. We have been able not only to press for the higher quality of design, but also to retain a strong brand, thus enhancing the corporate identity throughout the company.

DESIGN POLICY

While London Underground Limited is independent in its day-to-day operations, it is answerable to London Regional Transport in respect of design. For example, a recent stringent corporate identity audit carried out by London Regional Transport has confirmed the strength of these tools and has helped us consolidate our brand.

London Regional Transport has, at a senior level, a design director whose role is to co-ordinate design with its subsidiary companies, one of which is London Underground Limited. Having such a policy maker has important ramifications for the Underground:

1. It is of great importance to have a top-level designer, who is able to advise, and to direct the company's policy.
2. The design director's terms of reference encourage consensus, which allows the Underground to develop in its own manner.

The Underground's design policy is the responsibility of the marketing and development director. The main tasks with which he is charged in the design area are:

1. To translate LRT's overall design policy to the Underground,
2. To ensure that the corporate brand is properly used,
3. To ensure that all aspects of design maintain a high quality,

117

4. To develop design expertise within the Underground, in conjunction with the LRT design director.

This relationship means that the London Underground Director, who is charged with the implementation of design, is intimately concerned with its development.

PRODUCT INNOVATION

Our product innovation policy has been to concentrate on two inter-related issues. The first has been the development of a complete service package for our customers. The second has been a move in our marketing strategy towards an increase in off-peak traffic. This policy has been encouraged by the highly successful multi-modal zonal travelcard.

Our development of a service package has concentrated our minds on three particular features. These are:

1. Providing high quality customer-care attitudes at stations as a means of upgrading the product. Now the Underground has the opportunity to use the most successful features of others' efforts and to remodel them to fit its particular requirements.
2. Providing dynamic and constantly updated information. This is intended to make particular use of modern electronics; using dot matrix indicators and centralised public address equipment.
3. Greater and more effective use of information posters and leaflets.

Our efforts to brand off-peak travel have been most successful, as illustrated by:

1. The highly successful 'Great Capital Caper', in which 90,000 people took part.
2. A continuing campaign to promote child travel, because this is a generator of adult travel as well.
3. A series of poster campaigns where good communication

through high quality typography and illustration has culminated in a recent return to sponsored art on the Underground.

In developing these new product areas the management of a co-ordinated design policy has led to a product that is bright and appealing and which carries a strong London Underground identity in every aspect of its operation.

A DYNAMIC PROCESS

That I can be so positive about the design policy of London Underground does not mean that it is fixed and immovable. Far from this, we consider that design and product innovation should be carefully monitored to ensure that it accurately matches the customer's emotional needs.

Through market research we have been able to establish, for example, that passengers prefer to have more street-level related material on deep tube platforms. Moreover, in a recent survey into 'Passenger Security and Safety', market research has been used to determine which conditions customers perceive as being unsafe and what, in their view, would give an improvement. This information has been very important in creating a set of improvements that not only deal with the problem of crime and vandalism, but ensure that customers perceive that it is being dealt with.

I feel very firmly that passengers' anticipation of the quality of the service package that we should offer will continue to grow as they are presented with more and more sophisticated consumer goods elsewhere. The use of market research means that the Underground is able to match this growth in expectation with a corresponding development of our product and the continuing use of good design. With passenger expectation evolving, the management of our design effort is vital.

CONCLUSION

Design and product innovation are excellent tools, but they must be carefully managed. In recognition of this, the Underground has devolved its responsibility for the management of design to the client in order to ensure that the final product matches both the operational and customer requirements. While the creative element is under the control of our design manager the company's corporate interests are easily reviewed. Finally, London Underground acknowledges that a constant reference to the customer must be made to measure the success of existing ideas, and to determine how they should be developed for the future.

Many elements have played an important part in the success the Underground is presently enjoying. I believe part of that success must lie with the good use of design. This has manifested itself not only in the bright new face of modernised stations, and in good publicity material, but also in the cohesion given by the disciplined use of our corporate identity. I am confident that the future, with the further application of design to the innovation of our product — the service package —, will help to bring more success to the London Underground.

Design as a Management Tool for Innovation

Dr Günther Zempelin

Dr Günther Zempelin is one of Germany's leading industrialists who has lived for much of his working life in Holland. As one of the four members of the top management of Akzo, a major Dutch chemical company, he was also Chief Executive of Enka, its largest subsidiary, a Dutch/German-based manufacturing company with world-wide sales in yarns and textiles. He is now Chairman of its supervisory board.

His paper concerns the use of design as a management tool for innovation at Enka. His examples are not, as might be expected, taken from textile design, but from the technical areas in which Enka is involved: polymer structures for man-made fibres, dialysis membranes for kidney machines and the manufacture of texturising machinery. In all these areas he describes a significant shift in design focus at Enka, from research leadership to market leadership in developing new products.

Before I start this paper on design I should warn that I have never done anything like design work in my life. All I am going to say about design has been prepared by other people. I have only tried to manage the company in which this design has taken place.

Let me begin with a very short introduction of the company we are talking about. Akzo is a Dutch-based multinational company, active mainly in the chemical industry. It is a young company which came into existence only in 1969 as a result of several mergers. With six divisions the group is highly decentralised in its operations as well as its management.

Here I shall focus on Enka, which is the largest division

within Akzo, and in which I have spent my professional life. It is in fact a binational Dutch/German group of companies which originated from two man-made fibre companies: AKU in the Netherlands and Glanzstoff in Germany. The Enka group today is the largest man-made fibre producer in Europe and number one in the world as far as yarns for industrial applications are concerned. From this fibre basis, Enka has developed into a diversified group. It is this company that I will use to illustrate how design can be used as a management tool for innovation.

Before I start, I should clarify that in my country, if we talk about the 'design' of a car or a machine we think of its appearance, its face or shape — in other words 'design' in our language refers more to the aesthetics of a product rather than to its structure or its technical function. In the world of man-made fibres, membranes and plastics, there is no such thing as 'design' in this wider sense of the word. Nobody is interested in the shape or appearance of, for instance, fibres as we sell them. None the less, the Enka group does have a machine factory, and their machines, of course, look marvellous. This factory, called 'Barmag', has a small subsidiary called 'Artec Design'. Barmag management attaches great importance to the good design of their products because their customers not only buy Barmag machines and lines with the distinctive Barmag design, they 'buy' the size of the company, its quality, its good name, its reliability, the know-how and the competence of Barmag's engineers and technicians. A prerequisite for this prestige is, of course, that Barmag produces efficient machines that are suitable for the required process in a technically perfect manner.

But something else has to be added to ensure success in world-wide marketing. The development of the drawtexturing machine — on which flat man-made fibres are converted into yarns with textile properties — serves as an example to illustrate 'design' meaning the 'forming of products'.

When the Barmag texturising machine was re-designed several years ago, the company's designers participated right from the beginning. It was the designers who pursued their aim with skill and tenacity, to combine individual components into one unified and solid machine.

This design was not only a question of aesthetics. Barmag not only wanted their customers' workers to enjoy looking at their machines, they also wanted them to enjoy working at these machines, because this, as we know, has a positive impact on the quality of the yarn produced.

And the designer's contribution can even go further. Sometimes we even find that customers adopt a colour from a Barmag machine in designing the room where Barmag machines are installed.

This leads me on to another point. Previously the machines were green. This had been seen as a clear step forward from the undefinable, dull, bluish-grey that used to be the standard colour of machines world-wide. Today Barmag's machines are white. This change is not based on mere aesthetic considerations; it is a sales point. In today's fibre and textile production cleanliness is a critical and mandatory prerequisite for product quality and reduction of maintenance cost. Experience shows that white machines (and their environment) are instinctively kept cleaner by the workers than machines in other colours. Recently I visited Barmag and saw that their newest production machines (metal-processing machines bought from a highly specialised manufacturer) are also white!

The conclusions that we can draw are as follows: Design signifies more than the good shape of objects. Design also includes the prestige of a company and the value of its products. The terms 'corporate design' and 'corporate identity' can be defined by means of these examples. What has been shown here is that at Barmag the designer's contribution to innovation — meaningful innovation — effectively stimulated the growth and profitability of the company.

At this stage let us turn to Enka, where we have also found that 'design' in the broader sense has been an extremely important instrument of innovation. In the following examples I shall try to demonstrate how new materials are designed by our research people. First, some general background:

1. Until about 100 years ago all raw materials that were processed and used were supplied by nature.

2. With the emergence of modern chemistry, artificial products were invented. Man-made fibres and plastics are particular examples. The polyester fibre, for example, was invented by Calico Printers here in this country. But when our company acquired a licence, nobody could tell us what to do with this new fibre. We had to find fields of application for the fibre as it was.

3. A decade or so ago a new development began. Fibres, plastics and membranes began to be designed and constructed to serve certain uses that had been defined before. In other words: new polymer structures were tailor-made for specific end-uses. Designing new materials now means that our marketing people tell the researchers what properties they need and the researchers try to design those materials.

TEXTILE FIBRES

Let me begin with an example in the field of textile fibres. Here, 'designing' starts at the earliest stage of production, for instance by selecting a particular polymer in order to obtain specific properties. With natural fibres, designing must be confined to later stages of processing, such as yarn and fabric construction as well as chemical or mechanical after-treatments.

Modern man-made fibres are generally supposed to be perfectly 'designed' or 'tailored' for their particular application. But still, there is a constant challenge to offer improved properties in terms of optical appearance, drape and handle, especially in the traditional textile fields, such as clothing, household and home furnishing fabrics.

One of these challenges over the past years had been the perfect imitation of natural silk. For thousands of years silk has been the most desirable of all natural fibres. It was an equivalent for luxury — which means that the consumer was prepared to pay a high price for almost everything made from silk.

At this point, let me emphasise that innovation in industry is not just the art of creating something new. What we need in business is meaningful innovation, innovation that gives a company a competitive edge through higher value and higher profitability. This provided a major stimulus for the Enka management and the Enka research people to design a silk-like yarn on the basis of polyester. To achieve it, it very soon became obvious that drastic modifications of the inner and outer physical structure of the filament yarns would be necessary. The inner structure parameters included crystallinity and orientation of the molecular chains. A high crystallinity means high dimensional stability, expressed by a low rate of shrinkage under defined heat treatment. High orientation means high tenacity and high modulus and such inner structure parameters can be influenced by spinning conditions.

The outer fibre morphology can be tailored practically at will. Starting with the single filament fineness or diameter, its cross-section may be round or made into almost any shape, including hollow shapes in the form of a tube or other variations. Lengthwise, the many single filaments that form a filament yarn may be smooth and parallel, or entangled, crimped or twisted, textured into loops, helixes, zig-zags or other configurations. Finally, the filaments may also contain more, less, or no delustring agent, so that all shades from a deep dull finish to bright lustre are possible.

The experience of the textile engineers enabled them to use all these morphological and structural properties to 'design' a fabric in the true sense of the word. The properties of the designed fabric included optical and tactile aspects as well as physiological qualities.

It is unnecessary to describe in great detail how the textile engineers finally succeeded. But they did create a filament yarn about which you could almost say 'this is silk'.

However, even when we had this new yarn the designing work was by no means finished. In order to present to the consumer a silk-like blouse, an evening dress or a tie, practically all processing steps from spinning to finishing had to be individually designed by our textile engineers.

The ability to produce such a silk-like polyester yarn depends on mastering the process of spinning extremely fine filaments. In order to give you an idea of what we are talking about: the textile industry measures the fineness of yarns in 'decitex'. One decitex means that 10,000 m of this yarn weighs one gram! To be able to spin such fine filaments was a mere dream some five to ten years ago. Today we produce 0.5 Dtex yarns. But to arrive at this quite fantastic product, a completely new process had to be designed.

To demonstrate one means of achieving a 0.5 Dtex yarn without difficulty, consider a filament cross-section to be like a sliced orange. The experts call this a bicomponent matrix-fibril structure in a very particular configuration. The triangular sections of about 0.5 Dtex are the fibrils (in this case regular polyester) and the matrix is the material between (in this case polyamide). A method must be found to obtain as many fibrils as possible, each well separated from the other in the finished fabric. To do this it is possible to treat the fabric with certain organic solvents which cause an extremely pronounced shrinkage of one of the components, so that matrix and fibrils are simply forced to separate.

Now, let us discuss what effects were theoretically expected and what effects were actually found. The much larger inner surface of the fabric was expected to enhance water transportation. Experiments with ink or other coloured solutions actually showed a tremendous increase in the wicking effect. We also found — as expected — a very soft feel was achieved in all fabrics. Nevertheless, in this case the desired advantage of softness was accompanied by unwanted poor wrinkle resistance which was also theoretically to be expected.

I will stop talking about textile fibres. We will never solve the wrinkle problem. Why not? Because we don't want to. Our marketing people told us that wrinkling is a part of the luxurious image of silk: no wrinkles, no real silk — so we will leave the wrinkles without being forced to design them out!

MEMBRANES

Let us now consider another very different example of design as a management tool for innovation. You might be surprised to find a man-make fibre company in the field of health care. Looking back it seems to be a rather logical development. But having experienced a part of this process personally, I admit that in the first decades it was more or less incidental, by no means designed. Only in the past five years has our work in this field been designed; it was only then that design — at least in this case — became a management philosophy.

The cuproammonium process, which converts the short cotton fibres into endless, silk-type textile fibres, was invented towards the end of the last century. Since then the production process has been continuously improved. But until the end of the seventies it was still based on the experience of the production people rather than on detailed scientific understanding. It was not necessary to analyse the process more scientifically, because Marlene Dietrich was much more satisfied with her stockings made of Bemberg cuproammonium rayon than of any other material, as you can see from the advertisements of the thirties. In other words, this satisfied the market in the thirties.

In the thirties Bemberg, then a subsidiary of Enka, had also developed a film material to be used for packaging, based on the same process and using very similar production procedures.

During the fifties medical doctors recognised that this flat film packaging material was suitable for separating water and urea from the blood of patients with kidney failure, a disease that, until then, was equal to a sentence of death. The Bemberg material designed for packaging was used as a membrane in a device called a 'dialyser'. This treatment became a world-wide success and is well known under the more popular name 'artificial kidney'. Today there are patients who have already lived for more than 25 years on 'dialysis'.

The great success of dialysis in the sixties and seventies was based wholly on the availability of a man-made membrane that was able to replace the function of the natural kidney.

This situation changed dramatically in the eighties. Different dialysis membranes became available from different companies. Competition between membrane-producing companies started all over the world. The main question was no

127

longer 'Can the patient survive?' but 'How comfortable will his life be?' — a factor that became even more important as kidney transplantation became more successful. Not only Enka, but also the competitors practised the strategy of 'incidental' findings, but this offers only a very narrow basis for future developments and continuous success.

After the great success with the cuprophan membrane, Enka decided at the beginning of the eighties on a different approach concerning future membrane development and started to tackle three major problems:

1. To understand the opportunities and limitations of our production process and polymeric systems on a scientific basis in order to pursue more predictable developments, and thus overcome the dependence on the experience-orientated know-how of the machine-operating personnel.
2. To understand the total system of patient treatment and the factors that are directly or indirectly influenced by our product — a very challenging task to be solved in the environment of a yarn-producing company.
3. To anticipate future demands rather than defend the product with its limitations.

Setting up the know-how basis for this new strategy took between three and four years and was combined with a major adjustment in personnel qualifications, which involved highly qualified and motivated scientists keeping in personal contact with leading medical research groups all over the world. The most interesting fact was that many more properties of the final product and treatment procedure turned out to be influenced by the membrane than expected. Equally, properties that had hitherto been attributed to the membrane turned out to be dependent on other factors.

The re-orientation to design, rather than to finding the products of the future, has been solved to the extent that now membranes can be designed according to the special and changing demands of our customers fast enough to give us a leading edge over our competitors. At least for the time being, Enka seems to be the only company among the membrane producers to have achieved this, and has benefited from a world-wide market share of more than 50 per cent over the past ten years.

PLASTICS

As a last example of product design I wish to turn back to the world of plastic materials — this time not for textile but for industrial applications. We call these materials 'engineering plastics' — although recent developments have made 'engineered or designed plastics' a better name.

Since the early days of macromolecular chemistry an evolution in the development of polymeric materials has taken place, moving from important inventions of polymers more or less by trial and error, and even sometimes by accident, to a systematic approach that we now use.

In the past, polymers were invented with unknown properties. After evaluation of the performance, suitable applications were sought. Today, researchers have access to know-how which enables them to design molecules with predictable properties for the application they have in mind. They can prove the concept by a limited number of experiments, thus saving time and development cost.

What does Enka offer in this field? Let us begin by looking at the consumer market.

Take, as an example, the cross-country ski. Its sole may seem trivial. Certainly you might not imagine any innovative ideas behind it, but you would be wrong. For researchers an exciting story is hidden behind this application. I guess you would immediately advise the use of a suitable rubber formulation for the sole, and, in principle, you would be right. Ten years ago this was the solution. In the meantime cross-country skiing has become much more popular. Clever research work has developed new and cheaper techniques to produce ski, bindings and shoes. The sole material has to be tough and very flexible at low temperatures. It also has to be processed easily and should be assembled most economically. In order to fulfil

129

all these requirements the challenge was to develop a material with properties of natural rubber, but the easy processability of man-made thermoplastics.

Time is too short to explain all this in detail. The problem really was how to design a material which is processable at elevated temperatures (chemical crosslinks not being allowed), but which is also highly flexible at use temperature. This requires the presence of a certain mechanism, which will prevent the chain molecules from gliding off under tension.

The problem can be reduced to the question: Can we design macromolecules that form a 'highly viscous liquid' at use temperature, but interconnected by something that is thermoplastic at elevated temperatures in order to behave as an elastic and to avoid the chemical crosslink reaction for easy processing?

In short, is it possible to compose a polymer that is 'liquid' but also 'solid' and linear? The answer is YES. The need was to combine a soft polymer (the liquid at use temperature) with a hard polymer (the solid at use temperature) and make sure that both were thermoplastics!

This concept is very exciting and has generated great interest. The rest is chemistry — composing the molecules with the right performance. The polymer chemists were able to prove quickly that the concept worked, although at first the combination of hard and soft could not completely fulfil the requirements of our application. But by changing the structure of the hard and soft components somewhat and by playing with the ratio of hard:soft, we improved the performance quickly. Even more important is that the concept allowed us to design thermoplastic elastomers systematically for a range of different applications.

Today the market is served by several families of thermoplastic elastomers manufactured by many companies. For the polyetheresters, Enka has chosen Arnitel and continues to design special grades based on the same concept.

Returning to the title of this lecture, the Arnitel case may be considered as typical. The identified market demand had to be met by innovation and the management tool was managing the design of a new product.

I have tried to demonstrate this process of designing new products in different fields of the Enka Group's activities. One key question remains to be answered: to what extent did all this contribute to better profitability for Enka and what was the impact on the product mix of the company?

It is almost impossible to answer these questions in detail. But the change in the product mix of Enka over the last ten years is such that while the sales of textile fibres have shrunk by 40 per cent through drastic reduction of capacity, the remaining products have almost doubled their sales volume; our machine factory, Barmag, has more than doubled its turnover in four years! And textile fibres, in which we were making a loss in the 1970s, are now profitable again, thanks to a 50 per cent reduction of capacities plus the designing of new products such as silk-like polyester.

The best summary might be a quotation from a technical memorandum written by the United States Office of Technological Assessment in September 1986. It reads: 'With advanced ceramics and composites the very concepts of materials and structures merge together, joined by the new concept of integrated design. Such a design capability requires the development of sophisticated software for computer modelling and analysis. The diversity of structural trials available today offers many options to the designer.'

I do hope that those of you who are or intend to work as designers will make optimum use of all these options — provided that you stay in fields outside those of my own company's activities!

PART 3

Design, Retailing and the Business Environment

The Advancement of Design Awareness

Sir Terence Conran

Sir Terence Conran needs little introduction: a textile designer whose first forays into retailing were centred on food and the kitchen. He now runs Storehouse, a major retailing enterprise which owns a number of high street chains including BhS, Richards, Mothercare, Heals and, not least, Habitat, his original retailing base. However, in spite of his undoubted commercial success, his name will be best connected with his social influence on the life-style of the British middle class through the pioneering product development at Habitat in the early fifties.

His paper describes the explosion of interest in design since the encouragement given to it by government in the early eighties. He discusses the leadership of the retail sector in Britian in the field of design and the consequent benefits to the economy. He concludes with a discussion of future trends in retailing and a cautionary note about the limitations of design.

A second paper by Terence Conran, a case study of Storehouse, appears in the final section.

Mrs Thatcher has exhorted retailers, manufacturers, public authorities and the City to look to good design as the solution to many of the commercial, industrial and social ills of this country. And it has not been just lip service. The government has put up £20 million, spread over five years, to get things started — and this has encouraged those who are in a position to do so to invest heavily in this newly recognised resource.

As a result, a metamorphosis has taken place. Designers are rapidly losing the image of arty aesthetes who would never darken a factory door, and are emerging as vital components of the business scene. The design colleges are responding at last, producing graduates who have been trained to understand the needs and constraints of industry and commerce, who can design products which look as good and work as well as those produced anywhere else in the world, who can interpret fashion and mood. Designers of this calibre deserve and need to reach the highest level of responsibility within their companies.

Retailers are at the forefront of those seeking to benefit from the additional value design can bring to their businesses. One of the reasons for this is that they have direct contact with the consumer, they know at first hand just how demanding, fickle and sophisticated their customers have become. The public, educated by travel, the media and a growing band of retailers who recognise that well-designed, good-looking products will sell better, have a new-found taste for excellence, and will now settle for nothing less.

The role of the retailing industry in helping to bring about the economic recovery of this country has only recently been fully recognised. By stimulating demand, and streamlining distribution, retailers create opportunities for British manufacturers in the home market. Retailing today is a healthy service industry which can breathe new life into some of those manufacturing industries that have been afflicted and chastened by the recession. Close communication between consumers and manufacturers, via the retailer, is vital to Britain, because in the long run it is national economic madness to have high streets full of innovative and highly professional retailers who exist to distribute mainly foreign goods. This country needs a sound and profitable home market for its manufacturing industries. Even if it no longer employs such a significant part of the workforce, the earnings from manufacturing still account for a high proportion of the money in people's pockets.

So what has happened to retailing in recent years that has brought about its powerful resurgence?

In a word, competition. As the flab of high inflation was stripped away, retailers were forced to build real profit muscles. They looked to their image on the high street. Was it unique, sharply defined, and appealing to the target market? They looked to their products. Were they well made, well priced, attractive to the customer and, above all, exclusive? They looked to their stores. Were they creating the right ambience for the products, were they comfortable to shop in and easy to run?

Thus retailing, one of the most competitive industries in Britain today, has become a very active, innovative and exciting scene where businesses vie with each other to gain the edge. Design has proved a means of providing this edge — particularly in the hands of the larger retailers. Products designed and manufactured exclusively for the retailer cannot be sold at a cheaper price anywhere else, own brands can be developed, special store design can exactly fit the needs of the customer and the style of the products, the corporate image can be strengthened and sharpened through distinctive graphics and packaging. All this adds up to a shop with its own particular personality which will endear itself to its *own* customers.

Design is now recognised as a multi-layered discipline which should be built into all the marketing and promotional strategies of a business right from their inception. The good design of products and stores, and a strong corporate identity, has quickly become a prerequisite to retailers for survival. Those who understand the importance of design as an integral factor of their retailing philosophy and are prepared to make the financial investment in it, have quickly seen a return in increased sales. The retailer who brings in a designer to do a quick face-lift job on a tired product or concept is wasting his money — there are too many competitors around who understand the real contribution that good design can make to their businesses, and they know that every tiny detail matters. The old adage 'Retail is detail' has taken on a new relevance — price tickets, packaging, letterheads, every smallest detail must build and support an entire image, unique and exclusive to one company.

There are other factors too which have spurred the retail sector into handing out some of the largest design contracts. The recognition of shopping as a leisure time activity, rivalling holidays abroad, sport, TV and eating out in popularity, has caused an enormous upheaval in the retail trade. The public have made it quite plain that they look to retailers to make shopping a pleasurable activity in an atmosphere in which they can enjoy spending their money.

Hence, retailers have been strenuously considering how they are going to meet this expectation, and many new measures are in the pipeline that will revolutionise the shopping habits in this country — liberalised opening hours and Sunday trading are just two of these.

Following on from this, the design of store interiors, shopping precincts and malls, both new and old, has received a great deal of attention from retailers and property owners who already know that a pleasing and sympathetic ambience can have a remarkably beneficial effect on sales.

Store design is one of the first encounters a customer has with a retailer's image and its importance cannot be over-emphasised. All the major chainstore names, including those in my own Group, have in recent years carried out major remodelling programmes in their stores, and have seen their sales (and profits) rise dramatically as a result. In our experience the merchandise in a refurbished store takes added value from its setting, and customers frequently remark on the new ranges even where they have remained essentially the same. The ambience clearly has the power to alter the customer's perception of the offer.

In our own Group, sales in those Mothercare and Richards stores that were completely revamped have far exceeded those where there was no new design input, even though they were all selling the same merchandise. With Heal's the redesign of an old and failing department store into retail space for a group of our own related retail activities with offices above, has been a great success.

The out-of-town superstore complex is another phenomenon that is likely to become more popular, especially with a liberalisation of shopping hours. Served by excellent communications, free from traffic congestion and parking problems, these sites offer a chance for designers to create an environment in which it will be a pleasure to shop and work. The development of such complexes is obviously a major undertaking and large multiple retailers are finding it beneficial to work together to attract customers from considerable distances for a pleasant day out. BhS and Sainsbury's have formed such a partnership, and Marks & Spencer and Tesco have followed the pattern.

All this can be bad news for the small retailer who does not have the resources or volumes to achieve exclusivity or a price advantage over the large multiples. His future must lie in the quality end of the market, supplying a very high level of service to the customer, or in specialised areas of merchandise, or both. In these shops the quality and devotion to design will really have to reign supreme, and the liveliest new ideas must constantly be put before the public to provide an irresistible temptation.

To use design effectively in retailing it is essential that the retailer knows who he is selling to. This is particularly important in the fashion industry, as has been demonstrated by the continued success of the Next chain. In the female market the design of clothes, stores and advertising are very specifically targeted to attract 25–40-year-old women. In comparison, Marks & Spencer, who have introduced some excellent ranges for the same target group, turned in relatively disappointing results — the customer could not spot the fashion potential in garments dully displayed on racks lost in a sea of other clothes designed to appeal to just about everybody, and could not try things on without buying them first. Even good products cannot overcome bad presentation.

Similarly, the visible image, however powerful and cohesive, is of little use unless it is supported by a strong infrastructure of operational systems. No retailing business will survive with 'just a pretty face'. It needs to develop faster and more accurate communications — between shop and warehouse, head office and manufacturers and all the other possible computations, to bring a better service to the customer.

The large retailers have been experimenting with various electronic data-processesing methods for the past fifteen years or so. In some cases the learning curve has been painful and many found in the early days that the investment in cumbersome mainframe systems did not produce the hoped-for results. The rapid development of powerful mini and micro computer systems has changed all that. Micro-chip technology has now become so flexible and sophisticated that it makes economic sense for even small retailers to invest in computerised systems.

And here again design has a part to play. Systems, as well as merchandise and other visual aspects of a company, must be well designed if they are to work properly and not produce more paper than they do useful information.

The electronic and laser point of sale systems, which many large stores are adopting, will revolutionise the lives of shop staff too, releasing them from the drudgery of till ringing, picking lists, kimbal processing, and all the routine minutiae of keeping a store stocked with the right merchandise at the right time. Armed with immediate and detailed sales information, a retailer can be lighter on his feet and more responsive to the market he is aiming to serve.

Manufacturers must follow the dictates of the retailers. And so they are, but in many cases it is rather like watching a dinosaur follow a hare. Retailers are still too often having to look abroad for sources of merchandise which, with a bit of ingenuity and entrepreneurialism, could easily be produced in this country. If manufacturers can succeed in fulfilling the needs of the informed and discerning consumer in this country he will doubtless have a product that will be equally successful abroad. But let me make one thing quite clear, while retailers will lead, manufacturers must also expect to contribute with design and innovation — they must never allow themselves to take the easy route of just being told what to do, otherwise they will lose their spirit and essential entrepreneurialism.

But, one small word of warning. This new-found regard for design has its pitfalls. The danger is that we will expect it to be a panacea for all ills, that it will somehow compensate for weak management and unsound financial administration, or that having made an investment in design it does not need to be sustained. Products and corporate identities become outdated, the marketplace is continually evolving and competitors are always snapping at each other's heels; to be successful constant fine tuning is required to meet the mood of the consumer or, better still, to tell him what that mood will be before he has realised it.

Information Technology and Office Design

Dr Francis Duffy

Dr Francis Duffy is a partner in Duffy Eley Giffone Worthington, a design and architectural practice which specialises in space planning and the urban environment. He has recently undertaken two important studies into the effect of information technology in office buildings, entitled ORBIT 1 *and* ORBIT 2. *He has also been the leading figure in the establishment of the profession of facilities management in Britain. His paper deals with the recent growth in information technology and how it is affecting the buildings in which we work and more generally the urban environment of the City of London as it has emerged as a major international financial services centre.*

WHY SPEAK ABOUT BUILDINGS?

Architecture is frequently used by information technology specialists as a metaphor to describe systems of information technology but the ordinary, real, day-to-day architecture of the working environment is usually taken for granted. This is a mistake. Telecommunications are in one way or another affecting the office environment at least as profoundly as did the first primitive instruments of office work, the telephone and typewriter, when they revolutionised the office building in Chicago one hundred years ago, creating the prototype of the city of the 20th century. What we ought to be seeking today is a vision of what the new, intelligent city of the next century will be like.

Cities are aggregates of buildings. To understand why cities are the way they are and, perhaps more importantly what they could be like, it helps to make comparisons between different cultures. Compare, for example, Tokyo, London and New

141

York. It also helps to analyse the factors which intertwine to make office buildings:

1. Information technology ie the means by which office work, the storage, processing and transformation of information, is carried out;
2. Organisation ie the 'glue' that holds people together in organisations as well as the structures that motivate and reward them;
3. Building technology ie the means by which buildings are constructed and serviced; and
4. Facilities management ie the procurement and management of environmental resources to achieve organisational objectives through time.

Using such a framework it is possible to make comparisons between office buildings created by different organisations in different cultures. Such a comparative approach offers the extremely practical possibility, in a rapidly changing world, of helping organisations find the most appropriate kind of office accommodation to meet their needs, now and in the future.

In London irreversible changes have already taken place in the quality of office space being provided for the emerging financial services industry and, more importantly, in the expectations of the users of this kind of space. These changes are spectacular and in most respects are best measured by an order of magnitude rather than by a simple percentage increase.

A shock of this scale has had the beneficial effect of making everyone think harder — users about their needs, developers about their market, architects and engineers about their designs, builders about their methods of construction, institutions about their returns.

The most beneficial aspect is the closing of the feedback loop between consumers and suppliers — the realisation that there *is* a way of communicating emerging needs to the suppliers of buildings. Not all users are the same. Not all buildings are equally good for all purposes. Facilities managers, already enhanced by the new criticality of information technology in building design, now have available to them tools which can be used to match supply and demand.

AN ORDER OF MAGNITUDE

The scale of the changes taking place, not only in London, but throughout Europe in the provision of space for the financial services industry is summed up by the current proposal to build an enormous American-style office tower (architect Helmut Jahn) in the centre of Frankfurt. The function of the tower is to accommodate American banks and other parts of the financial services industry. The symbolic significance of the tower is the acceptance, for the first time on a large scale, of a North American style of office development, in a city where all the prestige has hitherto been found in custom-built offices, very often low rise.

What has happened already in London is similar. The stock of office space, which has gradually and painfully been built up on top of a medieval street plan and byzantine patterns of land ownership through incremental development — which has been influenced as much by planners as by the necessity to break investments into easily fundable chunks, is now obviously inadequate by international standards and totally unsuitable for the new business activity generated by the approach of Big Bang. The first warnings were expressed in the 1982 ORBIT study which charted the impact of information technology (IT) and diagnosed the phenomenon of premature obsolescence — defined as the moment when the cost of retrofitting a building to bring it up to modern IT standards exceeds the cost of rebuilding.

Big Bang is, of course, very largely the child of information technology. Without the possibility of moving vast sums of money round the world electronically and without the massive investments in manpower, communications, equipment and computers which are required to grasp the full potential of the financial opportunity, the more legalistic procedures of deregulation of the stock market would hardly be so significant.

Paradoxically the power of telecommunications to disperse information world wide is paralleled by the opposite tendency to channel and concentrate it into three or four major world financial centres: Tokyo, Los Angeles perhaps, New York certainly, and London, more than Paris, Zurich or Frankfurt.

What this means for architecture has become all too obvious. Instead of 50,000 square feet being considered a very substantial unit of space by large organisations, 500,000 square feet seems more comfortable; instead of being content with floors as small as 5000 square feet, big, simple, continuous, uncluttered office floors of up to 50,000 square feet are at a premium; instead of being content with electrical power loading of 1 or 2 watts per square foot, the call is for 10 or even more for trading floors.

Standards have increased tenfold in these and in other respects. More international competition has revealed the inadequacy of the traditional London speculative office building. More risk means that buildings cannot be allowed to fail. Far, far better facilities management is in demand because buildings are now part of the computer. They have become the infrastructure of services upon which commercial success and even commercial survival depends.

HOW INFORMATION TECHNOLOGY
IS REVOLUTIONISING THE OFFICE

Until recently the office building was considered to be an extremely simple device, easy to design and construct — even easier to use. The typical office user was a clerk using little or no electronic technology, apart from the telephone. Even the computer when it first arrived was an isolated phenomenon, dealt with in the basement, in an entirely different kind of office environment. Information technology in its newest forms is highly integrated. It is also wild, capable of cropping up anywhere in the office, not under one department's total control, constantly and inherently susceptible to change. Not surprisingly as the ratio of terminals to office staff narrows, the more work the office fabric has to do to accommodate a variety of demands for space, for cabling, for cooling, for security, and a whole catalogue of other special conditions. Less obviously, information technology is revolutionising the structure of the office organisation, getting rid of the lowly-paid clerks who used to be the bulk of the office population, and replacing them with acquisitive, demanding professionals and managers, all of whom tend to want *more* from the office environment. However, by far the most important consequence of information technology is the realisation that the office fabric, in all its manifestations — shell, services, scenery — must be capable of being adapted to meet changing needs. The office building is much more central to organisational success and survival because it carries the services upon which telecommunications rely.

BUILDING EVALUATIONS

The first ORBIT study (DEGW, Building Use Studies, EOSYS) carried out in Britain in 1982–83 was the first really coherent account of the fundamental changes being wrought by information technology on the fabric of the office.

One of the key ideas generated in ORBIT 1 was building appraisal — the careful comparison by standardised criteria of building performance. Since ORBIT 1 was concerned chiefly with the direct and indirect effects of information technology (such as the masses of cabling, the hot spots and the increasing demands of a professionalising office workforce) the emphasis was on *capacity*, the basic ability of any given building to provide, for example, plenty of vertical and horizontal ducting for cables, finely zoned air conditioning with back-up capacity to cool wherever a concentration of machines decided to settle, or to provide for demanding users the ability to mix cellular offices and open plan as required.

If organisational success is directly correlated with building form, then it follows that measures of building capacity are an essential component of architecture and facilities management so that the supply of environmental resources and the demands of changing organisations can be matched.

The follow up to the British ORBIT studies was a North American version, ORBIT 2 (carried out in 1985 by DEGW, Harbinger, and Professors Sims and Becker from Cornell University), which quickly developed into a technique for measuring the capacity of buildings to accommodate the new technology. ORBIT 2 recognised first the importance of users being able to determine their own mix of priorities, second the certainty that such priorities would be different from one firm to the next, or from one sector of the office market to another, and third that such profiles of demand are more than likely to change through time as firms develop, mature or decline. ORBIT 2's vision of demand is to describe all organisations in terms of their changing positions in a vast field made up of measures of varying degrees of change and of varying levels of complexity in the way organisations carry out their tasks. In this way not only can the present demand for environmental resources be charted but also now the trajectory of change is likely to affect these needs.

Two kinds of demand are obvious, neither of which varies greatly between the UK and the USA: first the direct impact of the changing technology itself and second the indirect social and organisational consequences. An attempt was made to categorise all office organisations in terms of their pattern of change (rapid change or relative stability) and the nature of their work (routine work or non routine, more complex, integrative tasks).

Such a typology allows us to place any organisation in an overall field, spotting where it is now, where it came from and where it is likely to be in a few years' time. Not only that, the ORBIT 2 method is designed to allow organisations to decide what exactly their priorities are, how these are likely to change, and what environmental resources are appropriate to accommodate these changing needs.

This all sounds complicated and a far cry from the City. It is nevertheless an essential precursor of any statement about what the future City office building should be like. *There is no perfect building. There is no such thing as a static organisation.* The task of the architect (and the letting agent, the developer, the planner, the facilities manager) is to meet changing demands with a changing stock of space.

In our terms it has led to three particular City office accommodation studies, carried out either for ourselves or for our clients, Rosehaugh Stanhope:

— *Eleven contemporary office buildings* (carried out for Rosehaugh Stanhope): a point-by-point comparison of the larger office buildings, available at a certain point in time, in or near the City, which would be suitable for the financial services industry.

— *Trading in two Cities* (also for Rosehaugh Stanhope): a comparison of trading floors in London and New York belonging to eight of the largest trading organisations. The comparison was of existing and planned facilities in both Cities.

— *The changing City* (DEGW): which extends the previous work on the requirements of the larger financial services organisations, into equally detailed studies of the requirements of a number of related but different kinds of firm — clearing banks, foreign banks, insurance, professional firms such as City accountants and solicitors. In this way the requirements for environmental resources of different sectors of City organisations are being systematically built up and compared. The idea of the *profile of requirements* is becoming a practical tool for building appraisal.

THE NEW CITY OFFICE BUILDING

So what is the new City office building turning out to be like? The most fascinating possibility is that an altogether novel and more convincing form of office building is being evolved — much better than the existing British stock, more flexible and adaptive than German custom-built offices — either *Bürolandschaft* or the new cellular format — and (most interesting of all) more functional and better serviced than the typical North American downtown office building. One great advantage which London enjoys is relatively low density of

147

development; the second advantage is the large simple sites which are becoming available away from the old City core — to the north and east, in Fleet Street, in Docklands, of course, and even in the West End.

It is worth considering the main criteria for the design of these buildings in turn.

The first set concerns location, accessibility and image — where the building is, how easy it is to get to, and what it says to visitors and staff. As the City changes, and as information technology loosens the bonds which used to determine location, more sites have become available, especially to the north and east, which are big enough to allow the planning of conveniently sized floors while retaining a high degree of accessibility to attract skilled staff from all around London.

The second set of criteria is about the overall quantity of space available in each building. Small units of space are no good for the financial services industry because the over-riding problem is to find the quarter or half million square feet that are necessary to house under one roof several, once separate, units and yet still allow space for growth. Space is precious and the efficiency of each building in providing usable space (exclusive of ducts, lavatories, stairs and circulation) becomes critical.

The third set of criteria deals with the shape and planning potential for each floor. Big floors are currently wanted (20,000, 30,000 even 40,000 square feet) which are clean and continuous so that artificial breaks within departmental units are avoided. Such floors will be largely open plan, at least at the beginning, but will also need to cope with an increasing amount of enclosure as the demand for individual offices and for specialised rooms increases. Intrusive columns are damaging to planning flexibility. Some floors will be used for trading, and there is a strong demand by a small number of organisations to bring very large numbers of traders (300–500) together in continuous, highly interactive, easily comprehensible, marketplace-like spaces. Aspect is not important for trading floors; for ordinary office workers to be able to look across the city or into an atrium is highly desirable. The cleverest building is one that is capable of providing, in shifting proportions, as demand changes, continuous bands of office space (60 feet deep or so) as well as trading space (up to two or three times that depth).

The fourth set of criteria takes into account the severe demands made on building services by this degree of planning flexibility. This is where the greatest pressure is evident. Individual local control of the environment is needed at the same time as greater overall cooling capacity; greater capacity for power and data has to be combined with generous vertical and horizontal distribution; movement of people follows quite a different logic from the distribution of services; new kinds of lighting are introduced to be compatible with heavy use of VDU screens. It is no longer enough to scatter a few, small lifts around and hope to meet the increasingly complex movement requirements in a large office building. The idea of one neat, centralised core for both movement of people and distribution of services is as anachronistic as the notion of universal, infinitely flexible office space which can meet any demand, anywhere. In other words, the design formula for satisfying the rapidly changing servicing demands of the financial services industry is quite unlike that of the conventional office building.

The fifth set of criteria is concerned with the complex of facilities — parking, shopping, restaurants, storage vaults — which support the modern office. The idea of the office as consisting simply of desks and chairs as far as the eye can see is no longer true. Any building for complex financial organisations must not only contain within itself adequate support but must depend on additional services in the vicinity.

Finally, timing and availability are critical in the financial services industry. Every minute counts — delay is measured in millions of dollars per hour. Hence the relatively novel concept (in London, at least) of shell and core. This issue concerns the freedom the incoming tenant has to negotiate with the landlord about the shape, servicing and fitting out of the new building. The more freedom, the less the chance of wasteful duplication of design effort, of constructional expense and, above all, of loss of time.

Tenant demand differs from one sector of the City office

149

market to another. Unlike a bank, a law firm might be content with an offpitch site and small, fragmented floors; it may very well insist on a very high degree of enclosure for private offices but be relatively relaxed about cooling and cabling systems. Landlord services may be a great attraction but timing may not be so critical because expansion is within controllable limits.

However, given what is known about the new financial services industry, the requirements are clear. The building blocks that combine to form the most appropriate office are:

— Central but non-traditional locations to the north and east of the old City core;
— Large aggregates of space with the potential for expansion and initial subletting without breaking security;
— Big, clean, continous floors of standard office space (60 feet deep) which are capable of being both open plan and cellular to a degree, some of which can be made (reversibly if possible) twice or thrice as deep to be suitable for dealing floors;
— A high level of electrical and mechanical services which can cope with high but fluctuating demands in different parts of the organisation; good access for people and goods; the capacity to subdivide; the ability to introduce new forms of lighting and local-services control;
— An excellent range of support spaces (ie non traditional office space for storage, machine rooms, restaurants, training centres) as well as the ability to zone ancillary space on each floor. Shopping and other amenities for staff should be adjacent.
— Availability on time to meet demand on time and to negotiate the exact shape, servicing and fitting out early enough to avoid duplication and waste.

These features have not happened by accident.

A catalytic role is being played by the new generation of facilities managers who have a new importance in the procurement of environmental resources because in operational terms buildings have become so much more important. Facilities managers in large international organisations have formidable purchasing power which they are using to good effect to ensure

organisational efficiency. Such features have also been ham-
mered out in prototypical form in such projects as the new
Corporation of Lloyd's building by Richard Rogers and Norman
Foster's Hong Kong and Shanghai Bank — the two most innovative office buildings of the late 20th century to be found
anywhere in the world.

WHERE NEXT? THE BUILDING AND THE CITY

The types of office building in common use in both Europe and
North America have remained remarkably static for at least 50
years since the last great burst of inventions in the 1930s:
lighting (the fluorescent tube) and air conditioning (systems
adjustable to small rooms). While it is true there is wide
variation between North American and European rooms, within
these local norms the prevailing reality in office design on both
sides of the Atlantic has been on the whole uninventive, even
minimalist. Such conservatism cannot prevail under the new
conditions caused by the widespread diffusion of information
technology.

Concentration co-exists with dispersal. Old commuting
patterns are being reinforced but traditional locational patterns
are being dissolved and replaced. Old buildings serve the
newest organisations but older, more established firms must
find entirely new buildings to survive. Rapid change is genera-
ting the need for simpler buildings but simultaneously for more
customised interiors.

The rich fabric of the City has always been able to some
extent to accommodate change. What is striking about this new
wave of rebuilding the City, which is stimulated by information
technology, is that it is not only the City but the buildings
themselves which must accommodate change.

London has not only the *possibility* of changing its
skin — it *must* do so if it is to achieve the infrastructure
required to continue to compete with New York and Tokyo (not
to mention Frankfurt, with its proposed Helmut Jahn tower).
Unfortunately, we may have lost the habit of urban coherence,

not having the rich North American tradition of urban design, nor a planning framework which can transcend such arbitrary boundaries as the City, the LDDC area, Islington, Hackney, Tower Hamlets and Southwark.

In Dallas a vision of a new City would come from a mixture of market forces and oligarchic manipulation by a handful of very rich citizens, immensely proud of their city and anxious to secure its future. No doubt in Frankfurt the vision will owe much to a strong Lord Mayor. Is it conceivable that such a vision — comparable to Lutyens's and Abercrombie's grand scheme for the reconstruction of central London in 1943 but with its feet firmly on solid economic and social ground — can be generated today?

The impact of telecommunications and information technology is nothing less than the rebuilding of both buildings and the urban fabric to create the cities of the 21st century. To accompany it what we need is good old-fashioned planning.

Impact of Design on the Retail Landscape
Rodney Fitch

Rodney Fitch is a designer who runs the design consultancy which bears his name. He founded the business ten years ago and it is now one of the largest in Britain and a publicly quoted company. Fitch consults in a wide range of design areas, but its reputation has been built on the design work for a number of major national retail chains.

Design and its impact on retailing is the subject of this paper. Fitch argues that the design consultant needs to take account of social and economic changes if he is to provide practical and successful solutions for his clients. He sees this as especially important in a business sector where competition is increasing and where too many retailers have too much space from which they sell too little undifferentiated merchandise.

INTRODUCTION

There is, at present, in this country an unprecedented interest in design. Design in the 1980s has captured the imagination as a 'tool for better business', in a way similar, it has been suggested, to marketing in the 1950s. Wally Olins also happens to have pointed out that the 'rise and rise of marketing coincided with the worst decline ever in the British economy'. Let us hope that there are no precedents there!

But why this interest in design, and what form does it take?

There are several interested groups, apart from the business community, including the government, the media, the educators, the public and the design profession itself. I will examine each briefly.

The government chief advocates are Mrs Thatcher and

John Butcher. You might have seen Mrs Thatcher on TV waving designer torches. Facile though that may have seemed, it is probably true that this government has banged the drum for design-led innovation like no other for 100 years. But what is the government doing about it? Its activities take a number of forms. There are those by the Minister — John Butcher at the Department of Trade and Industry — and his mandarins. The budget allocated to supporting design is approximately £20m, increasing at 5 per cent pa. There is the government-funded consultancy scheme which, at the time of writing, has helped some 3000 firms. There is the figurehead of the interested Prime Minister herself. There is increased help to the Design Council. And there have been numerous debates in the House of Commons, a conference on 'Innovation and Design', a NEDO working party on design etc, etc.

The media now features some twelve specialist magazines on design, six of which have been brought out in the past three years. There are regular articles in *The Guardian*, *The Financial Times*, *Harpers* and so on. Channel 4 has produced two six-part series on design. BBC2 has produced a number of programmes; and there is more to come.

If there is a growing awareness of design in business generally, the retail sector has used design in recent years like no other. Mintel has recently published an interesting survey into retailer attitudes to design. It found, for example:

1. Of those retailers using design, over 65 per cent had found the experience successful across a range of important criteria.
2. A staggering 86 per cent of respondents had embarked upon a design programme during the past three years. (A similar poll by *Marketing Week* indicates that 56 per cent of retailers will embark on a 'design experience' next year.)
3. That this design activity has been pushed across over 75 per cent of most outlets.
4. That an average of 60 per cent of polled retailers regarded those things which are at the heart of a retail design programme — namely environment, presentation and communication — as of the highest priority.

The educators include places such as the London Business School, with its Design Management Unit and various courses for its business administration and executive students. There are a growing number of general design-related and CAD courses. And of interest in this respect is the reorganisation of the Royal College of Art under Jocelyn Stevens, and the reawakened interest in design at the Victoria and Albert Museum (where it all started), where the Boilerhouse attracted some 1000 visitors per week.

Public interest is also manifested through its support of design-led businesses, such as Habitat and Next, among others; by the million visitors annually to the Design Centre; by the purchase of the 'Better by Design' General Motors car range such as the Astra models; and by the fact that the Boilerhouse had over half a million visitors since it opened in 1982.

The design profession is itself the marketplace example of design success. The fee turnover of the top ten design consultancies has quadrupled in the past three years. The same top consultancies now employ some 1200 people, and offer a diversified range of services, including the design of cars, shops, buildings etc. There has been a loosening of the traditional grip of architects and in-house design departments. Moreover the new designers are fêted, even knighted, and financially rewarded. The five design-related businesses which had a stock market quote in 1985 enjoy a combined capitalisation in excess of £100 million.

From this brief resumé, one might be excused for assuming that all is going quite well. The government is interested, the public are aware, and the designers are busy. But one area where precious little is happening — as you will well know — is among our manufacturing industries where design is not equated with added value but more with limp-wristed decorators, sharp copy lines and the fallacious macho belief that 'the British public doesn't fall for that design flannel'. Plainly, much needs to be done in this area. If we are to believe Lord Aldington, as I feel we must, time is urgent. We appear to be very good at selling things and rather bad at making things. The manufacturing sector can and must learn from their retail sector colleagues.

155

At this point I will turn to the core matter of this paper — the impact of the design factor on the retail landscape.

Retailers are at the sharp end of consumer affairs. The principal difference, it seems to me, between themselves and manufacturers is that retailers are in touch with the marketplace. They listen to their customers, and manufacturers do not. They are also aware of two principal issues which, I submit, have driven and conditioned the monumental changes now taking place in the retail scene. These are (1) the changing and developing nature of the society in which we live and (2) the increasingly competitive marketplace in which we operate.

In planning how to adapt to a society that, it has been suggested, is changing more rapidly than at any time since the 1840s, there are many fundamental issues of which I think we should be aware. Some of sociological issues are well documented. They include:

1. *Changing age profiles* There is a fundamental change taking place in the age profile of our nation. We are growing older. The number of 16–24-year-olds will decrease by 20 per cent and the over 25s will increase by 10 per cent by 1995.
2. *Changing household profiles* Household profiles are changing. We will see smaller families and a dramatic increase in single-parent households by the end of the century. Instead of asking how many children in the family, we will be asking how many parents!
3. *Urban decline* Our inner-city centres are declining at an alarming rate. In terms of the decline of urban fabric and social values, take the instance of the supermarket chain in Liverpool who have had permission to brick up their shop windows because of vandalism. In demographic terms, London's population has declined by 10 per cent and in other major towns by as much as 18 per cent over the past decade. Indeed, practically every conurbation above 100,000 is declining while those above 5000 are growing.
4. *Two nations* We must address the problem of an increasing polarisation of wealth and opportunities — the creation of 'two nations'. This is highlighted by the concentration of

wealth in the South and Southeast, and far higher unemployment in other parts of the country. This has important implications geographically for investment and 'ideas development'.

5. *Individuality* We find consistently in our research a new kind of individuality beginning to assert itself. People increasingly cry: 'Don't regiment me. Don't institutionalise me. Treat me as an individual.' You have only to observe personal fashion to see obvious examples of this. An appreciation of this particular trend is fundamental to any future ideas for successful retailing.

6. *Social class* Another discernible change is the way in which old ideas of social class are breaking down. In the old days there was a social class readily identifiable as the 'carriage trade', but now the equivalent people will happily shop at Harrods one day and in a street market another. They will buy Armani one day and second-hand clothing from Antiquarius the next. The idea that you can classify people by the old ABC1 rules of thumb seems to us to have gone completely by the board. We must find more appropriate ways of defining social class because in our view this will help us to understand and diagnose our customers' needs, life-styles and expectations more accurately.

7. *Women* Finally, over 50 per cent of women now work. The number has increased by 8 per cent, or over 1 million in the last decade. Women are becoming more powerful, more independent, vocal and discerning. As much as 80 per cent of discretionary retail spending may now be decided by women. Look at the launch of 'working women' magazines and shops such as Next, Principles, and others geared to the working woman.

It is the attitudinal shifts, however, which complement the dry demographic statistics of a society in change, which in our view are the most exciting and challenging for the designer and retailer alike. This is reflected in a substantial and significant shift by consumers away from 'the need for a better standard of living' to a 'demand for a better quality of life'. Whereas at one time people went to Butlins, it is now to Cosmos; in Virgin, there is now even a people's airline. At one time people would have been happy to have had any car, even without a heater. Now cars come with everything, there are two or three per family, and design really matters. It is the same with places to live. Flats, and particularly high-rise flats, are out. People want 'homes', and 172,000 of them bought council dwellings in 1984. What is more, they want to make 'homes'.

In other words, today's consumers take a more qualitative, more judgemental, more egocentric view. Our society will demand increasingly to be treated as individuals, rather than as retail statistics. These individuals will demand from stores more than just cheap prices. They will be looking for value — expressed in terms of:

new ideas — not the same tired old formulas
added value — not 'self service' as an excuse for no service
solutions — not more problems
service — which means not only 'stuff' — eg being in stock — but better 'staff', who are trained and more helpful
convenience — staying open, getting the department adjacencies right, recognising that customer convenience is not necessarily the same as retailer convenience
quality — as the American historian Barbra Tuchman says: 'Quality is *not* subjective. The judgement is subjective, but the condition is not!'
experience — hands on, and involvement in the process
choice — not just the 'two lines only syndrome'; for too long no choice has masqueraded as efficiency.

Competition is the second key issue. Clearly we all operate within a competitive environment. But, because we live in a democratic society where freedom of choice is imperative, with increasing consumer demands, a more or less zero-growth market, and the likelihood of further legislation towards de-regulation, competition is likely to become even fiercer. And there are other forces at play — all of which explain why design has been used by smart retailers to sharpen their cutting edge. These other considerations include:

1. *An overfooted market* There are too many shops. The market is grossly overfooted. If we take as an example the growth of superstores, in 17 years over 11 million square feet has been added to the stock of retailing. URPI suggests 800 to 1000 superstores will exist by the end of the century. Plainly somebody has to go.
2. *Shopping centres* The same applies to shopping centres. There are now 500, with 50 more under construction. We estimate that 80 per cent of the UK population now lives within a 15-minute drive of two. Many are growing old, and competition within the sector grows very fierce. In short, we now see competition not only among brands, but also between places.
3. *Undermerchandising* There is too little merchandise and too little choice. Confusion arises from the questionable idea that *wide* range means *real* choice.
4. *Undifferentiated shops* We see too many shops selling the same ranges of merchandise. There is too much similarity around, aptly shown in any one of a number of advertisements showing one product or range and an endless list of stockists alongside.
5. *Over-centralisation* Many shoppers say that there is too much uniformity in the high street and in retailing generally. The large chains have been successful on the basis of centralised organisation, but at the price of everything becoming rather boring. Clearly we understand the logic of distribution-driven repeat formats, but the customers does not. We should be looking at the alternatives.
6. *Sunday shopping* Future competition is likely to be fuelled by Sunday trading with its huge implications and opportunities, not just for the retail sector, but also for sport, leisure, newspapers etc.
7. *Armchair and teleshopping* These are likely to grow as will operations like Compucard.

Plainly, to be around in the future, tomorrow's winners will have to break out of this debilitating circle. But how? You'll not be surprised to learn that this brings us to design, and some examples of successful retail design in practice.

159

Burton

Burton has been design-led since 1977, based on segmentation or 'niche' marketing. They have a capital investment pro-gramme of around £50m pa and a devolved management style using operating divisions. They are heavy users of consultants and research to keep 'in touch'. They have approximately 1500 outlets and 5 per cent of the clothing market.

Top Shop

Top Shop is one of the first examples of retail market seg-mentation. It has succeeded in remaining contemporary, and has updated a successful formula.

Debenhams

A major department store chain which is using design to trans-form its image and upgrade its customer profile.

Habitat

An example of a design-led product and life-style story. Habitat has proved to be an accurate reflection of a changing society's tastes.

Next

Next filled a gap in the market. George Davis discovered that the 'mature' person could be credited by taking the spotlight off the young and by anticipating a return to more 'mature' values. With Next for Men and Next Interiors, to be followed by Next Lingerie, and Next Gifts, the Next stores are all examples of segmentation specialisms.

Asda

Asda, on the other hand, is a good example of northern stand-ards of presentation, perceived cleanliness etc. Here 'non-price' factors are still less important than they are in the South and

Southeast. It reflects the 'two nations' syndrome at work. To move south, an emphasis on 'better value' is required.

Woolworth

Woolworth's positioning statement says that you can't have 900 similar stores, so that various new concepts had to be developed. Two of them are 'Weekend' and 'General'. The intention is to have stores of 8000–15000 square feet, nothing priced above £25, convenient and product-led, to be based on core departments in areas where they are strong — eg records, sweets, electrical goods and so forth.

My conclusion is brief. People want design. If we use it to make shops, shopping centres and products places and things of interest, we'll come through these lean years in good shape.

Design and the Service Industries

Helen Robinson

Helen Robinson started her working life as a fashion journalist. After a period as Executive Editor of Vogue *she moved into retailing as Group Style Director of the Debenhams Group, with responsibility for all aspects of design. She is now a merchandise and design consultant. She is also a member of the board of London Regional Transport and chairs its Design Policy Committee, and has in the past undertaken similar responsibilities at the British Airports Authority.*

Her paper ranges over her experience in all these organisations. She argues for the importance of design in the service industries such as transportation, where a fast response to customer needs is the key to business success.

The subject of this paper is the importance of design in retail and service industries which is discussed in the context of the three companies where I chair, or have chaired, design committees. These are: Debenhams — where, as full-time Director of Group Style, I am responsible for the public face of the company; London Regional Transport — where I am a part-time member; and the British Airports Authority — where I was a part-time member for six years. I am also a member of the Council of the Royal College of Art.

The paper is divided into two parts. The first and shortest part will contain some worries that I want to share. The second part, in which I will try to be more constructive, will focus on STYLE and the particular components that contribute to it. After looking at some designed physical expressions of style, we shall consider some of the effects that current changes in thinking about the structure and scale of business has on the perception and management of design.

PART 1 — SOME WORRIES

The UK has a creative record in its manufactured goods, particularly consumer goods, that none of us can be particularly proud of. There are exceptions of course, but on the whole this is the case. We seem to be able to recognise the problem; but the solving of it seems to escape us.

I have been professionally interested in 'good' design for all my working life. In those years, and particularly in the last ten, I have listened to many speeches and presentations, read many articles and books, and sat on a number of committees, often composed of the same nucleus of people. We listen, read, discuss and feel all would be well if only *they* would listen to us. Perhaps it is self-delusion.

The 'bottom line' is success. We have volunteered to be shareholders in a company called 'Good Design'. But on the whole we are not yet producing a fair return on the amount of energy we are expending and the words we write and speak. Perhaps it is us, with our fixed positions, who hold back success.

I will talk later about the part I have played in solving some of the problems. But often 'solving' has meant moving things forward only a little. Most matters do not seem to be improved importantly. We just seem to chip away. Rather than progress, it is often simply movement.

What we need are clear objectives which we can monitor. The response of the executive who has failed, that 'he has worked very hard', is no answer. Maybe we, like the executive, work too hard. Perhaps we should be more concerned with nurturing roots which, protected by us, can go on growing.

One principle should be emphasised. Design is not an end in itself. It is a way of achieving something infinitely greater — STYLE. It follows the old statement: 'No one wants a drill — what they want is a hole.' Design is the tool for making style.

How do we achieve this style? Perhaps by teaching the bosses rather than the students.

Let me conclude this part of the paper with a paragraph or two from *The Dancing Wu Li Master* by Gary Zukav. He describes his book as an 'overview of the New Physics', and it is about Quantum Physics, although he is not a physicist.

'Wu Li' is Chinese for 'patterns of organic energy'. Al Huang, a Chinese physicist, was asked how he structured his classes:

> 'Every lesson is the first lesson', he told me. 'Every time we dance we do it for the first time.'
>
> 'But surely you cannot be starting new each lesson', I said. 'Lesson number two must be built on what you taught in lesson number one, and lesson three likewise must be built on lessons one and two, and so on.'
>
> 'When I say that every lesson is the first lesson,' he replied, 'it does not mean that we forget what we already know. It means that what we are doing is always new, because we are always doing it for the first time.'
>
> This is another characteristic of a master. Whatever he does he does it with the enthusiasm of doing it for the first time. This is the source of his unlimited energy. Every lesson that he teaches (or learns) is a first lesson. Every dance that he dances, he dances for the first time. It is always new, personal and alive.
>
> Unfortunately most physicists are not like Rabi. The majority of them do spend their lives doing what other people have told them is important. A technician is a highly trained person whose job it is to apply known techniques and principles. He deals with the known. A scientist is a person who seeks to know the true nature of physical reality. He deals with the unknown.
>
> [Technicians] are not interested in the essentially new. Their field of vision is relatively narrow. Their energies are directed towards applying what is already known. Because their noses are often buried in the bark of a particular tree, it is difficult to speak meaningfully to them of forests.
>
> . . . it is possible that scientists, poets, painters and writers are all members of the same family of people whose gift it is by nature to take those things which we call commonplace and to re-present them to us in such ways that our self-imposed limitations are expanded.

PART 2 — STYLE

Style and design are inextricably mixed. Style is wider than design; it encompasses attitudes as well as things. Before design policies can be established, the *style* of a business — any business — must be formulated. Design then plays a major role in announcing and making clear what that style is. It is the *physical expression of style* backed up by attitudes, relationships with staff and, where applicable, customers. It is about communication.

In retail and service industries the various elements of design — the stores, the stations, the buses, the trains, the gate-rooms, the graphics, the signing systems, the decor and so forth — properly planned and derived from a clear brief, should together make a statement about the business which emanates clearly from one source and which adds up to a picture of that business, its place in the market, its aspirations and its attitudes.

The design brief is made up from who you are, what you want to do, and where you want to place yourselves. It includes numbers and statistics. It is not an airy-fairy thing only to do with aesthetics. Good design works, looks as if it will work, and is a management tool to achieve profit plans.

A significant trend nowadays is for big companies to be decentralising into smaller units, and to be expanding by diversification. The issues of accountability and control then become of paramount importance — especially where they can conflict with entrepreneurial activities. Companies also need to attract bright high-fliers. One problem is how a large organisation maintains a total corporate 'face' while at the same time developing and retaining individual entrepreneurial spirit in the new and smaller business units (and, remember, customers don't care about structure). Companies should try to retain the strength of image of the single unit while having the advantage of being organised as a series of small ones. The British Airports Authority, Debenhams and London Regional Transport are well on their way down this route.

THREE CASE HISTORIES

BAA

BAA is a large business devolved into manageable sized units or bits — such as the Heathrow and Gatwick termini, the smaller airports and the various individual businesses. The whole organisation turned over £316.2 million in 1983–84, making a profit before tax of £49 million. It is a commercial business existing in a heavily service-orientated industry. The chairman, Norman Payne, set strong design standards, managed by Jane Priestman.

A design policy statement has been accepted by the board and written into the corporate plan. From this, design guidelines have been developed which are used for briefing, monitoring and so forth. A corporate identity programme has been carried out by Wolff Olins. The familar yellow colouring and distinctive brown or black letters appeared and was carried through from letterheads, literature, uniforms, to signing, vans and trolleys. The original work has stood up well to the diverse uses to which it was put, and to subsequent developments such as the opening of the Satellite and Terminal 4 at Heathrow, the growing importance of retailing in airports and the development of products such as the Jetsac.

The design-dominated ethos is not restricted to this straightforward use of colour and typeface style. Gate-rooms are designed to reflect a feeling of calm, peace and comfort — attitudes that help to make travelling begin pleasantly. Where possible, in new buildings BAA adds to the feeling of the beginning of the journey and the involvement with the airplanes by the use of large windows so that the interest of airport business can act as a source of diversion and entertainment for the passenger.

Because BAA is so far down the design management trail, it can develop individual products that meet very precise needs. For example, its upholstered seating worked ergonomically, economically and practically. It lasted, it looked streamlined, modern and comfortable — and it was. But in the aftermath of the terrible fire at Woolworth, where many people died because of fumes from burning upholstery, BAA felt that whether or not new standards of safety would be imposed by law, in the interests of passengers and staff it would develop seating that was equally comfortable and modern — but which also carried no fire risk. Again the results have been very successful.

The Tensabarrier is another piece of innovative design which resulted from BAA's needs to cordon off sections of its airports or to control passenger queues. Designer David Hodge did a bit of lateral thinking, and derived a solution which took its inspiration from car/airplane seat belts. The result won a Duke of Edinburgh Design Award. It is simple, foolproof and effective.

When BAA needed outdoor furniture, David Hodge developed a range which now adds lustre to the architecture of the airports. It is also marketed world wide through a joint company for a variety of non-airport uses.

When BAA was looking at people-moving systems for the Gatwick Satellite, we travelled world wide looking at every conceivable method, from walkways to plane-mates. The Westinghouse rapid-transit system won the day. It is a most elegant piece of design in terms of both engineering and appearance. Travelling on it is a highly reliable and entertaining experience. Although of American design, the rapid-transit system at Gatwick was mostly manufactured in the UK.

Similarly, in architecture the design ethos follows through. BAA's policy is to have airports that *look* as if they are part of the whole flying experience.

In short, design is deeply ingrained in BAA's management and staff. It is used both to spin extra profits and to give the organisation an even higher profile.

Debenhams

Debenhams in 1983–84 had a turnover of around £750m, with a trading profit after interest of almost £36m. Capital spending in 1984 was expected to be around £24m in the 68 stores known by the Debenhams name. The company also owns Harvey Nichols,

Hamleys, Lotus, Rayne, I Miller (US), Welbeck Finance Ltd, Freebody Property and DATEC.

In 1985 ten stores were refurbished and a new store opened in Aberdeen. Between 1980 and 1984 new stores were also opened in Cardiff, Telford, Cambridge and Edinburgh, as well as the first phase of the Croydon store. New stores are scheduled in Hounslow, Southend, Colchester, Preston and Glasgow. The ideal store size is considered to be 80–100,000 square feet. The working figure for refurbishment is £35 per square foot and for new stores £45 per square foot — to include lighting, decor, carpeting and signing. Display is budgeted at a further £1 per square foot.

The new look for Debenhams began in Cardiff, and stores since then — new or refurbished — have all been developments of the look and standards set there. In the next five years we hope to finish refurbishing all the existing stores as well as open a number of new ones.

The old organisational framework of Debenhams was horizontally structured into buying and selling, which resulted in problems of lack of control and accountability. Now a new and, in retail terms, unique structural change has been introduced, based on a vertical arrangement, with accountability for profit before rent for each buying and selling division. The number of divisions was reduced from seventeen members to ten, including three jointly owned specialist companies. The groupings are:

1. Womenswear and cosmetics
2. Menswear, lingerie, childrenswear
3. Footwear, accessories
4. Leisure
5. Home and garden
6. Home textiles and home sewing
7. Instore Enterprises (catering)

plus three jointly owned companies:

— Greens Leisure Centres
— Debenhams Furnishings
— Lighting

The new structure has great advantages. But it also brings problems, primarily of corporate identity and toeing the philosophical line. The problem is one of applying loose discipline.

The task of pulling these businesses together and presenting them to the customer as a coherent and exciting whole is that of my department — Group Style. It comprises forecasting and styling, promotions, advertising, visual merchandising, display, public relations and customer services.

Another department, Design and Development, is headed by Charles Sebestyen (who concentrates on property matters) and architect David Swann. The interface between David Swann and his team and Group Style is informal but tightly bonded.

We also make extensive use of the services of Replan, a company that breaks new ground as a planner in the retailing field, and one of whose most important functions is the proper use of our principal asset — space — in the UK and abroad.

These three arms, Group Style, Design and Development, and Replan work on behalf of store operations with the vertical companies and the designated store design company in order to ensure a cohesive presentation of what Debenhams is to our customers, shareholders and staff.

My job is to ensure that the company has a marketing strategy and that all the elements which clarify that strategy are taken care of within quite stringent budgets. Roughly, it splits into three parts — merchandise development and promotion, the environment in which it is sold, and customer service.

Merchandise development begins in Group Style, where mainstream trends are identified and forecast some two years ahead and then developed with the vertical companies according to their special needs. The design elements of this exercise include advising on the actual merchandise, recommending a designer when required, packaging, ticketing and fixturing. This carries on through to visual merchandising, display, advertising and public relations. Because the overview of all categories of merchandise is held in Group Style, the division plays an important part in merchandising new and refurbished stores.

The ethos behind our new look in the stores is simple. We

want to tempt customers in, and then keep tempting them when they are inside. We want the merchandise to star, not be overshadowed by the decor but enhanced by it. We want the customers to feel flattered by beautifying colours and lighting so that when they catch sight of themselves in mirrored columns they look and feel good. We want unobtrusive fixtures that carry temptingly the right amount of stock and are flexible for seasonal requirements. We want walkways that wind the customers through the merchandise. We want vistas with points of interest that lure people on, centres of excellence which are the best departments in town in terms of both merchandise and environment, clearly signed paypoints and service desks, attractive, easily maintained fitting rooms and loos, beguiling restaurants, and the ability to market concept merchandising. We want lifts and lavatories to make shopping easy for the disabled. We want our staff to feel valued and professional and to have excellent facilities, to know that when we spend money out front we take care of them too and recognise their contribution.

At this stage it is worth mentioning briefly some of the new developments and opportunities that we anticipate and the design implications. The concept of stores as precincts or malls is already being talked about, financial and property services are beginning to take off, and special areas such as chemists and opticians are fitting in happily and providing a needed service.

New approaches to food seem to be a recent opportunity. The food court is gathering pace in the USA, and is beginning to develop here. The British are now a multinational race, and therefore inclined to eat more adventurously. Restaurants and fast food outlets, a multiplicity of different sorts, from burgers to baked potatoes, from health food to ice cream, from curries to Chinese, are envisaged — each occupying a small specialist up-front area with low capital costs, and served by a central seating area. The idea is equally suited to airports, stores or precincts.

The concept of small, specialised food and drink bars scattered throughout stores requires special design treatment. Bloomingdales does it to perfection with small coffee shops or wine and cheese counters on fashion or home merchandise floors. The opportunities for high returns on small spaces are great. Food sold for home consumption is another customer turn-on, especially when accompanied by the delicious smell of baking bread, or freshly ground coffee. Many design lessons can be learned from old-fashioned street markets — still the most enticing places to buy food.

In short, stylish design in merchandise and in stores, the one enhancing the other, clearly signalling the kind of business to the customer, is the springboard to success. This is now recognised by the Group. There are no in-house designers of any kind. All design is bought in so that we are free to employ the very best designers for a particular job. Debenhams, to coin a phrase, is 'getting there'. We may never feel that we have arrived; but we are enjoying travelling in the hope of doing so.

London Regional Transport

London Regional Transport has sprung from that old friend London Transport. With a projected turnover in 1985–86 of £920m it is a large company broken down into smaller specialist units, covering buses, trains and property.

Many of the issues it faces follow the patterns already experienced by BAA and Debenhams. Which activities and controls stay central? What goes out to the newly formed companies? What about marketing and advertising? Who owns the properties? What about corporate style? What about the logo? What about the new ideas of licensing routes and joint ventures, and the consequences for logos? How to release *and* control? Where does design sit in all this and how should we manage it? And, to add to all this, there are the particular requirements of local and national government.

Peter Gorb has been helping us to think through the new needs for design management and how it might work within the new structure. With adolescent companies moving away from the central 'frame' the need for design management is even greater than before; but the tact with which it must be done makes it a complicated task.

The organisation started with probably the best-known

171

logo in the world. It has proved to be strong and flexible — a great starting point for a new corporate identity.

Half of our stations are scheduled to be refurbished or improved over three years at a cost of £150–200 million. The design brief for these has included the identification of the line and the development of a sense of place.

In train design, work continues on the thinking and development of new products. Considerations include how the train will look in a new station, how to identify the line, how to update the shape and improve the driver's vision (by making an ergonomic study of the driver's cab), what is the best seating arrangement for passengers, and how the colour and material will look in artificial light and in daylight, which materials are most practical in terms of wear and maintenance and, above all, whether every safety element is included.

With buses, the considerations have been concerned with balancing the need to update the look while retaining the best of tradition, as well as making them suitable for one-man operation and accessible for the disabled. A new look at the design of the driver's cab to make it ergonomically more efficient and to give a wider view, with better arranged instruments, and a reappraisal of security and safety aspects have been intrinsic parts of the work.

These are just a few of the big detailed design jobs constantly flowing through London Regional Transport. The complexity and size of the business is awe inspiring. So, too, is the management of design within it, especially since at the time of writing the management of design sits uneasily in more than one place. Part is located in the architect's department at the Aldwych, where building and engineering based design is dealt with; part rests in the marketing department at Broadway where all advertising, graphics and consumer-orientated matter is dealt with. Clearly this is a problem which will need to be given careful attention.

CONCLUSION

Summing it all up, the question that I started with remains — why, in general, is it all taking so long? Are we dealing with the right people? Are the right people doing the dealing? Above all, are we expanding our self-imposed limitations and widening our field of vision — starting up afresh each time?

The real subject of this talk, of course, has been the importance of design in the service and retail industries. I hope that the examples of these three different companies have persuaded you that informed, accurately aimed design is not just important: it is crucial.

Note: Since this talk was given, Helen Robinson has been reappointed to the Chairman's Design Group at BAA; Debenhams has been taken over by the Burton Group; and, at London Regional Transport, a Design Director has been appointed, the framework for design management is in place, and the first comprehensive design audit for the Design Policy Committee has been successfully held.

Observations on Architecture

Richard Rogers

Richard Rogers is an architect, a gold medallist of the RIBA and one of a handful of British architects with a world-wide reputation. Internationally he is best known for the Pompidou Centre in Paris, and more recently for the Lloyd's Building in the City of London.

In his paper he argues the case for the extension of the architect's responsibility into the public realm in the context of the political, economic, planning and technical constraints placed on buildings, using examples of his own recent work to illustrate these issues.

ART, SCIENCE AND IDEOLOGY

Architecture stems from our need to order the world in space and time which is a precondition to it being accessible to our understanding. It is problem solving in the environmental field, where logic is transported into form by art, combining science with art, the practical with the abstract, the measurable with the immeasurable. The science of architecture constantly progresses: science which proves more efficient supplements outdated science. Art in architecture, however, does not make linear progress. It is dependent on symbolism, and develops more randomly through philosophical and visual analysis.

Art encompasses our hopes and beliefs beyond the limit of the immediate. We affirm through architecture that beauty exists and beauty is timeless: perhaps of all our great achievements it is the only one that is always new and therefore transcends death. Beauty must be conserved, for it is our gift to the future and becomes our cultural heritage.

Although architecture is based on the knowledge of the

past and the hope of the future, it is rooted in the present. Architecture reflects our attitudes to society, equality, death, war, politics, freedom, and personal and public values. The architect's principal concern is for a better life, and from the awareness of the problems of the society in which he lives, the architect forms an ideology which determines his interpretation of the program.[1]

THE ARCHITECT'S RESPONSIBILITY TO THE PUBLIC

> Architect immortalizes and glorifies something. Hence there can be no architecture where there is nothing to glorify.
>   Wittgenstein

The architect's responsibility extends beyond the client's program into the public realm so that his buildings, large or small, give public performances to the user and passer-by — the audience of today and tomorrow. They are live theatre which, by means of appropriate technology, reflect and therefore make legible the prevalent social, economic, political and technical forces.

In the city today there is a crisis of public space, for it has been eroded by private needs, yet the two should be complementary. The public realm in London today, even considering its great 18th- and 19th-century parks, is steadily disappearing, especially at ground level, with the intrusion of the closed, isolated private building and the vehicle.

Traditionally public life has taken place at ground level along principal routes lined with shops, markets, theatres and restaurants, with entrances that give access to the more private activities above. The erosion of the street as a public place is the result of the replacement of street-level activities by those of a private nature, most commonly by the construction of office buildings. These private buildings stand isolated with no thought to the wider urban context.

[1] Throughout this essay I have used the American meaning and spelling of the word 'program', as its meaning is broader than the English word 'brief'.

175

Nash's Regent Street, for instance, clearly expresses the arcaded public realm at ground level and the private realm above. Compare the richness of this street with that of the totally inconsiderate contemporary development of the Albert Embankment, which is not only on the Thames, London's greatest public amenity, but also in full view from Westminster. Our proposed mixed development of Coin Street, a 13-acre site in Central London on the South Bank of the Thames, has been designed to return to the public the use of ground and access to the river. It includes approximately 1 million square feet of offices, but only the office entrances are planned at ground-floor level. This allows more than 97 per cent of the ground area to be given over to open space, pedestrian routes, pavilions, leisure areas, housing, shops, restaurants, workshop and river-related activities, as well as a pedestrianised bridge and floating pontoons.

Today it is the greed of the developer and his architect, especially those concerned with offices, that has led to a major loss of public confidence. Offices and their design are attacked by the public as being solely profit motivated and therefore inhuman. This ignores the fact that most buildings are built by and house profit-making concerns. The distinction lies in the architectural quality, for when buildings are well designed they become valuable assets to urban life.

In examining the reasons for the chaos of our present environment one cannot overlook the near total failure of the existing planning system. As it stands the system does not offer clarity of aims or continuity of purpose, nor does it encourage mutual understanding — all of which are essential if inspiration is not to be stifled. In seeking a way through the bureaucratic maze, the client is encouraged to select an architect whose strength is political rather than creative, resulting in loss of design quality.

London is still a great city, with its considerable business, educational and cultural activities, but if one examines how this is manifested in what should be beautifully scaled, continuous urban spaces full of grandeur and vitality, what one discovers in contemporary London is that the human heart of the city is formed by a series of roundabouts, scale-less blocks, and isolated ghettos of activities.

Traffic has become the single most important destroyer of the city fabric. Trafalgar Square, once the heart of an empire, Piccadilly Circus, Leicester Square — now a seedy, inconclusive conversion — Parliament Square, Hyde Park Corner, Marble Arch, Oxford Circus, places which were once the agoras of London have all been transformed into roundabouts. These are not essential to traffic flow; in the USA, for example, they are rarely used. They are dangerous, degrading, inhuman and unnecessary spaces where vehicles have replaced people. The servant has become the master and the square, the circus, the street and the park have all become containers for cars rather than places for people. In the light of the stated concern of the Modern Movement for sociology and the heart of the city[2] it is surprising that there have been so few significant urban squares created during this century where the public can meet in thousands for their pleasure, such as Rockefeller Center in New York or Beaubourg in Paris.

In spite of the complex planning legislation, modern London's built environment offers little to the pedestrian. Today the centres of many great cities in France, Italy, Germany, Austria and Scandinavia are closed to vehicular traffic, except at specific times or for those with special licences. Even in Paris, where Pompidou once stated that the city must make way for the vehicle, there is a new hierarchy of pedestrian routes which now extend six miles, inaugurated in 1976 with the area around Beaubourg. In Florence our practice is currently preparing a planning and conservation strategy based on the revitalisation of the Arno and specifically on the use of its banks for pedestrian activities.

With a better understanding of the nature of the city, based on the premise that people and space are more important than vehicles and individual buildings, cities, and London in particular, could be given back to the populace. Trafalgar Square, Leicester Square and Piccadilly Circus are within 400m

[2]CIAM *The Heart of the City*, José Luis Sert, London: Lund Humphries, 1952.

of one another and being on different levels offer scope for urban landscaping. Properly linked, they could form a great urban centre, a much-needed heart of London.

This concept formed the basis for our submission in 1982 for the National Gallery competition in which the Gallery extension formed a pedestrian arcade which linked Leicester Square to the lower Trafalgar Square, passing under Pall Mall.

Our plan gives a more comprehensive strategy aimed at weaving together this part of London and connecting it to the South Bank by introducing a number of revitalised and new urban magnets. The links would be created by well-defined pedestrian routes including two new pedestrian bridges, and river-related activities. This plan also includes proposals prepared with Ahrends, Burton & Koralek to link Trafalgar Square, the much-improved Covent Garden, and Charing Cross to Waterloo via a travelator across the Thames.

Further pedestrian routes could be easily woven through the city using existing urban infrastructure such as the river, the great parks, the squares, the small streets and alleyways; for example, from Waterloo to Holland Park and Highgate, or from Richmond to the Isle of Dogs along the Thames. What is needed to make this happen is conviction and vision enough to balance and weave together the existing infrastructure formed by past generations. A people's city could then be created which is more than the sum of its parts.

PUBLIC NEED AND PRIVATE BENEFIT

The outcome of an unacceptable economic disparity between the haves and the have-nots touches us all and leads to urban unrest and destruction, as seen in the USA in 1967, France in 1968 and England in 1981. In this context the architect must question and re-formulate the program so that new values may appear. It is part of the architect's role to reinforce and interpret social aims in terms which the investor-client can both appreciate and accept.

The beneficial link between social and profit-motivated development can often be proved to the mutual satisfaction of both the client and the user. For example, the proposed pedestrian bridge over the Thames at Coin Street was financially viable on the basis that a direct pedestrian link to the north bank would allow offices on the south to let for some £2 per square foot more, thereby easily justifying the cost on commercial grounds while providing an amenity for all.

The economic success of a city lies in its multifaceted activities, whether it is an opera house or a football stadium, for people choose to live in, work in or visit a city because of the enrichment it offers. Each visit to the coffee house, the museum, the shop, the restaurant, the cinema, the stadium and the club helps to fill the coffers of the state through the payment of taxes.

BEAUBOURG: PUBLIC PARTICIPATION AND LOST CONCEPTS

The achievement of the Pompidou Centre has been to make culture fun.

To make a city creative you have got to get culture out of the museum and into the streets, catch people off guard. You can't just sit back and wait for them to come to you. The Pompidou Centre has taught us that.

Jacques Chirac, Mayor of Paris, 1983

Do not forget I was for Beaubourg from the beginning for it is a people's place. François Mitterand, 1983

It is my belief that exciting things happen when a variety of overlapping activities designed for all people — the old and the young, the blue and white collar, the local inhabitant and the visitor, different activities for different occasions — meet in a flexible environment, opening up the possibility of interaction outside the confines of institutional limits. When this takes place, deprived areas become dynamic places for those who live, work and visit; places where all can participate, rather than less or more beautiful ghettos.

The popularity of Beaubourg, which draws more people than the Eiffel Tower and the Louvre put together is, I believe, primarily due to this overlapping of diverse activities ranging from the popular joy ride up the escalators across the façade, to the areas reserved for exclusive and quiet study. These are all contained in a joyful, easily understandable, multi-purpose, open-framed building set in a piazza full of spontaneous activities.

Beaubourg was intended to be, and is, a cultural fair-ground for all to participate in.[3] It is an urban catalyst in Paris so adopted and used by the French that it is now an inherent part of their culture. Yet for six years it was an all-consuming political and technical battle.

Rather than analyse the Beaubourg of today I would like to reflect on some of the concepts lost during its building. It was our intention to have no walls between different cultural departments so that works of art could be found in the library and books in the museum. To optimise accessibility, below-ground storage was to be minimised and instead books, painting and sculpture were to be stored in specially designed floating mobile mezzanines. Even today the structure can support more weight. The building was to be full of terraces, more transparent and articulated than it now is but the height had to be reduced due to planning regulations and therefore became more solidified.

Security regulations eliminated the possibility of a major internal vertical space and the aim of an easily penetrated building with numerous entrances fell foul of security control after the building was opened. The outdoor audio-visual information screen designed to cover much of the piazza facade was lost when politicians decided it might be used for political ends rather then purely for cultural information. Perhaps the most serious loss of all was the untimely death of President Pompidou and the ensuing reduction of motivation and funds which affected the quality of finishes, maintenance and operation of the Centre.

[3]See the description of Beaubourg by Richard Rogers in *Architectural Design*, May 1975.

An open-ended flexible concept such as Beaubourg contains many overlapping and changing activities, and needs constant tuning by a dynamic and professional team. The very size and popularity of Beaubourg endangers its independence from bureaucratic politics, yet without that freedom it would revert to being a traditional élitist cultural institution.

LEGIBILITY OF THE WHOLE AND ITS PARTS AND THE LANGUAGE OF TECHNOLOGY

It is not enough for a modern building to be something and do something. It must also say something.

Lewis Mumford, 1961

Nations, states, cities, neighbourhoods, streets and buildings are quarries of information and give off signals which can be read. It is our intention to make these signals easily legible both to the passer-by and the user. We arrive at the design of a building by understanding its essence, which must then inspire and infuse each element and detail. Each element in turn must affect the design of the whole so that the whole and its parts are totally interlocked.

I question the concept of sudden creative inspiration in design and believe rather in the steady process of creativity which can only be achieved through the understanding of the problem, and the process by which it is solved and transformed into built reality. This involves ranging back and forth between the general and the specific, from the whole to the detail, with each affecting the other.

Although a building must be complete at any one stage, it is our belief that in order to allow for growth and change it should be functionally, and therefore visually, open ended. This indeterminate form must offer legible architectural clues for interpretation by future users. The dichotomy between the complete and the open nature of the building is a determinant of the aesthetic language.

We design each building so that it can be broken down

into elements and sub-elements which are then hierarchically organised to give a clearly legible order. A vocabulary is thereby created in which each element expresses its process of manufacture, storage, erection and demountability, so that, to quote Louis Kahn, 'each part clearly and joyfully proclaims its role in the totality. ''Let me tell you the part I am playing, how I am made and what each part does'', what the building is for, what the role of the building is in the street, and the city.'

In architectural reality the measurable and the immeasurable, the private and the public, the interior and the exterior, the served and the servant, are one. They are separated as aids to the intellect but are fused by the same integrity, becoming unified steps in the process of architecture.

The benefits of industrialisation and its method of expression have had a profound influence on architecture. It is a process which when correctly used, gives cost, time and qualitative benefits and which must be maximised if we are to meet the needs of a world whose population currently doubles every 33 years.

GROWTH AND CHANGE: TRANSFORMATION AND PERMANENCE

We are searching for a system and a balance which offers the potential for change and urban control; a system in which the totality has complete integrity yet allows for both planned and unplanned evolution.

A dynamic relationship is then established between transformation and permanence, resulting in a three-dimensional framework with a kit of changeable parts designed to allow people to perform freely inside and out. This free and changing performance of people and parts becomes the expression of the architecture.

If buildings are not to 'strait-jacket' the developing activities enclosed, they should be capable of being easily adapted. In extending the life of a building by even a small percentage, considerable economy in materials, man-hours and rent can be achieved. Therefore the plan, section and elevation of a building should be capable of responding to the user's needs without loss of order. To date the Modern Movement has concentrated principally on the flexibility of plan, occasionally on the flexibility of a section, but seldom on the flexibility of elevation. Apart from the obvious economic benefits that longer building life offers, a further advantage is that building and places achieve a patina created by time which adds to the humanisation of the building.

The methodology by which we define areas designed for permanence and those designed for transformation is rooted in the program. A hierarchical system is set up based on the analysis of function and form, ranging from the most changeable elements such as moveable partitions, to changeable elements such as the services and the façade, to fixed elements such as the basic structure and outline silhouette.

In analysing the hierarchy of change, certain elements can be separated out. The basic framework of a building, if designed as an easily adaptable, well-lit, general-purpose space, offers the potential for a very long life. Even if the activities change there is rarely a need for different specifications between one activity and another in spatial terms. For example, a university, a block of flats, offices or light workshops have much the same spatial needs and so can be interchanged. It is primarily the mechanical servicing that is different and which therefore needs to be adapted to meet the change in building use and the demands of evolving technology. The most recent example of this is the extraordinary development and impact of the microchip.

The average life of a London building is approximately 75 years. However, 75 years ago there was no air-conditioning, telephone network, air transport system — Lindberg's plane first crossed the Atlantic 55 years ago — vehicular transport system, or copying machine. Electricity, lifts and vehicles were in their infancy. As a response to this we have developed a form of architecture which separates the long life, general-purpose spaces which offer maximum economic return, from the short life, technologically dependent activities.

In response to specific needs in buildings such as Lloyd's, Beaubourg and Inmos we have removed the normal vertical constraints which determine spaces, such as stairs, elevators, corridors, toilets, mechanical services and structure, and placed them instead on the outside of the building. This in turn allows ease of access, and simple maintenance as well as the ability to modernise the mechanical services which need to be constantly upgraded. This external framework also offers the potential for the play of light on the richly articulated façades. Although the external placement of structure is traditional and can be seen, for example, in Gothic architecture, mechanical services and movement systems have only been developed recently. Only now are they finding a true value in the orders of architecture, as they currently form an average of some 30 to 40 per cent of the volume and cost of an air-conditioned building and account for the greatest part of its maintenance and running cost. Mechanical servicing is a seriously under-rated and undeveloped science and to date has suffered a poor professional tradition. It still carries a stigma and is considered unsavoury so that, like the Victorian WC, it is placed under the stairs out of sight, out of mind. Yet it is exactly in this building area that the technological revolution is taking place.

This layering of served and servant activities, with its changing rhythm and potential for the play of light and shadow, offers the possibility for a controlled transformation of the building over time. In comparison the traditional concept of an architecture of total, finite perfection does not allow for transformation to take place without a considerable loss of quality.

Le Corbusier stated that life is always right, it is architecture that is wrong. From this we may deduce that a new architecture should be capable of both reflecting the ongoing changes in restructuring the process of life and transforming into three dimensions the perpetual dialectic between permanence and change.

LLOYD'S: THE LAYERING AND JUXTAPOSITION OF OVERLAPPING PLANES

After the Bank of England, Lloyd's is probably the most prestigious institution in the City of London, with an organisation that reflects a great tradition. If Beaubourg was designed as a people's cultural centre then the new Lloyd's reflects an English club at the end of the 20th century.

Our intention in the design of the new Lloyd's building has been to create a more articulated, layered building than the simple classical rectangular tower, by the manipulation of plan, section and elevation which would link and weave together both the over-simplified 20th-century blocks and the richer, more varied architecture of the past.

Approaches to buildings in cities are often along narrow streets, so that they are seldom seen front on. Lloyd's is designed to be approached on the diagonal and viewed in parts. As the viewer approaches the building, the form gradually unfolds, the overlapping elements of its façade opening up to reveal spaces related to the pedestrian scale, spaces that are sheltered from the passing vehicles. Contrast is thereby created by the juxtaposition in depth of different layers and elements. First there are the six strong, vertical, ever-changing, articulated towers; then the free-standing, more rigid but clearly legible structural framework. Behind this are the translucent glass walls while, finally, in the centre rises the glazed atrium. The building pivots around the highest tower which marks the principal entrance opposite Commercial Union Square and is on axis with the Bank of England. The towers and building decrease in height as they meet the lower, Victorian Leadenhall Market.

The towers also serve to anchor the building and define the lines of the street, giving scale, grain, shadow and interest to the building mass. A tension is thereby established both between the different parts of the building and between the building and its immediate neighbours. The tall serrated towers and the rounded atrium form are designed to enrich the skyline, placing the building in its urban environment among the spires, domes and towers of the past.

185

These techniques enable the viewer to participate in the dialogue between the different parts, between surface and depth, between tension and compression, horizontal and vertical, solid and void, and so his interest is revived and the form and meaning become easily legible.

SCIENCE AND ROGERS' PATSCENTRE

The choice is comparative richness on this planet or annihilation. It is our choice for we have the knowledge and the means.

Buckminster Fuller

Today problem solving involves thinking on a global scale and using science as the tool to open up the future. Science is the means by which knowledge is ordered in the most efficient way to solve problems. Each problem should be solved through the use of appropriate technology. The choice of technology depends upon the complexity of the problem and the traditions of the region, including what materials are most easily available. Appropriately used mud bricks can be as 'high' a technology as teflon-coated tents.

Correctly used, the new technology of communication is a process which could revolutionise the future in a way that will make all past technological revolutions look insignificant. It has the potential to help conquer unemployment and to come to terms with the limited resources of our planet, the two most difficult problems facing us today. It will allow us to be informed of the needs, the existing research, and development taking place in all relevant fields throughout the world.

At the same time one must beware of over-romanticising the image of science, for history and symbolism do not enter the pure science:design equation. Science has measurable results, while architecture is dependent, not solely on measurable decisions, but on more complex indeterminate ones. To ask what is the nature or essence of a building is all important, but hardly relevant in designing the form of a rocket floating through the universe.

186

Rogers' Patscentre is the testing laboratory for the practice and as such is the scientific arm of Richard Rogers and Partners. This has been set up in collaboration with PA Technical Science Centre, led by Gordon Edge, who is both a patron and a unique adviser. It allows the practice to develop its design language beyond that of normal architecture by extending the team's knowledge so that it covers not only the global macro- but also the scientific micro-end of the spectrum. Efficiency is thus increased and our architectural vocabulary is enriched.

TEAM IDEALS

The aim of the practice is to produce the best possible architecture in an integrated social, intellectual and physical environment. We have attempted to set up a team organisation so that all members can have the maximum opportunity to participate and fulfil themselves by sharing both the collective benefits and the responsibilities of the office. Although decisions are made by those believed to be most capable of making them, a constitution has been set up based on checks and balances to encourage maximum participation.

Ability, teamwork and control through personal contact are the keys to good architecture, so the size of the practice has been limited to 30 architects, except with the unanimous agreement of the partners. This implies the refusal of interesting work which arrives at the wrong time and limits the number of consultants working in the office.

There are no fixed hours as we believe enthusiasm produces better results than inflexibility. Holidays are encouraged varying between four to eight weeks, but when necessary we all work seven-day weeks. The aim is a balanced life-style, though in practice this is difficult to achieve.

We strongly believe in team design. The office is divided into teams led by team leaders (approximately one team leader per three architects) who run either a small job or a segment of a larger job, eg superstructure, substructure, mechanical services, cladding, internal systems, etc. The partners each have an area

187

of overlapping responsibility such as design, planning technology, science, programming cost, law and office strategy.

It is our belief that in a society split between the fortunate and the less fortunate, a socially responsible organisation cannot exist merely for its own interest and must look beyond the limit of the team and its work. We have therefore set up charitable trusts which receive part of the profits of the practice. Our constitution limits the salary of a senior partner to not more than seven times that of the lowest paid full-time architect. After providing for taxes and pensions, and staff bonuses, the residue of profit is allocated between reserves (one-third) and the charitable trusts (two-thirds).

The development of this type of organisation is not simple; either legally or, more important, personally. It involves a certain self-divestment of privilege and power on the part of senior members, and the acceptance of a share of responsibility by others, without compromising architectural quality.

Contrary to current beliefs, the success of urban public spaces is neither rooted in their continuity of form nor in their being continuously linked along a street or square, but rather due to the careful consideration of the topography, scale and continuity of the public realm at ground level together with the correct overlapping of activities.

A close parallel exists in the planning of early Renaissance and modern cities. The Renaissance city, whether ideal or real, primarily consisted of self-sufficient absolute objects constructed in the midst of the previously continuous Romanesque and Gothic architecture.

The interior and exterior of buildings may respond to different forces and therefore may need to be visually different but both parts must be infused with the same overall integrity. In complex urban situations, it is often impossible to express these different private and public roles by the use of modern, thin, taut skins. For the Modern Movement to continue to be valid it must be capable of development and adaptation in response to new information and considerations. It must learn from the past. Serious mistakes rooted in the revolutionary optimism of the first part of the 20th century, such as the belief that science could solve all problems, must be corrected. But it would be even more foolish to conclude that because science alone is not sufficient, it is not necessary either.

This current reaction has resulted in a spate of different 'isms', principally rooted in the belief that the aesthetic of architecture exists purely in its own right and does not need other validation; in other words, art for art's sake. This has lead to the abstract applications of historical forms, whether Egyptian, Minoan, Greek, Roman, Renaissance or Gothic. They have been dismembered from their original political, social and technical backgrounds and thereby stripped of the layers of accrued implications deposited by time so that their historical validity is lost.

EPILOGUE

Buildings are not idiosyncratic private institutions, they give public performances both to the user and the passer-by, therefore the architect's responsibility must go beyond the client's program and into the broader public realm. Although the client's program offers the architect a point of departure, it must be questioned as the architectural solution lies in the complex and often contradictory interpretation of the needs of the individual, the institution and the place.

A building is not a less or more beautifully proportioned finite object, for architectural problems are seldom simple and therefore can seldom be translated by a single form. Varied and overlapping needs must be interpreted by related building elements, which are influenced by the building process and are rigorously composed to produce a clear hierarchy of identifiable, legible spaces and parts, each with its own integrity. The inside of a building is interwoven with the outside and infused with the same integrity, but both the inside and outside need to be designed so as to be capable of responding to different private and public needs.

To meet changing needs, the building form should be dynamic, capable of responding to growth and change in plan, section and elevation, to allow people to perform freely inside and outside the building. This free and changing performance will then become part of the expression of the architecture of the building, the street and the city. Program, ideology and form will then play an integrated and legible part within a changing but ordered framework. The fewer the building constraints for the users the greater the success; the greater the success the more the need for revision and then programatic indeterminance will become an expression of architecture.

PART 4

Design, the Country and its Culture

On Design and our Industrial Future

Stephen Bayley

Stephen Bayley once taught art history, but took the opportunity to apply some academic principles to the study of every-day design when invited to do so by Terence Conran. As the first director of The Conran Foundation, Stephen Bayley set up the Boilerhouse Project in the V & A Museum, and is now creating the world's first Design Museum in London's Docklands.

His paper discusses the origins of modern industrial design and deplores the damage done to the design cause in Britain by the Arts & Crafts movement at the beginning of this century. He argues that the current technological revolution will produce its own aesthetic, and attacks the work of some of the current design consultancies for disregarding this. He concludes with some speculations about design in the coming age of robotics.

I've got two anecdotes about lecturing technique. One is from the Army Education Corps where, I'm told, the method is to

tell them what you're going to say,
say it,
and
tell them what you said.

But there's another one I prefer. There was a French sage who once said 'I always say the same thing, but I never repeat myself.' In talking about design I am going to try to say something different, but I cannot undertake to avoid repetition.

There seems to me no doubt — it has been proven to the point of boredom — that 'design' is good for business. Those companies that invest heavily in design — one thinks of IBM, Olivetti, Fiat, Ford, 3M, Honda, Sony — are also those that prosper. But there's little doubt that some companies that

193

don't invest in design at all prosper too. One thinks of BTR, Hanson Trust, British Telecom . . . I could go on. So what does this mean?

One problem seems to be that 'design', where it is understood at all, is thought to be a sort of synonym for a type of Scandinavian taste which was popular in the fifties. Neat, chaste ash furniture, a stainless steel platter — you know the sort of thing. Many people, when they are talking about design, are just thinking of transferring the values inherent in the ash furniture and the stainless steel accessories to their businesses. This can take many forms, but the principle is the same. No wonder 'good' design has got itself a bad name.

So, what *does* design mean today?

There is so much confusion, but it's really such a straight-forward subject. I suspect the confusion arises because the very straightforwardness is sort of illusory. Design is really not one subject, but many. Although the word has, in various forms, been in use since the 15th century, I would say that design is an essentially 'modern' phenomenon. When I say 'modern' I mean post 18th century. It is a process which has occurred since the manufacturing cycle got split up between maker, seller and user. Design combines engineering, materials science, inventions, art, commerce, anthropology, ergonomics and social science.

Of course, it's this essential richness that makes design so rewarding a subject . . . and such a confusing one. No wonder people are perplexed by what is and what is not 'good' design. Do they mean it's sound engineering, intelligent use of materials, an ingenious invention, a beautiful work of art, a successful commercial exercise, an efficient essay in ergonomics or a laudable and responsible social gesture? Perhaps it should be all of these things. But, certainly according to contemporary taste, it need not be ash furniture and stainless steel platters.

I think the reason the full possibilities of 'design' are not realised is two-fold. One lies in our historical and cultural inheritance, another in the way in which design is organised in the modern world. I would say that the present structure of both our inheritance and our organisation predisposes manufacturing initiatives to failure.

194

To simplify things before I confuse you further, in all its essentials I feel that the map of design can be divided into two territories:

1. Culture and Taste
    — human, emotional
and
2. Political Economy
    — technical, organisational.

Now let me tell you what I think is wrong with each of them.

CULTURE AND TASTE

I believe that the development of an efficient modern economy in Britain has been bedevilled by our cultural inheritance from the 18th and 19th centuries (and even before). I despise the Picturesque and the Arts and Crafts.

I recently saw an advertisement put out by a firm called Spencer Homes. They were publicising what is, alas, to many English people still an ideal: a brand new dwelling, which their copy described as a 'nineteenth-century home'. These are dishonest exercises in manipulative opportunism, slick exercises in the material form of the pastoral myth. Their strength lies only in the fact that the 'nineteenth century', as imagined by Spencer Homes or any other speculative builder, never existed. The claims made on our imaginations are uncontaminated by reality, and to the simple-minded are perhaps all the stronger for that.

Cottage architecture, the conservation movement and, I would add, the City are all symbols of the failure of technical culture in Britain. There is nothing fine about pastoral myths.

In architecture the existence of the cottage, and rampant, ill-informed, sentimental antiquarianism are witnesses to our ignorance and prejudice. In the City, institutions and the influence that they have over patterns of investment are betrayals of every hope that a civilised modern culture might be created on these islands. *Did you realise that London has not had a world class building erected in it for more than sixty years?* No wonder the world's financial centre of gravity is moving to New York (where, at least, developers can promise tenants buildings with decent, modern facilities). British culture is fundamentally suburban. And the stockbroker belt is no laughing matter.

This is the more depressing because we have the technical means to create, if not perfection, then at least the next stage on the journey towards it. Modern technology is able to provide us with a more agreeable, a more human and a more beautiful environment. But we have to understand *values*, and this is perhaps what interests me most in talking about design.

I rather agree with the renaissance architectural theorist, Leon Battista Alberti, who once remarked 'Beauty is never separate and distinct from convenience.' This argument for 'functionalism' seems such a laudable sentiment that it is unlikely anybody could fail to acknowledge its validity. But in Britain, the taste for the picturesque has combined with the parochialism of an insular nation to provide formidable obstacles to it.

William Morris, the founder of the conservation movement, who once said that you could do very well without coal mines, freely admitted to hating the (benign) innovations of the 19th century and wrote acres of unreadable verse about pack-horses strolling on the downs. He translated Icelandic sagas and wanted people to live in half-timbered houses, making corn dollies and singing refrains from 'The Clog Maker's Holiday'. To William Morris, industry was not a means of producing wealth, it was an agent for 'multiplying our distress'. He set the pattern for reactionaries of the right and of the left for the next century; as C P Snow once said. 'Nine out of ten English traditions date from the latter half of the nineteenth century.' Morris turned his back on the town, ignored the *real* distress of the Victorian urban worker and, instead, spent his time boating up the Thames to Kelmscott (where he frequently entertained other people's wives).

These 'traditions' are frequently admired by those with a vested interest in preserving the social order which the traditions exemplify. Our taste for the past is a form of negligence: the dialectic of cultural death. Sentiment for the past is a comfortable and indulgent form of nihilism. The Spencer Homes motif I began with suggests that we have *no* standards of our own, nothing to believe in.

Yet European culture has always depended on *rules*. The need for them continuously re-emerges in European thought. What are these rules to be in the future?

The historian, Correlli Barnett, once remarked that (no matter what else was achieved there) the struggle for Britain's economic survival was *lost* on the playing fields of Eton. Well, I believe that Britain's economic problems require a cultural solution.

Look around scrupulously enough and you may get a clue. I belive that industry is our culture and that technology should be our politics. By this I mean that we have to rid ourselves of 19th-century values. The only validity and interest they can have is to the antiquarian. Similarly, the role-playing of Parliament which passes for 'politics' in this country is a pathetic survival of a tired-out tradition. Politics is no longer about 'right' and 'left': that's another 19th-century idea. Technology is going to bring about unimaginably huge structural changes in the organisation of work, means and methods of communication, growth in services, patterns of travel.

POLITICAL ECONOMY

The first generation of designers were like Loewy. We are all his inheritors. However, if in the past, design was about *appearance*, I believe that in future design will become more than ever about *experience*. This is inevitable, because the old technological revolution, which brought about the system of values that created Scandinavian good design, is being replaced by a technological revolution which is affecting the organisation of work, rather than just the means of manufacturing.

But we still have to make things and decide what they must look like. I'd be the last to say that the role of designers is to sit around, musing about social structures. There seems to me really nothing very complicated about design. It's only a matter of *thinking*. What you have to do is to think about what it is you wish to achieve and set about finding a means of achieving it. This applies to your business, whatever it is.

The new technologies are making all the old assumptions about values redundant. Viewed purely historically, structural changes in the means of production have always brought about fundamental changes in aesthetic criteria. Marx's political economy and the aesthetics of the Modern Movement were brought about by mass production and the division of labour. The present revolution in 'communications' will be no less important than the old 18th-century revolution in mechanical means of producing iron gobbets. One revolution produced an aesthetic, another revolution will produce . . . well it's too early to say.

But some things seem certain. The existing design consultancies are like old sixties rock groups; they often have similar names, eg Hexagon; Yellow Brick Room. They have lead singers. They have hits (although increasingly fewer): forget the temporary triumphs of the USM. These people will not be with us for long: if the first generation was business consultancy with taste, the present one is shopfitting without carpentry skills. Like the rock groups, they will all end up on the end of Southend Pier: flashy and prosperous may be, but irrelevant to culture.

That's a shame because design is too important to be irrelevant. I have already said that I am convinced that to survive we must more thoroughly embrace technology and should aspire more consciously to 'functionalism'. This will also mean that managers and designers will have to apply a more 'functionalist' approach to their own professions.

If the picturesque tradition produced an image of the designer as an unworldly idealist, financially incompetent and politically naïve, the design profession as presently constructed contributes to the image. To be sure, the big firms are slick and successful, but their type of *styling* is only a cosmetic appendage and not a part of the whole process. Designers have opted out of the spectrum of activity that goes to create modern products. They are as ignorant in their way as philistine managers who go in for short-term accounting and disdain aesthetics as effete.

Architecture, again, supplies some useful metaphors of

the way things should be. The builders of the Acropolis were both designers and constructors and (in Periclean Athens) probably had to be politically astute as well. Alberti (who I mentioned before) could tell you not only how to design an attractive-looking chimney, he could also tell you how to stop it smoking. Brunel was an entrepreneur. John Nash was a speculative builder. Thomas Edison and Henry Ford were both engineers and dealers. The achievements we admire in the past were all the result of design-led processes.

Close to home, Terence Conran provides an outstanding example of a design-led process . . . although long ago Conran himself abandoned *drawing* as an expression of his vision. While his contemporaries struggle on to do this or that bit of quirky graphics, find a new radius for a food-mixer, Conran has raised the stakes and is designing whole retail chains. And I don't mean the shop-fittings, but the whole creative idea of what a shop can be.

Designers must accept the responsibility of becoming entrepreneurs and producers. Finance and politics will become as important as the drawing board to creative people in the future.

At least one designer in the United States has begun to realise this. Emilio Ambasz, an Argentinian architect living in New York, is already working the future today. Ambasz is not a blue-sky designer, sitting around waiting for commissions and new business to walk through the door. Instead, he gets his ideas himself. For instance, he developed an idea for an office chair. Instead of trying to sell his concept to a stern manufacturer, he sold tool-makers, die-casters and upholsterers a part in his business. He got them to make tools, dies at no cost (against a cut in future business). He was able to go to a manufacturer not with the 'Hey, you guys, I've got a great idea' number, but with a *fully costed programme*. He did market projections too. There was no risk for the manufacturer: the designer had handled it all. The manufacturer was 'reduced' to being merely the owner of the plant that actually turned out the hardware.

The new technology is going to offer more and more means of realising this. 'Flexible manufacturing systems' is the in vogue term for the modern, computer-controlled factory. In a flexible manufacturing system it is conceivable that intelligent machines will be so sophisticated that a factory will not be dedicated to the production of one particular type of merchandise. Indeed, the machine tools of the near future will be so flexible that it is conceivable factories will not necessarily be the property of a single manufacturing corporation at all, but will be installations owned by third-party service industries which turn out furniture one day and electromechanical widgets the next. And so on.

This potential change will make the designer even more significant in the future. Computerised tills will capture sales data from the stores and send it back to the computerised factory. The robot production lines will be flexible enough to respond to the market's every variation in demand. I imagine a designer, hooked into his CAD-CAM system, constantly monitoring sales returns and modifying his, his employer's or his client's product in response to every variation in popular taste.

Already the big institutions are acknowledging that there will be structural change in the way 'design' is practised. The old consultancies have had their day. Designers will, like Conran, either have to become integrated with retailing, or will have to get into a different sort of business. It's already clear that the big advertising agencies and the large firms of accountants are aware of this. Just as Emilio Ambasz offered a whole range of services to his clients, Saatchi & Saatchi (an advertising agency) and Coopers & Lybrand (a firm of accountants) are beginning to offer a whole range of services too. The manufacturers of the future, whoever or wherever they are, will not need to employ separate management consultants/accountants/advertising agencies/designers. Instead, I envisage a polarity: you will get capital-rich interests on one side, taking creative advice (be it managerial, fiduciary or aesthetic) from another.

The age of *mass production* is ended. The robot factories I spoke of mean an end to the old Cartesian economics of 'long lead times/high volume/low unit cost'. Technology makes a form of 'craft' production economically feasible for the first

time since the early 18th century. Mass production used specialised equipment to produce standardised goods; the craft production of the future will use the 'generalised' robot under the
control of designers or skilled artisans. These robots will be able
to make almost infinite varieties of different product.

But what will these products look like and who will want to
buy them?

That, I suppose, is where we come in.

CONCLUSION

John Ruskin once wrote an essay called *The Two Paths*. He was
comparing his nightmare perception of industrialised Britain
with his own fanciful vision of Britain in the Middle Ages.

Today there are two paths again and there is not very much
opportunity to sit at the crossroads. The alternatives to growth
and to change and the reorganisation of the means of production is not William Morris's or John Ruskin's vision of a Merrie
England, nor even Arthur Scargill's. The alternative is a country
with a pitifully inadequate health service, desolate towns, bad
roads and a worthless currency.

John Naisbitt, the American author of *Megatrends* (1983),
has just published a pamphlet called *The Year Ahead* in which
he says 'The challenge for industry in the information age
becomes not the retraining of workers, but the retraining of
managers.'

Managers and designers are going to have to learn new
means of production, but they are going to have to learn some
old lessons besides. Still, as I said at the beginning: experience
and history show that those manufacturers/retailers who 'flat-
ter' their public are those who prosper: here you need the mystic
ingredient 'X' . . . art.

The next generation of designers, like the first, will also
have to be business consultants specialising in taste. The only
problem is: what is taste? *Plus ça change*. Anyway, I did say I
never repeat myself. . . .

The Design Mind

David Bernstein

David Bernstein is an advertising man in charge of The Creative Business, a highly regarded and specialist agency which embraces a range of communication and design skills. He is the author of books on advertising, marketing, presentation and corporate communication.

His paper is concerned with the way design works and with what lies behind the creative impulse. In particular he deals with the designer's approach to problems and the range of skills the designer brings to bear on them. He stresses the visionary and multidisciplinary scope of design and the relevance of these resources to the world of management.

My talk on the design mind will be relatively unstructured — impressionistic, selective, subjective. Rather like a pointillist painting. Meaningless close up, but step back a couple of metres and it becomes totally . . . incomprehensible.

The word 'design' sometimes seems, if not incomprehensible, then too full of meanings . . . which is the same thing.

It's very difficult to be analytical when the term is so emotionally charged. Let me give you an example. You're in a washroom. The basin is . . . let's call it, modern. It's functional and pleasing. If you comment at all what do you say? 'That's nice.' 'That works well.' Maybe both. Do you say 'that's good design?' Do people say that? I doubt it. But I know what they do say when the opposite occurs. When there's no lip on the ledge and the soap slips into the basin. They say 'that's a design fault.'

When things go right few of us think of the design, or the designer. Maybe that's as it should be . . . .

I want to explore the design mind: the way the designer sees, the way he sees *his* role, and the way others see his role. I

202

want to explore his range of skills and his attitude towards design. And then, which is the point of it all, the implications for the organisation of the environment in which he works.

My talk therefore falls . . . crumbles . . . into several parts, but basically goes from design to management.

There are, I understand, some 26 definitions of 'design' in the *Oxford English Dictionary*. We'll meet a few definitions on today's brief journey. I'll put a couple down now as markers.

First Victor Papanek's
    'Design is the conscious effort to impose meaningful order',
And Buckminster Fuller's
    'The opposite of design is chaos'.
US management consultant, Peter Lawrence, defines design as
    'Values made visible'.

I like this last one because it works from the inside out — the word 'values' implies both aesthetic and commercial values, and the phrase hints at interpretation, at communication. And some of my favourite communicators — not to say my best friends — are designers. Alan Fletcher, who helped me considerably with this talk, is articulate, a stimulating talker, and a generator of ideas. His own definition of design may surprise you: a 'mental utensil'. He's one of a group of latter-day renaissance men called Pentagram.

As a wordsmith, working with a good art director or designer, I feel inadequate. The skills and knowledge the designer brings to the party eclipse mine. I know if the chips were down he would write the words. Whether a headline for an ad, or a verbal encapsulation of the values he's making visible. Or — and it's a point we'll come back to — write the brief (either for himself or a colleague). It might not be purist in style but it would use fewer words and those would fizz. Milt Glaser discussing the need for surprise and impact in a poster called it 'the disruption of expectation'. Art Kane called design 'putting flesh on the spirit'. And Gauguin (I don't know which agency he was at) described art as 'either plagiarism or revolution'. Magic words. All of them.

203

The design mind. The designer sees associations and makes relationships. The writer, of course, does that too. Both the writer and the designer possess insight and try to communicate that insight. The designer has a tougher job because the person to whom he is communicating is unlikely to be visually literate, and therefore the designer has to fall back on words to convey the insight. (And probably the experience has made the very good designers so articulate!) The writer on the other hand is communicating in the same medium in which he creates . . . to an audience brought up in a bookish culture.

The designer is critically concerned, obsessed, with perception. (Indeed a colleague of mine, Frank Sully, defines design as 'applied perception'.) Edward Lucie-Smith says 'the designer has to take into consideration the way things are perceived as well as the way in which they objectively exist.'

And of course the designer has to relate the two. He has to relate the thing to its perception. He also has to relate the object to its purpose, the object to the user, and, most importantly, he has to relate the object to the user to the environment in which that object is being used. It's very difficult. No wonder Buckminster Fuller contrasts design with chaos. No wonder even so brilliant a designer and thinker as Ettore Sottsass will momentarily cop out and express a 'commitment to the idea of objects as autonomous presences, existing in their own right *without external reference*' (my italics). A temporary phase. He calls objects 'catalysts of perception' but the description can be applied equally to designers and he's one of the best catalysts around.

The designer imposes order. He is a synthesiser. As Christopher Lorenz says in *The Design Dimension* 'The designer, trained to coordinate words, hands and visual imagery is still very much the exception. The skill of visualisation is most frequently used by the industrial designer to synthesise other people's ideas, and in particular to provide concreteness to marketing and engineering concepts.' And of course he synthesises his own ideas.

Often of course — the designer is called in too late. They are not his ideas or anybody else's. He is called in as a stylist to give some sort of surface appeal to another's 'design'. The problem has been solved and executed and he has to paint it. We might call him 'designer as prettifier'.

Alternatively, the problem has been solved but not executed and this is 'designer as executor'. There is more status and job satisfaction in this role. But not much. Hugh Conway (of Rolls-Royce, and a former deputy chairman of the Design Council) recalls an attitude which he laments 'is still about':

> I remember one meeting we held with a senior body of electrical engineers to discuss design matters, where a distinguished professor of electrical engineering expressed surprise that we 'Chartered Engineers' needed to discuss design, saying 'surely design is a matter for technicians'. He meant that if his researches produced some new idea, others at a lower level in the laboratory or drawing office would have the job of designing it as a task subsidiary to the laboratory work.

Designer as prettifier, as executor, or designer as problem-solver? Obviously. We'd all agree . . . wouldn't we? But if that's the case, why do those *other* people bring him in so late? And if design is about the relationship of object to user — of the interface, let's say, of the operator and the machine — how can an industrial designer in particular not be involved at the outset? And why is the company he works in structured the way it is? We'll look at that question later. But it's not sufficient to call the designer a problem-solver. As Alan Fletcher says 'solving the problem isn't the problem'.

The *designer* is an interface. He's an explainer. He is the link between the thing and the user, between the company and the customer. According to Milt Glaser 'he makes understandable things which are not understandable without his participation'. 'Design', says a colleague, Paul Eastwood, 'eases the conveying of information.' And my favourite definition of information is that of the communications scientists — 'anything which reduces uncertainty'. And the designer appreciates the needs of the customer and how the customer will approach the design. Rita Sue Siegel, a US design authority, calls the designer 'the user's advocate'.

Mike Smith calls his industrial designers 'translators, bridges and catalysts'. I stress this process because you cannot state too often that design is not an end in itself. Alas, to judge from the way it's talked about by the lesser practitioners, it still seems to be. The more designers do that the more they will be regarded as piecemeal and optional. The more they treat design as a means to an end the more they will be needed, integrated and called in early.

Take corporate identity. It's not a few squiggles and a choice of type face (end). It's an expression of the personality of the company (means). The means by which that company's personality is conveyed single-mindedly, consistently and coherently through all its communications with all its diverse publics. The designer conveys information about the company — to the company itself, and most pointedly to the chief executive.

But if the translator is to do his job — if he's a means rather than an end — he must not get in the way. Bob Gill makes the point:

> If you try to make an interesting statement *look* interesting, the way it looks competes with the statement. The look doesn't make it easier to see. It makes it harder.

Dieter Rams (Braun designer)
> I want to make things that recede into the background,

and Philip Webb, architect for William Morris
> I never begin to be satisfied until my work looks commonplace.

A word or two on the designer's skills, mainly from observation. He brings to the problem visual thinking, visual awareness. He certainly absorbs more visual stimuli than the average colleague or client. He is visually literate. He has an interest in and a commitment to things. And he's passionate, sometimes to the point of obsession, about products. Peter Gorb uses the phrase 'product passion'. Of course, the designer has imagination, creativity, lateral thinking, the ability to visualise what might be, the in-built curiosity that demands to know why something was done in a particular way, and to ask what would have happened if it had been done another way, and what might have happened if the question had been *asked* another way.

None of these skills or characteristics makes him easy to fit into a conventional working structure. However, one skill makes him very much an organisation man: synthesis, or what Lorenz calls 'the ability and versatility to synthesise all sorts of multidisciplinary factors and influences into a coherent whole'.

The designer *is* interested in order, which should mean some common ground between him and the administrator. Furthermore, he has to acquire other, more business-like skills and techniques, ergonomics (human engineering), marketing techniques, maybe retail pricing, and certainly knowledge of the consumer. He must be part social scientist.

A designer isn't versatile by accident. He has to deal with so many disciplines. The design mind comprehends various fields. And those minds may exist in other environments. G L Clegg in *The Design of Design* lists various inventions and their inventors' full-time trades

Invention	Inventor
Safety razor	Travelling cork-seller
Kodachrome films	Musician
Ballpoint pen	Sculptor
Automatic telephone	Undertaker
Parking meter	Journalist
Pneumatic tyre	Veterinary surgeon
Long-playing record	Television engineer

I'm not suggesting that designers don't have to be trained as designers. What I wish to point out is that designers, like inventors, don't take kindly to pigeonholes. Nor, as I've hinted, do they take kindly to the standardised linear approach to their jobs or to problem-solving, which of course is one definition of their job. The standard routes, formalised in work flow diagrams — analysis, synthesis, appraisal — make sense only if you appreciate that they are repetitive steps: analysis, synthesis, appraisal, analysis, synthesis, appraisal, further analysis, synthesis, appraisal and so on — and if you appreciate that synthesis can actually precede analysis.

One of the problems that administrators find difficult to get their minds around arises from the term problem-solver. Since the problem must by definition precede the solution then analysis must precede synthesis and by extension the solution of the problem must precede the entry of the designer. This is particularly the case in any organisation where the work flow diagram is more important than the work — or the 'organogram' more important than the people.

The unimaginative administrator looks for logic — not only in the solution but in the process of problem-solving. The designer on the other hand will argue for the logic in the solution but may get there by any number of seemingly illogical means.

Here again there is a confusion of means with ends. How the designer gets from the problem to the solution may puzzle even the designer, let alone the administrator. The lateral thinker may not even know he's being lateral. The thought may come as a result of interaction or collision with something totally irrelevant. The scenic route may be the most direct.

I believe there are only four means of getting to a solution:

Centripetal Analysis, followed by patient working out.
Centrifugal Deliberately going away from the problem.
Parallel Simultaneously considering something analogous.

And the one we've been discussing:
Random collision, where thoughts come into contact, either by accident or by design. And the accidents are perhaps not so accidental. They say about a good footballer that 'he makes his own luck'. Pasteur said it more eloquently perhaps: 'Chance favours the prepared mind.' Arnold Palmer said 'The more I practise the luckier I get.'

The designer doesn't simply question the process. He also questions the expression of the problem. He is not necessarily being difficult or obstructionist. The brief is, after all, his travelling companion en route to the solution. He wants to make the journey as interesting and stimulating as possible. But more importantly the two of them are going to work together.

'The initial expression of design problems may often be quite misleading', says Bryan Lawson in a very good book *How Designers Think*. He tells an amusing story:

> A client once asked me to design an extension to his house. The initial brief was rather vague with various ideas of adding an extra bedroom or a study. The real purpose of this extension was difficult to understand since the house was already large enough for all the family to have their own bedrooms and still leave a room which could have been used as a study. The site was cramped and any extension either had to occupy some valued garden space or to involve considerable expense in building over a single storey garage and removing a rather splendid pitched roof. It seemed that any extension was almost bound to create new problems, and was not even likely to prove a worthwhile investment. The client's thinking was still unclear and at one meeting, ideas of being able to accommodate grandparents were being discussed to the sounds of rather loud music from one of the teenage children's bedrooms. It then gradually emerged that this was really the source of the problem. In fact the house was indeed already large enough but not well enough divided up acoustically. The problem then shifted to installing some better sound insulation, but this is by no means easy to achieve with existing traditional domestic construction. The actual solution was suggested initially as a joke. Buy the children some headphones! Thus by treating the cause of the problem rather than fixing the symptoms the client kept his garden and his money. The architect regrettably lost some fees, but gained a very grateful client.

Design problems *are* often misleadingly expressed. And the reason? It's very common. We do it all the time. You see the brief was expressed not in terms of needs but rather (and I use Lawson's term) as a solution image. This is a common fault in design, advertising, everyday life. The designer's job is to find as well as to solve problems.

Now, just in case I've misled you, the designer is not opting out of hard work. He's not trying to make his job easier by widening the parameters. Indeed, quite the opposite. He's focusing the brief on the essentials of the problem to ensure that the problem he solves is the right one — not how to add an extension or even how to insulate the room but how to isolate the sound. Trafficators were a solution to replace the motorist using his arm. They were not a solution to how to indicate you were turning left or right — flashing lights solved that problem.

The designer is not breaking out of a prison but substituting one brief for another, which could, as I said, indeed be tougher. The designer's job is to exploit the constraints of his craft: the graphic designer (two-dimensional composition, colour, texture, form, contrast, proportion, line, shape etc), the ad art director (the product, the format and medium of the ad, and the production processes). And, of course, there are also the constraints of the brief itself.

But a brief is more than a statement of the problem. That's only the first of its three roles.

Its second role is that of a tool, an ally, the partner in the journey to the solution which the designer embraces in creative conflict. 'Embraces' — I use the word advisedly. Milton Glaser cautions: don't treat the problem as an enemy, treat it as a friend. 'The solution', he says, 'is in the problem.'

No wonder many designers go back and work on the brief together with the client. No wonder designers take time to ensure the brief is correctly expressed.

The brief's third role is as a checklist. Just as it begins by stating the problem so it provides the criteria which have to be satisfied. Or, should I say, the minimum criteria to be satisfied. Because, as Alan Fletcher has said, 'solving the problem is not the problem. The problem is adding value.' One of those values for Alan is wit — another, surprise. His colleague

Kenneth Grange talks about adding pleasure. He tells Christopher Lorenz that whereas he accepts 'fitness for purpose', 'I do believe in a bit of cheerfulness and glamour.'

Terence Conran, in the preface to the book which bears his imprint (and what artefact today does not?), says 'good design starts from the premise that living is more than just a matter of existing and that everyday things that are both effective and attractive can raise the quality of life.'

Form or function? Clearly, today's designer says 'both'. The ascetic interpretation of Sullivan's dictum 'form follows function' has mellowed. Sottsass says design must 'help people somehow'. Form or function? Either/or? Why not both? It seems a pointless division. A chair must work as a support (function) and look good (form), and be comfortable. Or, as Ken Grange says, 'add pleasure.'

A design curator asked Charles Eames 'Mr Eames, do you design for pleasure or for function?' Charles replied 'Whoever said pleasure wasn't functional?'

Either/or? Why do we always seem to force a choice?

There used to be a firm of estate agents on the south coast called Reason and Tickle. If they didn't exist I would have invented them. Every advertisement, for example, consists of both Reason and Tickle.

Creative people, designers, don't separate out — rather than categorise they synthesise. They operate idiosyncratically, haphazardly, yet observe strict disciplines.

A designer is a paradox. And design structure must take notice of that, must itself be a paradox. Which brings us to management.

Management which uses design, either from within or from without, must be sympathetic to, and understanding of, how the designer thinks and works. It means initially making sure that design features in the company objectives, that more than token attention is paid to it (eg in the company philosophy and on the board agenda). Design has to be seen as a vital resource and central to the company's activities, present *and* *future*. Imagination. It's a rare commodity. It needs to be harnessed. The designer is like a poet — a seer:

El poeta puede contar,
or cantar las cosas
no como fueron, si no
como debian ser . . .

But just as a designer is not a stylist at the end of the process, his
role as imaginer of the future should not be conducted in some
hermetically sealed box, let alone an ivory tower. The design-
orientated company must be structured to encourage collision — because ideas happen when thoughts collide. And just
as the designer must impinge upon the work around him, the
various disciplines of the company must impinge upon and
stimulate the designer. Ideas should be encouraged from every
source.

Design above everything else is a *multidisciplinary activity*.
(I have no less an authority than the Department of Trade and
Industry for that statement. And I heartily concur.) The implications are obvious. Dividing lines, barriers, need to be broken
down. Structures should be horizontal rather than vertical,
plateaux rather than pyramids. The design-aware companies
experiment with structure. The results bear at best a superficial
resemblance to traditional formats. Some are surprisingly anar-
chic. But business has to be done, products made and profits
gained. There is thus paradox. A discipline from within (the
brief, the self-discipline of the professional) and imposed by the
management cadre on the company . . . plus a complementary
anarchy. A creative tension. Disciplined anarchy.

Or, should I have said *multidisciplined anarchy*? Companies with a design function or design element within them, and
those with development engineers or a significant R&D
element, all suffer from the tensions induced by the traditional
vertical structure and seek either to replace it or accommodate it
in some way. When a project is begun in one department (eg
R&D or planning) and handed over to another (eg market development or design) then inevitably some of the impetus is lost,
much of the continuity and sense of ownership. The answer is
frequently to create a matrix structure, a horizontal band across
the vertical divisions, a project group, for example, cutting

across the departmental divisions and consisting of members from each department.

There is nothing quite so disconcerting as seeing the company structure in a new way, as if for the first time. For example, take a piece of A4 paper and draw your company's organogram, but do it landscape. On the extreme left indicate the chief executive. Then the people directly next to him and so forth. Now take a further piece of paper and draw on the extreme left a customer. Next arrange the people from the first chart on to this chart according to their proximity to the customer. You may find that some of the people on the second chart aren't on the first and that some on the first aren't on the second and so on.

The designer has his own hierarchy, independent of the organisation chart, in his head. Similarly, the project group exists independently of the organisation although feeding upon it. The project group is project-driven. The team exists as long as the project exists. Its decisions are concerned with the progressing of the project. They are not concerned with the day-to-day administration of the company or the minutiae of the departments. Their timetable is that of the project not the company. And the industrial designer is in many companies the key member of the group. As Lorenz says

> the industrial designer remains the only person directly in touch with both technology and the consumer. Despite the introduction of product managers and various other types of co-ordinator, he or she is often involved with a new product throughout the entire development and production process, from concept to market launch. Equipped with uniquely inter-disciplinary attitudes and skills, the designer sits at the centre of a multidimensional matrix, with an eye (and an influence) on every dimension. With the arrival of shorter development cycles, and the need radically to improve communication between different departmental specialists, his or her multidimensional skills become even more invaluable and influential.

A creative organisation conducting many different projects is notoriously hard to fit into the conventional company structure.

In my book[1] it has more in common with artistic rather than business structures, with the theatre for example. The creative company is like a repertory company. For each play there is a new cast and the hierarchy of one cast may be totally unlike that of another. Charlie's Aunt may carry a spear in *King Lear*.

Thinking of the company as a repertory company encourages you to avoid preconceived solutions to the question of progressing work through the organisation. Every problem is a new problem and demands a new solution. How, then, can you possibly structure on mass-production principles which presume consistency, indeed permanence, of both problem and solution?

It's time to step back from the canvas. Is there a pattern to all this, a message even? I believe so. We've talked of paradox, disciplined anarchy, Reason and Tickle, rejection of the tyranny of either/or.

Peters and Waterman's excellent companies are able to manage ambiguity. The designer manages it — lives it. As an interface, and interpreter, he must. Olivetti designer Ettore Sottsass, according to his biographer Penny Sparke:

> realises that to design the body of a calculator one needs to know and to understand how it functions internally, and yet he still manages to keep technology at arms's length in order to see how uninitiated users will 'read' the forms of the complex mechanical objects that surround them. It is the ability to combine both knowledge and innocence that makes Sottsass such a successful industrial designer.[2]

The designer is both maker and user. He is multi-disciplined — both artist and engineer.
The designed — the object — is ideally answering more than one question at the same time. The award-winning Radion Backlite aerial which utilises the rear window heating element simultaneously avoids the ugliness of the external aerial, the

[1] *Company Image and Reality*, New York: Holt, Rinehart and Winston, 1984.
[2] *Ettore Sottsass Jnr*, London: Design Council, 1982.

damage to the car, prevents vandalism and cuts the drag coefficient. Very often the design is an answer to an otherwise either/or situation. The designer, the inventor confronts the challenge of either/or. He says 'why not?' Consider Nick Butler's Durabeam torch, Alex Moulton's 'Advanced Engineering Bicycle', Alvar Aalto's Stacking Stools, Herb Lubalin's logos, and much of the work of graphic designers.

Inventors have always rejected the either/or mentality. Let's face it, most of us want to have our cake and eat it — to change the programme and stay in our seat (remote control), to watch a TV programme and go out (video recorder), to go out and still hear a programme (Walkman radio), to go out and still be in contact (all manner of bleepers and phones).

Design, the concept of design, is equally both — not either/or. Form and function are not alternative options. They are interdependent needs which the designer must satisfy without compromising either.

Finally, the *design environment* must simultaneously satisfy the twin needs of commerce and design: discipline and anarchy.

I made an observation earlier which, on reflection, I believe is the key to the central subject of how to manage design and designers. You'll remember that I said a designer was concerned with meaningful order, with making sense of relationships. And I suggested that surely there lies common ground between the designer and the administrator (between the creative and business elements, if you like).

The problem lies in that word 'meaningful'. The administrator believes that something which exists and has been proved to work represents meaningful order. The designer, on the other hand, is still seeking a meaningful order, looking for new associations, new relationships. We've seen that the thing designed and design itself, are about new relationships. Not either/or but both.

The design mind is synthetic. Like the poet he entertains new entities. Any structure which fails to appreciate this crucial aspect of the design mind will fail to get the best out of the design talent it employs. And he tackles the problem idiosyncratically. His order may seem meaning*less*. It certainly won't be that of the administrator.

The administrator craves meaningful order . . .

. . . so does the designer.

But what is meaningful?

Any structure that fails to appreciate this duality, that fails to harness the design mind, will fail to get the best out of the design talent it employs.

Design and the National Interest: 1

John Butcher MP

John Butcher is a Member of Parliament and the Minister in the Department of Trade and Industry responsible for design. To him must go the credit for implementing the design policies of the Thatcher Government, including the financial support of a wide range of design activities and particularly the design consultancy scheme which has introduced design to a wide number of smaller companies in Britain.

His paper, the first of two on this subject, deals with the contribution that design makes to the creation of wealth. He stresses the value for money which good design brings to products, describes how government is able to help promote design, and argues for a more effective use of design in the manufacturing sector in both domestic and overseas markets.

A discussion of 'Design and the National Interest' presents an almost insurmountable task, for it involves speaking about the relationship between two topics for neither of which is there an agreed simple definition. I propose to deal with that hurdle in the way Alexander dealt with the Gordian knot — arbitrarily.

I am going to set out briefly what each topic means for the purpose of this talk.

First, design. Peter Gorb defines design as 'a planning process for artefacts'. He has since, I am told, extended the meaning of 'artefact' to include 'service' by arguing that services depend on artefacts such as pens, pencils, paper, promotional literature, and that they are offered in a context of artefacts — tables, chairs, carpets, offices, showrooms. Dr Burchfield will, no doubt, take note of this extension of meaning when he next revises the first volume of the *Oxford English Dictionary*.

For my purposes the definition misses out one essential thing — the marketplace. I would prefer to use *this* definition:

'good design is the planning process for products or services that fully satisfy the aspirations of the customer.'

Those of you who follow the design scene closely will realise that the last phrase owes a lot to Merrick Taylor, Chairman of Motor Panels (Conventry) Ltd, who has argued for many years that it is no good producing something that responds to what the customer thinks he wants now — you have to aim for what he will discover he wants in the future — by which time your product or service will, of course, be ready!

Second, the national interest. This is a little easier. I am going to take the broad brush approach and define that as 'the creation of wealth'.

I could spend much of my time justifying my definitions and we could no doubt generate a lot of intellectual heat debating them. But I suggest that would be a waste of our time in this context. In our own ways we all have a common appreciation of what this discussion is about. And that it is far more important than a debate about semantics, however stimulating that might be.

So, what is there about design that means that it is in the national interest for government to be so concerned about it? Stripped down to the basics it's about the survival of the fittest. As a country we have to pay our way in the world. If we don't, then we don't create national wealth and over time the very fabric of our society will wither. Wealth creation depends on national competitiveness and company profitability. And both of these depend in the long term on producing what the customer wants at a price that offers value for money. Design, properly allied to quality and marketing, is one of the most important factors which influences people.

In 1984 I said that, whether you run a bank, a bakery or a bus factory, you must get the design right. If you don't, you will not be producing what your customers want; and what you are producing will be unsatisfactory — you will be producing it uneconomically, your workforce will be unhappy, your premises will be repellant, your literature will be confusing and your identity will be incomprehensible. And your company will go to the wall.

I'm still saying it.

Yes, it is true that companies fail for many other reasons — not least poor financial control. But, given that all other aspects of a company are satisfactory — quality control, finance, production and marketing — given *all* that, if you do not design to produce what satisfies the customer, *you will fail*. Not necessarily in the short or even the medium term. But over the long term certainly you are doomed. And there are plenty of competitors ready to take your place.

It is clearly not in the national interest for that to happen because on present trends the gap that is left is more than likely to be filled by imports. And then we are not just importing goods — we are *exporting* jobs.

We have seen it happening. But that trend can and is being reversed. And some of the more vivid examples are in manufacturing industry. Let me move on from the rhetorical to the practical and give some real-life examples to which I hope you can relate directly.

In the area of design for economic production, a consultant, Tim Sumner, quotes these two cases:

Wadkin Vertical Spindle CNC Machining Centre

The redesign of the Wadkin Vertical Spindle CNC Machining Centre resulted in a reduction in the number of components by some 37 per cent and enabled the machines to be built in 20 days instead of 20 weeks. Other design changes led to greater efficiency and a doubling of the power transmitted.

Although the number of man-hours to make the new machine has been reduced, the competitive price at which it can be offered, together with its improved performance, has increased demand to such an extent that Wadkin has taken on an extra 150 people — an increase in the work force of around 12 per cent.

Ferguson TX Colour Television

In the case of Ferguson's TX colour television, the company has reduced the number of components from just over 1000 to just over 300, and reduced the number of joints to be soldered by around 85 per cent, of which about 80 per cent are now made automatically. This in turn led to the power consumption of a set being reduced to about 40 watts and thus led to much less heat being generated inside the set.

In both these cases not only were costs significantly reduced, but customer calls were reduced by 75 per cent. These and various other examples are described in more detail in the booklet *Twenty Companies and Design*, published by the Design Council in 1985. Other cases include:

Camborne Fabrics

A range of co-ordinated screen and upholstery fabrics has increased turnover at Camborne Fabrics by £500,000 and a recent specification from an international furniture manufacturer is set to boost sales even further.

Stellar Components

Stellar Components redesigned their battery charger and reduced assembly time from 35 to 15 minutes. In the first year alone Stellar saved £760,000 on manufacturing costs and generated sales worth £7,500,000.

Clarence Clothing

In 1982 Clarence Clothing had 45 employees on a three-day week, producing 900 pairs of trousers a week. Now they have 90 employees producing 4000 pairs a weeks.

Pyrex

Market research revealed that the consumer saw Pyrex as outmoded and inconsistent with modern cooking requirements. The design and launch of their 'Classic' range in 1984 increased volume sales by 80 per cent and has led to a doubling of Pyrex's market share.

Ross Electronics

Finally, Ross Electronics, a company that has for a second time succeeded in persuading the Japanese to buy from us in a product area where they excel. They expected to sell over 10,000 of their new radios in 1986 in the UK alone, and one Japanese customer has placed an order for at least 10,000 units a year.

Here is design at work. Improving competitiveness. Winning markets. Increasing profitability. Proving in the flesh my basic point — that if you design a product (or a service) that satisfies the customer you have taken a critical step on the road to success. That's what design is about and that's what is in the national interest.

The report *Design and the Economy*, published by the Design Council in 1983, makes some more telling points about how design contributes to our national economy. It included a study on the influence of non-price factors on exports from, and imports to, Britain. It found that non-price factors account for 45 per cent of British export performance and are responsible for the decisions that influence up to 80 per cent of British imports. What these figures say to me loud and clear is that if British industry is to regain its competitiveness, both domestically and internationally, then companies have no choice but to generate products which are competitive in terms of design and quality. Aiming to be just the cheapest will not do.

This was reinforced in a report in 1985 by The House of Lords Select Committee on Overseas Trade. It too showed that the success of manufacturing and trade depends not just on price but also on non-price competitiveness.

A further survey published in 1985 which monitored the effect of the Department's 1983 'Design for Profit' campaign found that 98 per cent of respondents agreed that 'good design can increase company profits'. An admirable outcome, you might think. But how many of them are actually doing something about it?

221

Despite all the available evidence of the benefits, we are still having to put massive efforts into convincing managers to act on this belief and treat design as a function that is as important as marketing or finance. I think we are winning slowly and am encouraged to see design finding a more prominent place in some boardrooms.

I am encouraged too that the same survey revealed that over half of the companies were now holding more discussions on design than they were a year earlier. What worries me though is the other half — this is one area where I can only see the glass which is half empty rather than half full.

As Government we are trying to do something about this. So are our allies in the Design Council, the professional bodies, the educational establishments and the many committed individuals who help us to spread the design message.

And we don't just deal in messages. We offer practical help too. The Support For Design element of my Department's Business and Technical Advisory Services is perhaps one of the best known of our activities.[1]

Through this scheme we have provided over £20 million since 1982 to assist firms with the costs of design consultancy. That is a lot of money and you may ask if it is being well spent. I can answer that with a categorical 'yes'. Although the scheme offers quick advice on a particular design issue, its long-term aim is to change attitudes. To show companies how good design can help to improve a product's competitiveness, increase sales and profits, reduce manufacturing costs.

But, aside from financial assistance, if I were to use one word which I thought summed up our activities I would use the word 'education'. Educating industry in the need for greater awareness of the importance of design. Educating the public in what design is all about. And getting design and design-related activities established as valuable components of curricula at all levels of education.

---

[1] Since this paper was prepared, the Support For Design scheme has been replaced by Design Initiative, which forms one of the elements of the new DTI Enterprise Initiative.

That is why we have supported the LBS's Design Management Unit which plays such an important role in providing design management training to business graduates. It is encouraging to see that the courses are over subscribed. It is also why we supported the CNAA in the implementation of recommendations from their report, 'Managing Design'. These proposed more inclusion of design modules in post-graduate management courses and has led to the establishment of pilot courses at six selected polytechnics.

We have also tried to influence the attitude of industry's top managers by campaigns and other awareness activities. In 1985, for example, there was a series of design management seminars organised by the Society of Industrial Artists and Designers (now the Chartered Society of Designers). These looked at four industrial sectors — textiles, vehicles, information technology, and leisure — and discussed how companies in those areas benefit from good design. My Department was happy to support those events. Four books covering the seminars were also published (we supported those as well).[2] Get hold of them if you have not already done so. They offer further evidence of design at work in the economy.

In 1986 we supported a management awareness campaign, organised by the Design Council. This consisted of a supplement on design which appeared in two major magazines, aimed at increasing senior management's awareness of the benefits of good design. We shall be building on this with a further round of awareness campaigning.

When I last spoke to the London Business School in 1984 I was able to report that there was some indication of increased awareness in industry. Much of this came about because of the 'Design for Profit' campaign which the Department ran the previous year. This time, while I can report further progress in the right direction, I will tell you frankly that I am still not satisfied with industry's response. We are still not using anything like enough design to win back substantial markets and give the international competition a sound drubbing.

[2]*Directors on Design*, edited by Beryl McAlhone, London: Design Council, 1986.

But that is not to say we do not have our success stories. Many of those are among our larger companies. So we have convinced the chairmen and women and chief executives of our top performers that they can help us to spread awareness of the need for good design.

In January 1986, my Department held a Design Commitment Conference at Lancaster House. This was chaired by my colleague Paul Channon on only his second day in office. That itself demonstrates the Government commitment to design. We were delighted with the response of those invited to attend the conference. We aimed for the top, and wrote to chairmen and chief executives from the country's top industrial companies. Nearly seventy of them turned up, their combined turnover totalling almost £100 billion.

The aim of the conference was to get a commitment from those attending to hold similar seminars for their principal suppliers and so spread the design message by a multiplier effect. The vast majority of those attending agreed to hold such a seminar or to consider holding one. This has resulted in more than twenty seminars being already held or confirmed, and I confidently expect that number to grow.

Figures from a recent survey of our leading directors' attitudes to design confirm this feeling. Of directors from the country's top 500 companies, 65 per cent agreed that 'effective design management at board level is of increasing importance to the country'. I am sure that that figure too will rise over the next year or so. But I still say there is a long way to go to translate sentiment into wealth-creating action.

I am immodest enough to be proud of this programme of activities aimed at bringing about the change of attitude in industry necessary for increased competitiveness and an economic recovery.

We have gone down many paths and will go down many more. Perhaps you yourselves can think of other routes we could be taking — I would welcome your views. When the Prime Minister held her seminar in January 1982 I was surprised by the number of constructive ideas that emanated. A similar seminar was held in 1987 to discuss our progress since then.

The Government has been playing its part on all fronts. Our expenditure on design has trebled from £4 million in 1982 to £12 million in 1986. What other country can boast that? What other country has received an award from the Congress of the International Council of Societies of Industrial Design for its unparalleled commitment to design? The British Government is unique in that. Praise, though, must also go to our allies who have supported us so strongly in our efforts. Together we have made a substantial investment. I want to see a better return on it. Not for me personally. Not for the Government collectively. But for the national interest.

The gathering pace of international competition means we are at war in both our domestic and export markets. There's a weapon which can help us win. It's not a secret weapon. Nor, by itself, is it so potent that we can throw all our other competitive weapons away. But it is strategic and unless more of our firms pay better attention to it then I fear many of them will find themselves on the losing side.

That weapon is design. It's a powerful national resource and to see the proof of that you need do no more than look at the part it has played in regenerating large parts of the UK retail sector. But I have no wish to see a powerful UK retail sector which flourishes to a great extent on the sale of imported goods. What design has done for our retailers it *can* do for our manufacturers. The national interest depends crucially on putting that into more widespread practice.

Design and the National Interest: 2
Sir Simon Hornby

Simon Hornby is Chairman of W H Smith, one of Britain's largest retail chains. He is also Chairman of the Design Council, the body through which the government promotes design in Britain. As a professionally trained manager with a wide range of design and design-related interests he is well equipped to lead the most powerful and the most influential force for good design.

His paper complements that of John Butcher, in arguing the national cause for design from the viewpoint of the individual and the community. He deals with the contribution that design brings to quality of life and how that in itself, directly and indirectly, through its influence on the economy, adds to national well-being. He sees education as the key to ensuring that this process works well and describes a range of educational changes that need to be made in order to bridge the gulf between design and industrial society.

John Butcher has already tackled this subject — Design and the National Interest — with a directness and vigour which delighted us all. Invited to treat the very same subject I feel a bit like the chap who went to a village in Norfolk during the war and found a banner across the street proclaiming the Annual Strawberry Fete. Going closer he found, pinned to the pole supporting the banner, a note which explained that 'owing to the emergency prunes will be served instead'.

John Butcher defined good *design* as the 'planning process for products or services that fully satisfy the aspirations of the customer', and he defined the *national interest* still more crisply as 'the creation of wealth'.

As Chairman of a public company and as Chairman of the Design Council, to whose function I shall refer later on, I certainly buy the Butcher definitions but it would be prodigal to produce a mere paraphrase of the earlier speech.

It dealt with the vital *need* for good design as a marketing force in the country. I want to deal principally with the value and pleasure to be had from design by each human being; for me, therefore, *the national interest* relates to the well-being of the community — design and the quality of life, design as part of the culture of our national life. All other things being equal this should lead almost naturally to design for profit — the national commercial interest.

I want also to deal with *design and how to get it.* You see, there is a lot of the king's new clothes about; there is a dreadful fad these days for describing expensive items as designer radiators, designer shorts, designer garden furniture, using the word 'designer' as an adjective to differentiate the high-ticket item from, I suppose, *undesigned* design. Martin Amis in 'Money' sent the habit up beautifully by having his main character drink glass after glass of designer water, and a friend of mine, on being offered a Ritz by St Laurent, accepted, remarking 'Oh, designer cigarettes'. It is a misleading use of the word by advertisers who, wielding the power they do, should be more responsible. I remember, in this context, a woman who swore by Brown & Polson cornflour because, as she put it, 'the advertisements speak well of it'.

So this word 'designer' needs to be treated with caution; it is analogous to the king's new clothes. You'll remember that the person who spotted that there were no clothes, new or old, was a child who had not succumbed to the hype in the kingdom. The child simply used its eyes; no motes or beams nor any received opinion. I now come to the point

> We must open the eyes of the community to the benefits of good design and to the benefit and pleasure it should bring.

There should be no mystique about design and, while of course good design is not created by people who haven't been trained for it, good design can be appreciated by anyone with their senses — and common sense — in working order. The trouble is that design is not at present an informed topic in our society, nor a general subject in our schools. More often there is complaint about bad design rather than an awareness of what is good or original.

It would, I grant you, be tiresome to dwell upon the virtues of your shoelace, your ballpoint pen, your mousetrap, your toothbrush — each designed and redesigned down the years; they represent the category of product whose design, like good manners, should be and remain unobtrusive. But the graphics on an electric light bulb should not be unobtrusive since I have to read what sort of bulb it was that died in order to replace it correctly. In another context, the space for me to write my name and address should allow me to do so without the use of a mapping pen.

We should be aware or made aware of the winners of design awards as we are aware of the winner of the Booker Prize. We may not discourse on the Inmos transputer but we can discuss new cars or fabrics, furniture or appliances, aircraft or waterproof clothing.

Good design works and is pleasing; bad design fails in either or both areas. I am sure that everybody, however unconsciously, is quite capable of making a judgement but it doesn't occur to them to do so any more than they stop to ponder how they breathe or walk or sleep. Forced to an *opinion* on design, many will have difficulty in articulating what they think and that's the second stage.

First we must bring design to the front of the individual mind and then we must supply the vocabulary and the idiom with which people can communicate about it.

I think nature as a designer is a more than reasonable starting point and the simplest stimulus for just about everyone.

It was Gropius, I believe, on an afternoon off from architecture, who went to the zoo and redesigned the animals — all of them, that is, bar one. It was the seal which he found functionally and aesthetically perfect, and it is not surprising that this anecdote immediately sparks off discussion. How brilliantly the seal functions, and who can deny its beauty.

Another approach to the same end of stimulating thought and conversation about design is to encourage people to give a value to certain inventions (and 'invention' is frequently a synonym for 'design') in terms of their contribution to the well being of mankind. How should we rate the plough, the wheel, the bridge, the loom, the brick, the violin, movable type, the telescope and steam engine, the metalled road, the dynamo and camera, the thermos flask, the recording of sound, aeroplane, refrigerator, body scanner? And which in their time were best designed? And have they actually improved?

Apart from those whose work is design, I believe it unlikely that any of you regards it as a subject for consideration outside meetings within your own company; yet we all talk to our friends about money, dividends, sales trends, staffing and training policies, investment, advertising, corporate image of our own and other people's organisations.

So far as I know it's not a conspiracy of silence and it isn't because it is so esoteric that designers can only talk to designers. It is just not a conscious part of life from the start.

Let us now consider two propositions. The first is that we all have a right to good design. It should not be an extra, an expensive option for those who can afford it, but a 'given', a right which we should demand because human experience has developed to a stage where the specialised knowledge available can always produce good design. The second proposition is that we are unable to establish this right because we haven't been educated to recognise it.

Let us examine design in our own lives and start with our house. A house should be a perfectly designed object because all of us use it every day. If we consider a house and then some of its contents from the aspects of design, function, maintenance and beauty, we can ask how many houses get high marks on all three.

One key element of design should be innovation — and how little innovation there has been in the design of a house over the past fifty years. Materials have altered, some of the components have been improved but apart from a bit of tinkering little has changed. I don't believe there has been an attempt to redesign the house as a product; if there has, failure is the result. Just think about function. I challenge anyone to write an instruction manual for a house without breaking down in despair at the realisation that the 'sanguinary thing doesn't work'. If you were writing a design brief for a house, I think you might put in a requirement for a constant temperature, with a reasonable toleration, and a circulation of fresh air. Yet to get into a house you have to open and shut a door which, apart from blowing papers about and breaking the occasional object, almost invariably lets in air of a different temperature to that which you are trying to establish inside the house. The same applies to opening and shutting windows, and what about windows, both from a functional and aesthetic point of view? Fenestration has done more to wreck the appearance of houses — and why should not all houses be beautiful — than any other single feature. (If I had my way, there would be a bit of defenestration of the main culprits.)

You will be relieved to know that we are not going to continue a guided tour of the house, but before leaving it, consider two rooms: first, the bathroom. Just think about the design of the bath and the shower. Why should you bend over to put the plug in, why are taps so inconveniently placed, why can you only get a proper shower in America, why can't you turn on the shower without getting water all over your head, and so the list goes on. The answer is because the bathroom has not been designed as a product but as a series of independent components.

When you stand in the kitchen you may experience more satisfaction, as much effort has been made to make kitchens and their appliances efficient and good looking. If you are wise enough to abhor nouvelle cuisine, which seems to me the designer cooking of the yuppie generation, you should have the equipment to cook simply, like Brillat-Savarin, which not only works well but looks good too. You may, however, think that the country of origin of the most effective gadget is not in the national interest, and you may wonder why, in the middle of so much good design, it is still impossible to open a bottle or a tin without cutting yourself, or toast a crumpet crisp and golden.

Now turn to the maintenance of the house. Consider how difficult it is to maintain and how expensive. There is, for instance, no focal point for dealing with plumbing, heating, electricity. Each is placed in one of the most inaccessible areas. A house was not designed with maintenance in mind and frequently an expert has to be called in because it is outside the competence of the ordinary householder to carry out even apparently simple maintenance.

I have described enough to make the point. But finally, what about beauty. Are you proud of the housing estates which have swamped 20th-century Britain? As you drive round the towns and villages, do you make a detour to look at good, new housing? Have you ever taken a foreign visitor to look at a housing estate in Britain as you may take them to look at an 18th-century market town? I am not going to answer this for you as I know the response.

My intention is certainly not to knock the architectural profession, but to illustrate vividly why I made the claim that good design should be a right. It would be easy to argue that a component of good design is to develop the product at the right price for the market and that a perfectly designed house would be too expensive for most. Yes, the *perfectly* designed house may be too expensive, but I am certain that well-designed houses could be produced at a price that all could afford. This should be our right.

Within the past three years, W H Smith commissioned a new office building in Swindon. The brief was long and detailed and the result is a most efficient and pleasing building. It works, it's a good place to work in, it looks good, it was built on time and within the budget and it is not too hard to maintain. It was shortlisted for two national awards.

I claim that it is in the national interest that we live in and with well-designed products. Therefore it is a matter both significant and important that the BBC and Channel Four recently have given television time to the subject of design and, in particular, I am encouraged by the initiative of the BBC design awards with which the Design Council has been closely involved. One of the three categories chosen for awards was the environment. In the countryside it is rarely possible for man to equal the design of nature, whether on the sweeping scale of the Dorset downs or in the delicate tapestry of the country hedgerow. Man

231

can produce great landscape design, as did Brown at Stowe or Hoare at Stourhead, but now the need for environmental design must stretch from the countryside into the town. It is desirable that we improve the setting of White Horse Hill or Stonehenge, removing fences, siting car parks and shops and other conveniences out of the sight line; it is important that the creation of new landscape, reservoirs, dams, roads, sheltered belts, are designed so as to damage the natural landscape as little as possible and occasionally even enhance it.

But it is essential that our housing or industrial estates, our streets, stations, airports, should be designed to please and to function. Design of any environment must be a prime constituent of national interest, and it is vital that we all have the education to demand it as our right. As an example of a universal approach which is succeeding brilliantly look at the Docklands development. Compare it to the lost opportunity of the Barbican. I commend Nan Fairbrother's classic book *New Lives New Landscapes*, written in 1970, as a sensitive, scholarly and intelligent examination of the problems posed to designers by the changing use of and demands on land. It is not only the moulding of the various elements of the new landscape and the demands of its multiple uses that must be understood by the designer so as to produce an area which is both functional and pleasing, but also the objects in it, the street lamp, the litter bin, the bus shelter, the seat, the ticket kiosk.

I do not believe that 'beautiful' is an adjective we can expect often to use of the urban environment. There is no reason, though, why we should suffer an egregious mixture of ugly objects producing a visual cacophony as the attack on the senses develops a loud crash of angry discontent. But we do, but less than we did, because in the past ten years there has undoubtedly been a greater awareness. We cannot quickly eradicate the barren areas of subtopia created in the past, but we must not allow them to be produced again.

Good design should produce contentment. Pleasure is sensual but it is not only a direct appeal to the senses that gives rise to it but the satisfaction which comes from good performance. It is in this cerebral context that I believe design is also significant to the national interest. It goes without saying that efficiency in all its forms is productive. John Butcher considered the commercial and economic benefits of good design. Acknowledging these, I want to suggest also the social benefits. I believe contentment is productive, not the hedonistic and ephemeral gratification of Noel Coward's 'Design for Living', but the deep comfort which derives from the well-ordered life. The instances of pain or distress are frequent; many are caused by the temptations or stress of life, but we need not be subjected to the stress of malfunction nor ugliness. I am confident that a world in which simple appliances used in everyday life work because they are designed well and, where beauty is supreme, will be much more productive than a subculture served by ugliness and non-performance. It is that world for which we must educate ourselves.

Most children love to make things — just as many seem to want to break them too, or at least seem to be quite skilled at it. In my far-off schooldays teaching woodwork contained about as much creativity as the teaching of the Bren gun by an army corporal to squarebashing recruits. I remember making an egg stand, which was the standard alternative to an occasional table or pipe-rack. Nostalgia brings back memories of the glue pot bubbling on an old iron stove, mixed with the high-tech sniff of balsa wood cement. I was taught to make things — badly. An egg stand was a rectangle with twelve holes in it — there was no question of a skyscraper or a duplex or a round or a semi-circular egg stand. It was: that's an egg stand — make it. We made other things as children. We played with Plasticine, put together Lego, had Meccano sets, bricks, drew pictures. All these things we were encouraged to do, but never at any stage were we, nor are most children now, educated in the relationship between design and making things and the true meaning of design and its benefits to us. Of course, things have changed since my childhood and quite clearly one of the things which has changed is that education at primary and secondary level in Britain has in many ways got worse.

We want to develop a society in which design is part of the culture, the tradition of the country, as it is in Italy, or as is music in Wales, food in France, gardening in England. I considered three countries where design seems to be part of the culture, and it's part of the culture for different reasons. In Italy I believe it is part of the classical tradition. Greece, where design was pre-eminent, has latterly lost it, but somehow in Italy the tradition of good design has remained, and you can see it in products and in fashion. In Finland, design is the child of economic need. The Finns have been educated of the necessity of good design. A small country, it has to have good design if it is to compete in the commercial world. So design has been inculcated through the educational system, and has spread through the country. Japan is a mixture of the two. There is a tradition of good design, based upon craftsmanship and beauty. There is a new commercial ethos of design produced in the past thirty years, which has made it so strong economically. They started copying others but quickly learned the disciplines and developed the integrated approach.

I believe, long term, that this is the most important task of the Design Council. The DES accepts that design should be a key element in curricula at primary, secondary and tertiary level. Reports have been written, people congratulate themselves, heads nod, it should all be about to happen and in certain cases it is. There has definitely been progress, but our greatest enemy in Britain is lip service. There are innumerable barriers — the quality of teachers, disinterest, lethargy, money — but these barriers mean that if we attempt a gradual approach nothing much will change.

Thus we start with a great disadvantage, to which I have already referred.

I am involved with a campaign of great significance to get children to read books, and although it is hard to get recognition of the crisis, at least people know what we are talking about. If I talk to a group of parents or teachers about books we are immediately on the same wavelength. If I talk about design, many may think they know what I am talking about, but few do. So if our ambitions, and by 'our' I mean the government and all those responsible for formulating the policy to improve Britain, are to be met, I believe that the Design Council has to lead a campaign with evangelical fervour and total commitment to the cause. Who else will do it? This government does act. There are good signals, a radical change to improve education. This government also seeks to enable things to happen, reckoning that if something ought to be done about it, then the people should get on and do it. It may be thought that I am being over-ambitious in saying that the Design Council should lead the crusade, but what is the point of a Design Council if it does not lead. We are charged with three main objectives — to continue to increase awareness in industry and commerce of the benefits of good design, to encourage greater consciousness of good design by customers, both in the public and the private sectors and to reinforce the importance of design education and training at all levels.

At the Design Seminar held at Downing Street in January 1982 I outlined what needed to be done in education. First, design should be an essential part of the education of all children at all stages from primary through tertiary education. It should not only be taught but examined in that light. More teachers of design must be found and should be trained in the importance of the cross-curricula approach. Second, a major drive must be made in the education of engineers, both to increase the number of good engineers and to develop their understanding through education of the multidisciplinary approach. Third, design for product development should be taught as a core subject in all general business management courses. It is as important to success as accounting, marketing or human behaviour. Finally, all design and arts courses should include management for profit as a core subject in their curriculum. Implicit in all of these aims is the need to open the eyes of the entire community to the significance of design.

James Pilditch's word INTEGRATION is fundamental. C P Snow would have liked it, for he was a notable advocate of the need to bridge the gulf between science and the arts; to bring the aesthetic designer and inventor, as it were, together; to eliminate once and for all the mutual suspicion which prevails when the products of two quite separate educational streams first confront each other at the factory.

235

But not only in education — industry, too, must improve its training. All managers, senior, middle, lower, must understand what is meant by design — what can be achieved by it and how to practise it. Designers and engineers, particularly those in authority, must be made to think about the business application of design. More companies should follow the lead of a few to establish links with schools, polytechnics and universities to help plan curricula, assist with teaching and to give student placement. Industry should encourage and inspire children through competitions, visits and other imaginative ideas. The London Business School was alone in pioneering design management in its courses. Now, thanks to the efforts of many, including the CNAA, the DTI and the Design Council, at least six polytechnics are developing design management courses within their curriculum. The Royal College of Art and others insist on business management in all design courses. These are all milestones which are being passed, but my concern is that although it is all most commendable, and I mean that very sincerely, although many excellent things are being done, progress is too slow.

Britain has some exemplary companies, and many outstanding designers. Unfortunately the good companies are outnumbered by the mediocre which do not use the designers available, as do the wise Japanese, Italians and Germans. John Butcher talked of the Design Council's management awareness campaign. In summer 1985 advertising got a depressingly poor response. This year, a new and imaginative mailing programme is getting mild success — good if you relate it to mail order statistics but pitiful if you relate it to the absolute numbers approached.

So the Design Council must be prepared to lead, to be outspoken, to criticise bad design and show up good design. Although paid by the government, it must not be the servant of the government but of the nation, who really provide the money. As servant of the nation, it must behave not only with the subtle persuasiveness of Jeeves or the impish ingenuity of Passe Partout, but it must follow the polemicism of the young Churchill or the statesmanship of the experienced Talleyrand.

It must use any means to succeed. And success means achieving a culture where it is accepted that good design is a right, that good design enhances life, that good design creates wealth, and that good design is a quintessential component of the nation's well being.

PART 5

Case Studies

Design and the Building of Storehouse
Sir Terence Conran

Sir Terence Conran's second paper is a case history of how design works in his company, Storehouse. He claims it has invested more in design over a longer period than any other retail chain in the world. The case history describes how this has happened. He begins with the Habitat decision to design its own products for manufacture and goes on to show how this design-led strategy has been implemented as the group acquired the retail chains that currently make up the Storehouse Group.

The recognition of the commercial value of design is a relatively new phenomenom, and is one that is still not fully understood by some retailers, and even more manufacturers. In the Storehouse Group, however, design has always been a fundamental part of our own-brand retailing philosophy, and we have invested heavily in it. I would like to talk about how we came to develop this philosophy, and how it has proved its commercial value.

Habitat was unquestionably pioneer in the application of retail design. When the first Habitat store opened in London 24 years ago, it differed from other furniture stores in several, very significant, respects.

First, and perhaps most importantly, it did not try to satisfy every taste. In fact it did not set out to satisfy *any* taste. Instead, it created a new one through the application of the principles of good design in the selection of products, and their display. By selecting products to this criteria, a collection was built up which was extraordinarily harmonious and individual in style, and quite unlike anything else on the High Street at that time. In furnishings, it focused on natural finishes and materials such as earthenware, rush matting, basketware, wool,

241

cotton. In furniture it set the scene for contemporary classic taste by selecting simple shapes and forms which were comfortable and not so extreme in style that they quickly dated.

Second, Habitat differed from other furniture stores at that time by selling furnishings and furniture together to portray a complete furnishing style. This again was a radical departure from the normal practice of the time, when furniture shops looked like mausoleums for three-piece suites during the week, and only came to life briefly on Saturdays. The inclusion of non-furniture items in the store kept the shop busy at all times, and greatly benefited furniture sales. The shop displays encouraged people to feel, try and select for themselves (another innovation at the time), and the ambience was relaxed, light and welcoming.

As Habitat grew, we continually sought new products made to high standards of design that we could sell at prices people could afford. We bought goods from all over the world, but it often proved difficult to find reliable sources that were exactly what we wanted in terms of design and quality. So we decided to design the products ourselves and have them manufactured to our requirements.

This was an important stage in our development, but one which was not easily achieved. In the UK, manufacturers had traditionally made the decisions about what or what not to produce for the retailer, and not the other way round as we were attempting to do. Initially many were sceptical. After all, their products had sold perfectly well in the past, and those same products were still selling. What was the point of changing just for the sake of it? Why should they risk the cost of tooling up for a product of unproven popularity, for a relatively new retailer who could only guarantee small volumes?

Well, of course, people can only buy what they are offered, but as retailers, we could see many opportunities for improving the home furnishing products of the time. We felt confident that if the public were offered well-designed goods at the right price they would buy them. 'Good Design at Good Prices' was the slogan that was firmly nailed to the Habitat mast, and we have sailed under that banner ever since.

Although, at first, it was hard to convince many manufacturers, a few smaller, younger companies were eager to co-operate and I am glad to say that many of the products we developed
with them in the early days laid the foundations for profitable
and long-lasting working relationships to the great benefit of
both companies. Initially, some larger suppliers would grant
little more than a special colour or pattern applied to their
existing products, and it is only as we have grown in size that
they have come to trust our judgement.

The development of products made to our own design had
two very beneficial effects. First, it gave us exclusivity, thereby
protecting us from price wars with competitors, and preserved
our margins. Second, it enabled us successfully to develop our
own brand (rather than the manufacturers), which has been
perhaps one of the most important trends in retailing in the
past two decades, and a natural consequence of retail-led
manufacturing.

So far, I have talked mostly about product design, but now
that I have come to 'uniqueness of identity', I must talk about
the value of design in a wider context.

In 1983, Habitat merged with Mothercare, the mother and
baby specialist retailer. The two companies had many paral-
lels — they were both founded in the early sixties; both were
specialist, their own livery, stationery etc, were all redesigned in
a fresh, new spirit, and sales responded vigorously.

Of course, the application of design principles in retailing
can only be effective if it is sustained and becomes an integral
part of a company's philosophy. It's no good putting in an
enormous one-off effort and then sitting back until profits
start to slip again. Creative designers who are 'commercially
aware' — that is knowledgeable of the market they are working
for, and who never allow budgets, costs and final retail price to
stray far from their thoughts — are essential components of
today's successful retail management team.

Now, I certainly don't pretend that designers are perfect or
will automatically ensure a company's profit and success (excellent operational systems and well-motivated staff are equally
essential), but I do think that what they have to offer is

fundamental to modern retailing. They have the power to create the unique products and special identity which will separate you from the shop next door. They should be an equal part of the team with buyers and marketing people and store operations and, in large organisations, they must be represented at board level.

So clearly has design-led retailing demonstrated its success that there is scarcely a retail chain in the UK which has not, during the past five years, embarked on some level of modernisation and redesign programmes. Many millions of pounds have been spent by the retailing companies during this time on design fees, and in the same period the number of major design consultancies has increased fourfold.

At Storehouse we invest approximately 0.3 per cent of our turnover on design and product development through our own in-house design teams. This doesn't seem much when it allows us to create our own branded products, which we sell at margins that we determine in environments that are unique to us. Through the design process, we are in control of our own destiny.

Following the merger with Mothercare, the Group acquired two businesses which were in a fairly advanced state of decline: Heal's, the long-established furnishing business, which occupied huge premises in Central London, and Richard Shops — a chain of approximately 200 womenswear shops which had badly lost its way in the fashion world. Once again, the design-based approach to retailing was applied. The market was studied, the target customer identified, and the designers used their skills to create exclusive new products and shopping environments aimed specifically at these customers. In both cases, the results have been very successful.

The most recent application of our design-led strategy has been in BhS, which merged with the Habitat Mothercare Group in January 1986.

What has been done at BhS since then shows just how much can be achieved in a very short time by efficient use of the design process. Following the merger, it quickly became clear that there was a lot of good merchandise in BhS, but not enough customers knew about it. The immediate and urgent task was to create an atmosphere that would help to adjust their perception. A three-pronged strategy was devised, to give British Home Stores, as it was then called, the new identity it needed. First, we shortened the name to BhS, created a new logo which retained something of the reliability and solidity of the old but incorporating a colourful 'flying h' which hinted at a new excitement within. In the stores the changes had to draw customers to the merchandise, which we knew they would want to buy if only they could find it. Exclamation poles riding high over the displays marked defined areas within the store, and acted as landmarks to guide the customer to their desired destination. Fashion displays, mood boards, attractive fittings and better graphics all combined to give the stores a colourful, modern image.

To create maximum impact at minimum cost, we decided to change all 128 stores in one weekend — a massive logistical exercise, covering 3 million square feet of space. All the fascias were changed. Over 3000 exclamation poles were erected, and 150,000 mood boards put up. All the price tickets were replaced with the new ones carrying the redesigned logo, and all the hanging fittings were altered.

The third part of the strategy was to communicate these changes on two major fronts. First to the staff through a redesigned and renamed staff magazine, *Storetalk*, so that they would be well primed on the new direction of their company. Second, we told the public through a vigorous advertising campaign involving posters, press advertisements and television commercials. Immediately, sales started to respond — the wheel of change started to turn.

But this is just a beginning. What we will do in the future is to ensure that BhS is selling merchandise that customers want, and to a certain extent, aspire to. As with all the other companies in the Storehouse Group, we will constantly research all aspects of the operation. With BhS we are reviewing all the existing merchandise, and searching for new opportunities. At Conran Design Group we have set up a fashion studio dedicated to BhS, and have extended our products studio to cope with the vast amount of new work.

No other retailing group in the world has invested in design resources so heavily and over such a long period of time as we have. Our design teams working at Conran Design Group have a wealth of creative talent and collective experience second to none. We service *all* the design needs of all the Storehouse companies through Conran Design Group. The Group also has many outside clients in all fields of commerce which further enriches and stimulates the creativity of our designers.

This, then, is what our future will be — constantly striving to offer customers better designed, better quality products at good prices. We must not allow ourselves to be deviated from this goal. The search for new ideas and new retailing formulas, the investment in technology, and the need to attract and motivate staff gathers pace as this new retail philosophy gains strength and conviction, and the marketplace becomes even more competitive.

The Columbia-Presbyterian Medical Center, Identity Program

Colin Forbes

Colin Forbes is a designer and a founding partner of Pentagram, one of Britain's leading design consultancies. In 1978 he set up their New York practice, and Pentagram now operates from both New York and San Francisco. A graphic designer by training he has always had a deep interest in management. His paper reflects that interest by describing a case study of the first major corporate identity scheme with which he was involved in the USA. It deals with the design contribution to the identity problems of a major US hospital and medical centre. It describes the analytical process behind the scheme, the problems encountered and shows how they were resolved.

The Columbia-Presbyterian Medical Center is not an organisation but the name given to the joint activities of two separate entities: the Columbia University Department of Health Services, and the Presbyterian Hospital. The overlap occurs because the Hospital department heads are also professors in the University's clinical departments. The Hospital and the University have different organisational cultures — distinct hierarchies, payroll structures, etc. The problem of a unified identity is made more complex by the fact that the Hospital has grown by incorporating numerous specialist hospitals, often very highly regarded names in their specific fields.

IDENTITY ELEMENTS

The purpose of this paper is to illustrate the development of an identity programme as it was presented to the client. The case is

247

that of the Columbia-Presbyterian Medical Center. It leads on from an initial investigatory report presented to the client in April 1983, and focuses on the recommendations put forward by Pentagram to the client.

Briefly, an identity programme is based on four basic elements. These are:

1. Nomenclature and identification policies
2. A logotype and/or symbol
3. Ancillary alphabet and typefaces, and
4. Colour

Nomenclature

Our earlier research findings showed that the objectives of the identity program should be to project a) the *breadth* of the Center, which makes it *a* medical centre and b) the *depth* of the Center, which makes it *the* medical centre. The proposals stemmed from this. It was therefore necessary to develop a method to communicate a correct blend of breadth and depth.

The approach also had to be modular in order to:

1. Cater to the various needs of the Medical Center's constituent parts.
2. Amplify the uniqueness of each constituent.
3. Personalise the Medical Center's approaches to its various external audiences.

In order to establish a policy on the structure of the Medical Center to be communicated, the following had been recommended and approved at the meeting of the University and Hospital senior administrators in March 1983 (see Figure 1):

1. The name 'Columbia-Presbyterian Medical Center' identifies breadth, and would always appear on graphic items.
2. Columbia University and the Presbyterian Hospital were distinct institutions and therefore both would be identified.
3. As 'The Presbyterian Hospital' would never appear without 'Columbia-Presbyterian Medical Center' also appearing, 'in

the city of New York' could be omitted after the Hospital's name, except on letterheads and legal documents.

4. Rather than identify the university component of the Medical Center as the Columbia University Division of Health Sciences, the University would be identified as four parts without expressing the hierarchy between the College of Physicians and Surgeons and the Schools of Public Health and Nursing:
   a) Columbia University College of Physicians & Surgeons
   b) Columbia University School of Public Health
   c) Columbia University School of Nursing
   d) Columbia University School of Dental and Oral Surgery

5. The third institution to be identified would be the Columbia-Presbyterian Medical Center Fund, Inc.

6. The New York Psychiatric Institute would be included in the identity programme.

7. The word 'department' would be used Center-wide, and not 'service'. Therefore, for example, the 'Department of Urology' would exist in both the University and the Hospital.

8. The Medical Center had within its structure departments, centres and institutes which had a promotional value and should be clearly recognised. These included 15 clinical departments, 7 basic science departments, and 9 well-defined research and teaching centres.

   In addition, there were centres, programmes and institutes within the Medial Center which fell into three categories but which needed to be more clearly defined. These included: a) Private doctors' offices, b) Billing for radiologic services, and c) Service centres or programmes (patient care programmes).

IDENTIFICATION POLICIES

It was decided that the identification system should be based on four different functions for names, combined with appropriate emphasis when used in various applications. These were:

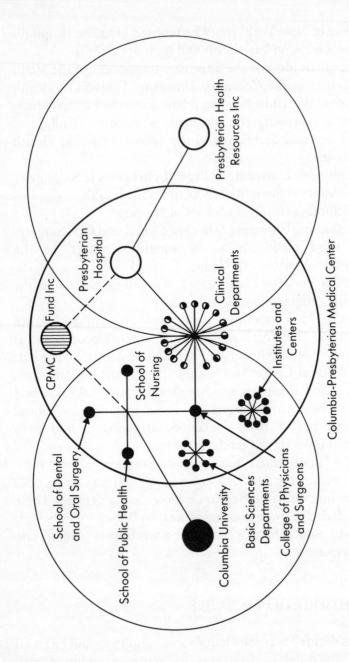

Figure 1 *Structure of the Columbia-Presbyterian Medical Center*

Presbyterian Health Resources Inc

Presbyterian Hospital

CPMC Fund Inc

Clinical Departments

Institutes and Centers

School of Nursing

School of Dental and Oral Surgery

School of Public Health

Columbia University

Basic Sciences Departments

College of Physicians and Surgeons

Columbia-Presbyterian Medical Center

1. An umbrella function
2. An institution identification function
3. An activity identification function, which for the University included:
   a) Administrative and alumni offices
   b) Basic sciences departments
   c) Centres and institutes
   for the hospital:
   — Administrative offices
   for both the University and the Hospital:
   — Clinical departments
4. A place identification function.

The latter included examples such as the Dana W Atchley Pavilion, the Bardhaven Towers, The Julius B Armand Hammer Health Sciences Center and The Neurological Institute of New York.

It was suggested that to help clarify the distinction between institutions and places, the Presbyterian Hospital and College of Physicians and Surgeons buildings should be renamed Presbyterian Building and P&S Building.

In terms of signage, it was thought that it might be necessary for 'place' to be further delineated into 'subdivisions' in cases where a clinic, centre, institute or other large entity was located within a building, for example, the Squire Urological Clinic, The Babies Hospital, The Augustus Long Library.

These issues needed to be further discussed.

Logotype and/or Symbol

Due to the broad exposure which the umbrella 'Columbia-Presbyterian Medical Center' would receive, it was important that it appeared consistently in only one format. In order to design the format, several approaches were considered.

The first option was to have the name appear as a logotype: Columbia-Presbyterian Medical Center. This approach was rejected due to the fact that, with the subsequent hierarchical addition of names of institutions, activities, places and addressed on letterheads, too many names would be difficult to read.

A second approach was to use the initials 'CPMC'. This too, was rejected, for two reasons. First, initials generally do not communicate except to members of an organisation, profession or trade. To someone outside the Medical Center, 'CPMC' would just be another set of initials, not unlike VDU (visual display unit), LED (light emitting diode) and REM (rapid eye movement), which tend not to have any meaning until they are spelled out. Second, because the Medical Center did not have the level of exposure of a company such as IBM, the initials could never appear unless accompanied by the name written in full. The work undertaken to combine the initials with the names did not result in a design that fulfilled the criteria of simplicity and memorability.

For these reasons, the possibility of developing a symbol was explored. There are two essential criteria for a symbol: it should be a simple and memorable 'visual shorthand', and it should have the most positive associations with the activities of the organisation.

First, the development and amalgamation of the existing symbols of the University and Hospital were considered. Despite the coincidence of each institution having a form of shield as its emblem, shields did not have any symbolic medical emphasis; they are so extensively used that in any form they would not be unique; and they have old or heraldic associations.

An extensive investigation into symbol sources showed that two primary symbols have universal recognition for medicine or medical care: the Greek serpent/staff and the form of the cross used by the Red Cross. A study of shapes that have visual recognition was undertaken and the cross was seen to be one of the basic forms.

To combine recognition value, medical connotations and a unique form, an adaptation was made to the Celtic Cross with the proportions of the Red Cross to make the symbol of the Columbia-Presbyterian Medical Center.

The same arguments for including the full name of the Medical Center applied to a symbol. Therefore the name was included in the design. By positioning the words in a circle around the cross, the total device became a single unit. The device also had associations with an academic seal or badge. The symbol proposed by Pentagram is shown in Figure 2.

In order for the new identity programme to be effectively implemented, the new symbol would have to be used exclusively. No other symbols or logotypes for the Columbia-Presbyterian Medical Center were to be used unless there were legal or historical precedents.

Symbol Connotation Research

To test that there were no unfavourable associations and to verify Pentagram's opinion that the proposed symbol would represent the desired Medical Center image to most people, a survey was conducted by Marketing Service Associates, Inc. The key points are summarised below.

Figure 2 *The symbol proposed by Pentagram*

The primary objectives were to determine:

1. What the design elicited on a spontaneous basis.
2. Whether there were inappropriate associations with this design that might detract from its usefulness (for example, military, political or religious associations).
3. How closely the design was associated with the appropriate organisational types (for example, medical centres, hospitals, universities, research organisations and scientific organisations).

Personal interviews were conducted with 45 physicians, nurses, donors, recent in- or out-patients and medical school students. Respondents were first asked for spontaneous reactions to an assortment of symbols, one of which was the Pentagram proposal. The majority were more favourable than anticipated although there were, of course, a few unfavourable comments.

Respondents were then asked on a scale of 1–10 the degree to which they would associate the symbol with specific types of organisation. Figure 3 shows the average responses to the symbol proposed by Pentagram.

On the chart a median score of 5.5 indicates no strong association or non-association of the proposed symbol with the organisation category listed at the side. The results showed that associations of the symbol with military, industrial, legal, governmental, political and financial groups fell below the average of 5.5. Through the level of religious association was above 5.5, it did not rank as high as medical centre, hospital or university associations, nor as high as scientific and research associations.

During the interviews undertaken with doctors, nurses, administrators, medical staff, students, community residents, local politicians, alumni, patients and donors in February 1983, there was not a single case where the name Presbyterian was considered a disadvantage because of its literal religious meaning. Therefore, it was considered that the level of religious association in this survey was easily outweighed by the very positive medical associations.

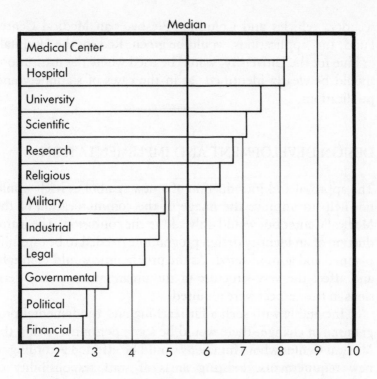

Figure 3 *Average responses to the symbol proposed by Pentagram*

Typeface

The typeface Times was recommended because a) it is a serif face b) it has a wide range of weights c) it is clearly legible and d) it is readily available in almost every typesetting system. It was recommended that Times should be used on all stationery, building signs and other standardised items, but should not be mandatory for such promotional publications as the Annual Report and magazines.

Colours

We proposed that a colour-coding system be used, partly to support individual identities and partly for decorative reasons. General Medical Center applications, such as building signs, security, vehicles and Columbia-Presbyterian Medical Center Fund, Inc. applications, would be green. Red for the Hospital, or blue for the University, would be used where the institutions should be clearly identified, as in the cases of stationery and publications.

DESIGN DEVELOPMENT AND IMPLEMENTATION

The approval and introduction of a new symbol in itself would not help to improve the image or the communication of the Medical Center but would only add to the confusion. The introduction of an identity design programme needed to be carefully planned and administered. As the programme would highlight and affect the very structure of the organisation, policy decisions in this respect were required.

Inevitably with such a far-reaching and fundamental programme of change, there would be some personnel within the Medical Center whose functions would be affected according to new requirements. Existing areas of staff responsibility or creative freedom might have been removed. Therefore, it was important to communicate the need for a new identity and to demonstrate how everyone would benefit from it.

The following steps outline the procedure that we recommended:

1. Appoint a Design Steering Committee whose purpose was:
   a) to implement policies agreed on by the joint management of the Columbia University Division of Health Sciences and the Presbyterian Hospital, and
   b) to control budget.
2. Appoint a design officer who would have a thorough understanding and enthusiasm for the scheme in order to promote and explain it to all levels within the Medical Center.
3. Divide the total programme into categories of activities and appoint committees:
   a) to obtain detailed information on the total inventory and specific applications of the programme.

b) to provide information for implementation.
c) to control standardisation of design details for each category: stationery, publications, signage, vehicles and uniforms.
4. Based on the presentations made to the University and Hospital senior administrators, present a motivational programme to senior doctors and those executives who would be responsible for implementation.
5. Produce detailed design specifications or manuals for each category in order to set standards for the future.
6. Set a date of introduction:
a) to achieve maximum impact.
b) to minimise confusion between the old and new identities.

At this stage, steps such as the following were to be taken:
a) withdraw old stationery
b) issue new stationery
c) issue a typing guide
d) design new publications to carry the symbol, and
e) erect signs on the campus.

The implementation programme would extend over a minimum of three years and priorities of items within each category of activity would be established. For example, stationery, business cards and other items normally held in a secretary's desk would be a first priority and the most important forms received by donors, students or patients would become the next priority. Publications and uniforms would be changed on a replacement basis, however, and a major study and investment required for signage to undergo any significant changes.

It was proposed that Pentagram continue to act as a consultant on an ongoing basis and that budgets be developed for design work in each category of activity, not necessarily to be undertaken by Pentagram.

Design Management Policy at British Rail

Jim O'Brien

Jim O'Brien is joint Managing Director of British Rail and a member of the British Railways Board. He was converted to the value of design as a management tool during the tenure of Sir Peter Parker as Chairman of British Rail. Since that time he has actively encouraged the development of design, run a number of important design promotional activities with the organisations; ensured that design has a formal place within the policies of the business, and appointed a new Director of Design with comprehensive responsibilities reporting directly to him.

Rather than reproduce his talk at London Business School he has chosen to present as a case study a documentation of the process by which the present position of design at British Rail has come about. A short introduction to BR precedes the five documents in the case.

INTRODUCTION

The British Railways Board, the senior management of BR, sees good design as central to good business. Thirty years ago, 20 per cent of Britain's passenger kilometres and 50 per cent of her freight tonne kilometres were on rail. Today the figures are 7 and 11 per cent, even though the market for inland transport has more than doubled. BR has had to reorganise in order to be more responsive to customer demand. In this reorganisation, the benefits of good design policy are clear.

The late 1980s allow us to make a major updating of our physical apparatus and in particular of our rolling stock. At the same time our engineering and catering organisations are now asked to submit tenders which are competitive to those offered by outside firms. Overall, we are more conscious of market needs; and, having embarked this year on Britain's biggest investment programme since 1985, we can demand the best of our suppliers. These various factors have pushed design to the centre of our marketing strategy, with fresh significance.

The design panel of the British Railways Board was set up in 1956. The panel has always counted distinguished independent experts in design among its members. In the 1980s its tasks are more important than ever.

We have recently established a newly structured role to make design implementation more effective in British Rail. Jane Priestman, as Director of Architecture, Design and the Environment, is directly responsible to me for all design matters in the railways.

What follow are a number of documents which deal with design policies and their implementation. The first of these is concerned with the background to design at British Rail. It is an excerpt from an article by James Cousins, our recently retired Director of Design, and is taken from a recent book on British Rail design, published for us by the Danish and British Design Councils. The book was the outcome of a year's active commitment to design at both British Rail and Danish State Railways. Two conferences were held by the two railways, one in January 1986, and the second in January 1987. The first conference set in motion a wide range of design-based projects, the outcomes of which were reported to the second conference. Documents two and three are examples of two of these projects, the first a strategy statement, and the second a specific project on stations. Since then, our thinking about design has culminated in a design policy statement which has been approved by the British Railways Board. Document four is the memorandum which introduced the policy statement which is itself attached as Appendix I to the memorandum. Appendix II is the statement of responsibilities of the Director of Architecture, Design and the Environment. Finally, document five is the widely circulated management brief on British Rail design policy.

I hope these various documents will illuminate the practical route we have followed at British Rail in recognising design as central to our business.

DOCUMENT I:
BACKGROUND TO DESIGN AT BRITISH RAIL

Pioneers

Great Britain invented the railway and so changed the face of the world. To operate the railway Britain built steam locomotives.

The 2nd of September, 1825 saw the beginning of a competitive and much duplicated endeavour in this innovation. It established that triumph of art and industry — the steam locomotive — which reached a quality of functional and aesthetic design that became part of the British psyche.

Perhaps the most spectacular early performance was that of *Firefly* built by Daniel Gooch for Brunel, which reached a speed of 58 mph on its first run in 1840. The *Actaeon*, of similar design and class, in 1844 travelled 387 miles to Exeter and back in one day, at an average speed of 40 mph. Thus began the InterCity business.

Conquest was the dominant motif of the railways in the late 19th century. They became the key to opening up the American West and the vast territories of Africa. A hundred years ago, trains were the only fast mode of transport. Competition existed only inside the industry. More than 100 railway firms vied with each other for expanding markets, and it took but six months to design and build a new locomotive.

As the careers of the Stephenson and Brunel families showed, design for the railways was very much a fusion of civil engineering, mechanical engineering and knowing how to draw. While he established the physics of modern transatlantic steamships and so went on to build the *Great Eastern*, Isambard Kingdom Brunel was also a superb draughtsman in his own right. He insisted on working with informative drawings, and made extensive use of industrial photography in his design and project management decisions.

Brunel and Broad Gauge

In the days of Brunel, railway design meant practical mastery of both graphic image and of materials. With pencil and lathe, the railway designer was someone who got his hands dirty in one of the world's first systems of industrial management control. Design decisions took on a truly epochal scope.

Isambard Kingdom Brunel's broad gauge rail systems, in which lines were no less than seven feet apart, meant that trains could reach 60 miles per hour as early as 1848. Broad gauge was a visionary design concept: it allowed steam engines to take more fuel, carry heavier loads and travel with great stability at high speeds. Discontinued in 1892 as Britain went over to a four feet and eight-and-a-half inches national standard, broad gauge could have done much to reverse the complacency about innovation that came to characterise Britain's railways in the early part of the 20th century.

The Birth of Railway Graphics

Railway companies had begun to identify themselves by distinctive liveries since the early 1840s. The product design qualities of their trains were enhanced by the creative application of what is now described as graphic design, from basic signage, through commercial posters and staff uniforms, to tickets.

In 1922, just before it was grouped into four main-line companies, the railways in Britain counted 27 main companies and 94 subsidiary ones. All the larger companies, and many of the smaller ones, had special liveries and crests. *Corporate identity* was a design issue very early on in the railways.

The graphic design of this era is marked by a sureness of touch. Before nationalisation, corporate identity could be a fresh, exciting and characterful business. It was not until the 1960s, however, that railway graphics began to regain its former clarity and quality.

Corporate Identity and the Corporate Identity Manual

In November 1964 the British Railways Board agreed a series of proposals on corporate identity for its whole operation. The proposals, which were made by the Corporate Identity Steering Committee of BR's Design Panel, covered a new symbol, name-style and alphabet, plus a schedule for their introduction. Early priorities for change were advertising and printed publicity.

The new scheme was publicly unveiled at the opening of a special exhibition at the Design Centre, London, in January 1965. It quickly established itself as a metaphor for the concurrent modernisation of BR. Later the same year a *Corporate Identity Manual* for staff applying the scheme was published: it was drawn up by the independent consultants Design Research Unit (DRU). This manual, which at one time ran to four separate volumes, forms the basic plan of campaign in the graphics of BR.

The manual defines BR's symbol, logotype, lettering and colours, and gives detailed directions about their use in everything from brochures and timetables to signposting and station fascias. Users of the manual are given regular help by the Corporate Identity Steering Committee. It is vital to note, though, that use of the manual must be flexible. Independent reports by the designers Pentagram and Herbert Spencer have recently confirmed that our basic graphic scheme is sound, but our new move to management by sector: Freight, Parcels, Inter-City, Provincial, London & South East, is just one of the continual changes which make it sensible for BR to apply its corporate identity flexibly. Flexibly, but with added vigour.

The British Rail Alphabet

Jock Kinneir, the man who designed the British Rail Alphabet, has seen it adopted widely. Denmark's and Norway's state railway systems use it, and, in a different context, the British Airports Authority has adopted it, as has Australia's. Why? Because, as alphabets go, it is based on the sound ergonomic principles of maximum legibility. Kinneir's tests, performed at the Road Research Laboratory, determined that letters with an x-height of 55 mm could be read at more than 40 metres. What was more, Kenneir showed, such letters could be put on flap-type displays of 990 x 113 mm for the station names and information display on station indicators.

Kinneir is one of a special generation of British graphic designers. He trained in the late 1930s and went on to create much of the nation's graphic dynamism in the 1960s. His road alphabet upheld the new motorways of Britain as landmarks of modern signposting.

Station Architecture

For an organisation as big and as complex as BR, corporate identity includes *everything visual*. The architecture of our stations therefore forms an important aspect of our corporate identity.

Long before *user-friendly* became a buzzword it was clear that our passengers looked for a sense of space and light in stations, for clarity, reassurance and cleanliness. Whilst designing to give just that we also have to exercise imagination and flexibility in aiming at well-mannered buildings: not those which project an artificially old or nostalgic image, but those which, by their sense of style, vigour and freshness, are clearly of today and ready for the 21st century. Stations which will happily merge with their habitat, whether urban or rural, yet at the same time, proclaim their business.

At the same time we need to take care of our old building stock, of our often splendid heritage. That may often prove time-consuming and expensive. But the returns, whilst not immediately apparent in financial terms, promise well. Response from the communities is encouraging as also is the positive effect on our own self-respect.

We use colour in a spirited and occasionally witty way to decorate and maintain our old buildings. But as the example of London's enormous Waterloo Station shows, the liveliness we seek to develop in our city-based stations nevertheless needs discipline if passengers are to be presented with information of a high degree of clarity.

Rolling Stock

The exterior style, the interior decor, the seating, fixtures and fittings of a carriage, the organisation of the driver's cab, all these different aspects of a train are bound up in the industrial design of rolling stock.

At BR we have clear evidence that good industrial design when combined with the higher speeds that passengers now demand, can contribute to higher passenger revenues.

At the high speeds proposed the front end design of British Rail's power cars have been designed with a view to aerodynamic efficiency. Pressure waves and turbulence from trains passing in close proximity at high speed must be avoided.

The driver's cab of the High-Speed train is an interesting construction in that it is formed of glass-reinforced plastic to a thickness of 50 mm. It has been manufactured as a complete module with all conduits, air pipes and ventilation ducts incorporated in the wall thickness.

The Journey

Comfort, convenience, safety and speed — with customer care. BR has an ongoing commitment to provide a better service for the passenger. Passengers are people — a pleasant journey by rail requires more attention to seat design and the environmental control of the carriage interior.

BR has adopted ergonomic principles in seating design. The aim is to accommodate 85 per cent of the population comfortably. It is quite wrong to design for the *average man*. If average dimensions were applied, seats would be unsuitable for half of the population.

People do not sit still. Sitting involves a constant search for a stable, comfortable position. Any one position is only comfortable for a time. A well-designed seat allows for a great variety of change of posture.

Passenger travel by rail requires an interactive system embracing the quality of graphic design in providing train information, whether by timetables, posters or electronic displays. It requires clarity in the promotion of the railways fare structure and consideration of the problems experienced by special users, for example, the disabled. For safety and convenience, a clear graphics system of signs on stations and notices on trains has been developed as an important part of the Corporate Identity Programme.

James Cousins 1986

DOCUMENT II:
DESIGN STRATEGY

The second document summarises the strategy statement contained in the brief given by the Anglo–Danish Railway Design Conference in January 1986 and covers BR and DSB positions, with comment on the present situation in BR and DSB (Danish State Railways) and proposals for the future.

Present Situation

BR design strategy now
No formal design philosophy binding together the business sectors of BR exists at present, though the Director of Industrial Design had been striving to help the sectors to achieve 'diversity within unity'; BR at this moment presents an image of design confusion.

With fundamental changes in management structure and procurement policy, there have been problems in carrying out in detail the implementation of a centralised design policy, particularly for rolling stock.

Having endowed the BR design panel and environment panel with power and prestige, there is no doubt that the BR Board expects vigorous action in the fields of design co-ordination and execution. This can only be achieved by way of a new design management programme that sets out the Board's intent and lines of responsibility for all aspects of design of the rail environment.

Some of the latest developments in BR reflect a lack of understanding of the natural rhythm in which the various parts of a co-ordinated design programme can be carried out. New styles in advertising may be launched overnight, but it takes years to renew rolling stock. A design management programme will need to reflect these variations in timescale in all strategic planning.

DSB design strategy now
During the past fifteen years, DSB has been following the way pioneered by BR — first adopting a comprehensive design

programme, and then fighting it fiercely. The struggle is not caused by negative sentiments in the organisation, but rather by the particular dynamics of a big bureaucracy. This tendency has not been diminished with the emergence of sector management in DSB — again a British model.

The situation highlights the classic dilemma of design management: on one hand it is necessary to motivate and stimulate innovative thinking, on the other hand to keep the overall image consistent and in some cases restrictive. The difficulty is to maintain a balance between the two conflicting demands.

In DSB the design balance is influenced by three factors

a) Most of our design results have been achieved in the field of house style and corporate identity.
b) Most DSB trains are still old-fashioned, the first significant technological leap forward being the IC/3 train in 1988.
c) This gives marketing and advertising a very meagre basis for promoting DSB products, most of them actually being created within the existing framework of advertising.

In other words, DSB is torn between the inertia of the apparatus itself and the impatience of those who must market it. This situation is being felt more strongly after sectorisation, because the business sectors wish to show results and to make themselves immediately visible.

To illustrate how corporate design can work for the sectors, DSB will issue a pamphlet for the conference giving examples of design solutions as they might be in the future. It is not a side-line but rather a debate book to be used during and after the conference, both in DSB and, if relevant, also by BR.

Design Philosophy for Sectorised Railway Administrations

Future action by BR and DSB
It is not intended that BR and DSB follow the same lines of thought in their future corporate planning. In fact the scale and corporate cultures of the two administrations are so different that a common model of action is hardly applicable.

However, the corporate design problems of the two organisations show many similarities so that a common philosophical approach seems relevant. This assumption forms the basis of the following proposals for future action.

(i) Boundaries between overall corporate identity and design business sectors

Overall corporate identity should be based upon the established BR and DSB corporate identity manuals, with amendments to bring them up to date and with the addition of chapters on design objectives and procedures to follow for all design work. Design by business sectors should follow these principles, building on visual assets. Individual profiling and creative work should relate to an agreed central framework, thereby providing visual clarity and continuity.

Creative people, particularly those of the advertising community, complain that a corporate identity programme straitjackets their creativity. This is not so. A good corporate identity programme provides a base-line from which creative work can expand and flex to meet commercial requirement.

(ii) Principles of design management

Design management is a matter of building an efficient communication network and establishing firm lines of responsibility and procedure throughout the system. It involves four distinct, yet closely related activities

— establishing overall design policy
— implementing that design policy
— monitoring the implementation of those policies
— auditing and policing.

(iii) Co-operation of design development in business sectors

Because of the scope and complexity of the design process in the railway systems there is a range of design tasks which must be controlled centrally. In the interests of maintaining economic, consistent and cohesive standards of design excellence throughout the businesses, a formal procedure for advice and

267

control will be set up by the Director of Architecture, Design and the Environment.

Already in BR, to deal with a controlled application of corporate identity, the industrial design graphics section has developed a computer program and service to deal with the requirements of 500 'clients' within the railway.

(iv) Creative interaction between marketing and design

Marketing has a two-sided responsibility in the design context. First, marketing must provide data from the marketplace that product developers require to produce solutions that fulfil the purposes of the business. Next, marketing must understand and know how to use corporate design philosophy in its extrovert activities, especially in advertising. Advertising has a powerful and immediate impact on the public's perception of the business. It must be careful to maintain this image consistently and careful not to promise more than can be fulfilled.

This means that there must be close interaction between design and marketing executives in order to maintain and develop a common understanding of the aims and scope of a corporate design and marketing philosophy, and to build a consistent approach between expectations and actual results. Lines of responsibility and procedure must be defined clearly. A permanent design and marketing forum, where the two disciplines — design and marketing — meet to discuss development strategy, is proposed.

3. In-house and external design consultants

Architecture and environment are as much part of a corporate design philosophy as are industrial design and graphic design.

The proportion of in-house designers to external consultants will vary according to the type of project in question. For instance, rolling stock design requires railway engineering expertise, whereas graphic design and architecture will benefit from creative input from external consultants.

External consultants bring a fresh analytical approach to projects and their relationship to internal disciplines can be healthy and beneficial in both creativity and cost effectiveness. However, strong internal design management is required to achieve results that conform to an overall Board design intent. Advice on the most effective in-house or external design resource will be given by the Director of Architecture, Design and the Environment.

Conclusion

Regardless of the branch of design, there will always be a requirement for an in-house nucleus of highly professional and qualified staff. It is the management of their skills and those of outside consultants that will produce co-ordinated results for the future.

A forward-looking, positive design policy statement from the Railways Boards can form the umbrella for development of this principle. The training of line managers in how to use design and communication of the scope and effectiveness of this resource within the business can be the only method of ensuring it.

DOCUMENT III:
STATION DESIGN

The following is a report of the Anglo-Danish project on station design, prepared by Dr J D C A Prideaux, Director of BR's InterCity sector, in January 1987.

Background to the Project

British Rail, InterCity sector, since the last design conference has focused attention on its key stations. It has commenced a major study of its business philosophy as applied to the operation of its stations and how this business philosophy can best be expressed through a design philosophy.

Aims

To produce a report setting out in clear and concise terms a design philosophy for the reconstruction or partial reconstruction of existing or 'green field' stations.

BR/DSB Links and Co-operation

Joint conferences have been held in London and Copenhagen at which background papers have been tabled: From DSB 'Policy to Modernise I-C Stations', and from BR; 'InterCity Stations'.

The papers and exhibitions produced for this conference will be complementary, DSB using a single theoretical station to illustrate its aims, BR using examples from current work and experiments carried out during the year.

Activities

Three part-projects have been carried out: a survey of existing stations and two experimental projects to test in practical terms the validity of design ideas. A report has been produced setting out a design philosophy for stations.

Results

The report has been prepared and issued for the use of InterCity Managers and their technical consultants (both in-house and external). This, together with case studies for each station, will enable future reconstructions and 'new build' stations to be planned as a coherent whole under a unified design and business philosophy. This will provide the best consistent image for InterCity stations while at the same time ensuring that the best commercial advantage is taken of the opportunities available.

The condensed report reads as follows:

ANALYSIS OF THE FUNCTION OF AN INTERCITY STATION
— An InterCity station is the 'point of sale' of travel by InterCity. While the 'sale' aspect of a station may decrease in the future, due to technical innovation making it possible to buy 'travel' other than at the station or

even at home, it will remain a significant point of sale for the foreseeable future.

— An InterCity station is a physical and informational entry point to the InterCity network.

   An InterCity station is a transport interchange within the InterCity mode and between InterCity and other modes.

— An InterCity station creates a quality of environment for rail travel. This must be consistent with the environment of the *best* InterCity trains.

— An InterCity station creates an opportunity to develop additional income by a judicious placing of retail outlets and commercial advertising. These must be developed to fulfil their full potential but should not dominate the station's other main functions.

The development of retail outlets should form part of the overall plan for a station both in financial and physical terms. Proposals should demonstrate how the retail activity is to be managed, to attain consistent high standards of environment.

The overall concept of station planning must be applied to an InterCity station before alterations or improvements to its various functions are carried out, which, while praiseworthy in themselves, may be abortive or in the *wrong* place when an overall concept is achieved.

Inevitably the functions listed can at some point be mutually inconsistent and hence a balance must be struck.

THE OVERALL CONCEPT — THE STATION PLAN

A 'Station Plan' should be prepared for all InterCity stations. The 'Station Plan' should include the physical, financial and managerial aspects of the station. The physical and financial and managerial plans are interdependent.

PHYSICAL

The physical aspects of the design of new, reconstructed or major improvements should as far as possible emulate the principles set down in this report.

Design Talks!

FINANCIAL

The appraisal of the 'Station Plan' must justify the capital expenditure. The improvements required in the environment of InterCity stations must be justified in terms of increased revenue (passenger *and* commercial). The extent to which the improvements in the environment can be pursued will depend on the appraisal of particular options.

The role of trading is a key factor in the improvement of InterCity stations. The revenue from trading must be maximised.

The 'Station Plan' must include station trading as an integral part of the concept.

The aim of an InterCity 'Station Plan' should be to fund the improvement of the station environment from station trading.

MANAGEMENT

The 'Station Plan' should also include a clear statement on the management of the station. It should be clearly indicated how the maximum revenue will be obtained in management terms. Whether the commercial aspects will be managed separately. Whether this management will be 'in-house' or by outside management through competitive tender. A clear management structure is required for each station.

THE STATION PLAN — PHYSICAL

InterCity stations should as far as physically possible and within financial constraints, be planned to the concept of zoning areas of function.

ZONE 1 Access
ZONE 2 Arrival and Ticketing
ZONE 3 Waiting and commercial area
ZONE 4 Departure area (to trains and from trains).

It will not always be possible within site constraints to define the area of the zones exactly. They will tend to merge one in to another.

Certain entrances into the stations may not come into the right zone.

A sequential movement throughout the zones is implied but passengers, greeters or shoppers may choose to use the facilities in any order or indeed pass backwards and forwards several times.

The principle, however, is that the zones are recognisable as such and the customer can easily pass to that part of the station he requires. (Gatwick and Heathrow's Terminal 4 are good examples of the zoning philosophy.)

ZONE 1 — ACCESS

The catchment area of an InterCity station should be determined by conducting a survey of the existing station users' starting points and access modes of transport. Consideration should be given to the extent the potential market is inhibited by limitations in facilities provided to cater for these modes of transport (eg parking). A projection should be made of the potential increase of traffic that could be generated from the existing catchment area (and a potentially larger one) if the facilities provided were improved.

Each type of station user: passenger, greeter, weeper and shopper, should be examined separately. Each category should be examined by mode of access.

The current arrangements for the mode of access should be examined in terms of convenience (or inconvenience) or whether it is provided at all, under the following headings: pedestrian, bus, underground (if applicable), local rail, taxi, short-wait car parking, long-term car parking. The area external to the stations' entrances is part of the 'interchange' function of the station. This area should be carefully designed or altered so that the utmost convenience is given to passengers changing their mode of travel.

The entire area external to the station should form an integrated design. Too often the station is not part of the design for the urban centre.

The environment of the station should be made an

273

attractive area with a judicious use of attractive paving, signing and landscaping.

The station approach should in essence reach out into the surrounding town or city, especially where the station is near the urban centre. The customer should be made to feel he/she is approaching a highly organised and efficient business, and one where the customer is welcome.

ZONE 2 — ARRIVAL AND TICKETING

An area in which travellers arrive by foot, car, taxi, bus, underground, and are processed for travel. This area should have attractive entrances through which passengers pass from whichever form of transport they arrive. This is the 'Entry Point' to the InterCity network and is the point at which first impressions are formed. The reception area as its name implies is the area in which passengers are received into the system. The ambience of this area is very important in that it creates in the passengers mind the efficiency (or otherwise) of InterCity. Passengers should be welcomed and then treated with respect. This area is concerned with the mechanism of travel and is also the railway sales outlet.

Travel Centre and Ticket Office should be seen as one total design concept, they are both selling travel but not necessarily as one single unit. The best retail practice should be applied.

However well signed and simple to operate the ticket machines are, there will still be a demand for over the counter ticket transactions by passengers who are timid and require reassurance.

In addition the complicated transactions, seasons, privilege, special offers etc will also require over the counter transactions. These should be dealt with at normal ticket office counters, strategically sited adjacent to the ticket machines. Passengers should not be separated from the ticket clerk by glass screens: change machines and mechanical removal of incoming cash systems are available to overcome security objections. Staff objections will need to be overcome. Electronic signing over these positions should clearly indicate which transactions are dealt with at each position.

Left-luggage lockers are a more convenient way of storing luggage than the traditional office but they have two disadvantages

1. Security (the major one)
2. Oversized luggage.

Left-luggage facilities should be designed mainly in the form of lockers but with a narrow security entrance which would be permanently manned and be provided with anti-terrorist monitoring equipment.

Luggage trolleys should be allowed into this area to allow unloading adjacent to the selected locker. Space should be allowed for parked trolleys so that they are available for withdrawals. This system would be self circulating. The manned position should have a small lockable area for abnormal luggage (skis etc!).

Travel information and timetables on display boards should be readily accessible in Zone 2 but grouped together in attractively designed fittings.

Free-standing 'temporary' notices should be avoided. Monitors of all information on main indicator boards should be distributed throughout Zone 2 (see information section, Zone 3).

IMAGE OF ZONE 2

The design image that should be created by good design is twofold. Firstly the entrances should reinforce the brand image — InterCity. The public should perceive that they are entering an efficient, sophisticated and successful travel system.

Secondly, the passenger on entering the reception area must feel a 'customer friendly' ambience. The area must be well designed, colourful and attractive. It must be well signed, but not over signed. The services the passenger requires must be readily at hand and he/she should be processed efficiently and speedily by helpful staff.

On leaving the reception area the passenger should feel relaxed, having had all his/her wants taken care of. They should have their ticket and any other required documentation, they should have their luggage on a trolley and they should know their train time and thus how much time they have to spare in Zone 3 — Waiting and Commercial.

ZONE 3 — WAITING AND COMMERCIAL AREA

Major opportunities exist in all InterCity stations for a major investment in retail trading. The tatty image typified by the flower shop trading on a trestle table surrounded by buckets, the newsagent whose too-small premises are expanded over the concourse with trestle tables, the down-at-heel bar etc must be swept away. Retail trading at InterCity stations should be planned on the concept of the right facilities, at the right place, at the right time.

The customer must be identified, the competition identified, and the age and range of the customers identified. A high quality of design is essential in this area. Good design will enhance business performance and improve the environment. The value of design is that it 'communicates an idea'. The disposition and type of trading outlets must be a conscious decision of railway management (and its advisers). The criterion that a space should be let to whichever retailer will pay the highest rent should be discontinued. The long-term benefit to the InterCity business should be the criterion. The retail outlets must be judged on what are the needs of the the passengers and other shoppers. In general there should be not more than one outlet of any type of merchandising. The public must be given the widest choice. Space should no longer be let on a rented area basis, unless good financial reasons justify it.

The Waiting and Commercial Zone should give an overall impression of efficiency, theatre, occasion. Control of the overall design of the area will manufacture an ambience in which the individual shops will be subordinate to the whole. (Terminal 4 at Heathrow is a fine example of this philosophy). Within the above framework, an exciting prospect emerges of a partnership between InterCity management and station trading which will revitalise many

InterCity stations providing an improved environment and increased revenue, which will provide the funding for the improvement of the station environment outside the trading area.

Advertising both in this zone and the other two must be strictly controlled. It must no longer be sufficient to sell every available space with small, irregular sized advertisements, plain and illuminated arbitrarily mixed. Advertising must form an integrated part of the whole design. Well-sited, large, illuminated advertising will provide better profits whilst at the same time enhancing the station. The long-term benefit to the InterCity business should be the criterion on which installations are judged. The central feature of Zone 3 should be the waiting area. This area must be designed to the highest standard, and must be a true 'centre'. Landscaping, palms, fountains, sculpture, special lighting should be sensitively incorporated.

Information at InterCity stations varies greatly in volume, quantity, design and construction. *Full* details of arrivals and departures and other helpful information is an essential focal point of this area. Information on stations must be standardised to present an acceptable minimum standard on the platform, the waiting rooms, the concourse and the entrances/exits. Consideration should be given to eliminating large main indicators at the departure point and substituting monitors throughout the station.

Station toilets are an essential adjunct to InterCity station facilities. They should be available for passengers use from any of the four zones. Ideally the siting of toilets should be adjacent to the waiting and commercial area. Permanent supervision of toilets should very seriously be considered. The evils of graffiti, wilful damage, general abuse and occasionally intimidation will not be cured other than by permanent supervision.

Constant cleaning and the removal of rubbish are essential if high standards are to be maintained.

Each series of telephones should be grouped together in a well-designed unit, free-standing preferably. Telephones should not be tucked away in odd corners where they become abused and subject to graffiti. There are plenty of well-designed groupings on the market which can be an asset to the environment. Low height units each with its individual stool, with a common set of directories which cannot be removed are one such example. All telephones should be inspected at least once a day. All unofficial stick-ons (which deface practically all telephones on stations, at this time) should be removed daily.

ZONE 4 — THE DEPARTURE AREA

This area should be one of relative calm, even a haven of peace. Passengers should not have difficulty in finding their departure barrier because it is sandwiched between commercial outlets. It should be a place where the passenger can draw breath before plunging into his journey.

The atmosphere to be created by design in this area must actively remove from the passenger's mind any thought that he is being institutionalised or regimentalised. The passenger should feel an individual being treated as an individual; that the business cares and welcomes him as a person who has consciously chosen this form of travel.

ZONE 3 — THE BARRIER AND BEYOND

'Barrier' is an unfortunate word in our new philosophy; 'Gate', as used by the airlines, is a better description of the function. The gate must be attractive in design. It should not be surrounded with placards giving last minute advice to intending passengers (this should have been done before), but it should have a clear indication of the time and destinations of the departing train on monitors. The gateway to the train should be inviting, rousing the intending passengers' anticipation of the travel experience.

Platform surfaces must be perceived to have a high-quality finish (not necessarily high cost). The platforms, the canopies, the auxiliary buildings for public and staff, the seating, the vending machines, the technical equipment, the lighting and the colour must all be combined into a coherent whole by a careful design reflecting the Sector's image.

THE SECTOR IMAGE

An essential prerequisite to the launching of any upgrade of the InterCity image will be to upgrade the quality of Inter-City. The marketing thrust should be to present InterCity as a total package *but* as part of the BR family. A total branding package must be introduced. The existing striking brand name must be supported by a distinctive style which must permeate the system. InterCity should work towards the public perceiving it as efficient, sophisticated, successful and accessible. The initiative will increase staff pride which will improve their attitude to the public.

The rolling stock should have the brand image displayed inside in suitable places as well as outside. The stock has established house colours which should be developed throughout the sector image. The InterCity image should be recognisable at all InterCity stations, not by treating them all in the same way but by having certain easily recognised common items.

Selected items of station furniture should be well designed, of distinctive colour and in some cases incorporate the words 'InterCity'. Suitable items are station seats, litter bins, luggage trolleys, fascias of indicators, barrier line gates, notice boards, travel centres, ticket offices. These items must be seen, therefore, as part of colourful, brightly lit, efficient and sophisticated stations.

PROPOSALS FOR FUTURE ACTION

It is proposed to continue the indepth study of all aspects of individual stations until all important stations have been covered. It is proposed to continue the experimental application of design solutions at individual stations. A corporate image will be chosen from one of the consultant's proposals and eventually applied to the system.

DOCUMENT IV:
MEMORANDUM TO BRITISH RAILWAYS BOARD
Subject: Design Policy
Sponsor: J J O'Brien

Purpose of Memorandum

In September 1986 the Board issued an instruction which promulgated the amalgamation of the Industrial Design, Architecture and Environment interests under one director.

This director was asked to take an early opportunity to
redefine the direction and policies of a design directorate for
British Rail. The memorandum seeks to carry out that task.

The paper identifies the major strategic elements of an
integrated design management department and continues with
guidelines for the organisational structure needed to deliver a
highly professional, business-oriented design service.

Recommendations

The Board is asked to support:
a) The design policy statement shown in Appendix I which
   outlines the concept of an integrated design strategy for
   British Rail as part of their corporate plan.
b) The responsiblilities of the Director of Architecture, Design
   and Environment, shown in Appendix II.
c) A detailed review of the directorate's organisation, structure
   and procedures, within the framework of (a) and (b) above.
   The report will be presented to the Chairman's Group by
   April 1987.

1. Introduction
British Railways and its Principal Subsidiaries have succeeded to a
unique architectural and design heritage. With this responsibility comes the need to establish a policy for the protection,
custody and development of all environment and design aspects.

By integrating Architecture, Design and Environment,
there is an opportunity to bind these respective disciplines
closely together and provide a cohesive approach to all design

responsibilities. Such a policy would ensure that goals are clearly defined and that design management fully contributes to business success.

The impact of design excellence on business results is well recognised today and the challenge for British Rail is to ensure that it contributes fully to the success of its corporate strategies.

2. Existing policies
Prior to their amalgamation each of the three design functions followed individual policies to serve the various business interests.

Whilst having to approach three different design responsibilities the business director saw this as, at best, a hindrance to progress, if not actually creating conflict.

3. Integrated design strategy
There are five key areas underpinning an integrated design policy. They are:
a) Contribution to corporate communications
   To utilise fully the pervasive nature of good design practices to communicate corporate expectations accurately to customers, the public and staff.
b) Support to strategic business
   Early integration of design in decision making can consolidate the development of a corporate image and help define business aims.
c) Contribution to change
   Innovation and new attitudes are transmitted and encouraged by carefully managed design solutions. These must be harnessed for success by the design directorate.
d) Design and marketing
   Positive results from marketing depend on a close relationship with well-formulated design policy.
e) Education, appreciation and promotion
   In order that a strong position of co-ordinated design is maintained, a continuing programme of education in the importance of design in the businesses must be available to

281

senior management. It will be necessary for all staff to understand that design can be a strategic tool in the future success of British Rail.

4. *Structure and organisation*

The design directorate aims to develop a professional service both corporately and to the business. This aim can only be achieved with a highly responsive, business oriented organisation and well-directed, professional staff. The overall direction and strategy of the design function will be set by a Design Policy Committee. It will consist of no more than five people, chaired by an Executive Board Member together with the Director of Architecture, Design and Environment, and will meet monthly to monitor design projects and to ensure that the design input is introduced into business projects at an early conceptual stage.

Reporting to the Design Policy Committee will be four or five specialist design working groups. The Director of Architecture, Design and Environment, or delegate, will attend each group for continuity. Each group will take responsibility for environment, architecture, industrial design and graphic design respectively, and will be responsible for developing their own terms of reference and working procedures.

Details of the restructured organisation were required by the Board by April 1987.

5. *Conclusions*

With the continuing stimulation from government to raise the standards of design in industry and the public sector, the perceived status of British Rail through its Architecture, Environment and Design becomes increasingly important.

British Rail will need to be perceived by both the public and its employees as taking this responsibility seriously. An integrated, highly professional directorate will go towards achieving this.

4 February, 1987.

APPENDIX I

Design Policy Statement

— In line with other major UK service industries, British Rail will continue to develop and maintain a high standard of co-ordinated design in every aspect of its operation and business.
— Design is seen as fundamental to British Rail remaining an efficient enterprise and as an essential ingredient of passenger, freight and parcel services and good working conditions for employees.
— In its widest sense, design is seen as a corporate resource such as finance, or personnel, and must have clear central policy and guidance.
— For this resource to be successful the importance of design in the business is a factor which managers must understand, acknowledge and promote. British Rail will ensure that effective training and education is delivered.

The breadth of design in British Rail encompasses all disciplines. It is not only concerned with appropriate visual requirements but takes proper account of planning, cost effectiveness, flexibility, maintenance and on-costs.

Design in British Rail covers four main areas:

1. Architecture
Stations, depots, workshops, office buildings etc, the design of which is mainly the work of architects, design engineers and interior designers.

2. Industrial design
Locomotives, rolling stock, ticketing, station products and display, which are mainly the work of design engineers and industrial designers.

3. *Graphic design and communication*

Corporate identity, signs, advertising, timetables, promotional literature, mainly designed by graphic designers and typographers.

4. *Environment*

All areas surrounding railway land and linesides, station approaches, listed buildings and structures, car parks and transportation access — mainly the responsibility of civil engineers, architects, landscape architects and planners.

In addition the CEF encourages and sponsors community involvement and participation, local government involvement and partnership and sponsorship of the Arts.

The effective process of management of all these elements will secure a recognised British Rail identity — recognised by passengers, customers, staff and the media.

Design standards are to be kept under regular review by the Design Policy Committee and upheld by the specialist design working panels.

APPENDIX II

Director of Architecture, Design and Environment

Responsibilities

The Director of Architecture, Design and Environment is responsible to the Joint Managing Director (Railways) for the following:

1. To formulate and implement a business-oriented corporate design policy for the British Railways Board.
2. To integrate the three main design departments of architecture, design and environment.
3. To manage, advise and direct staff of the three disciplines and to raise professional standards.
4. To ensure the provision of a comprehensive, professional and integrated design management service to the business

sectors, regions and corporate functions from inception to project completion.

5. To establish, monitor and maintain design standards and criteria throughout British Rail which meet the corporate design policy, statutory requirements and business sector needs.

6. To select within a competitive framework all external architects and design consultants employed by British Rail and to act as a service procurement executive for the Board.

7. To provide a climate of understanding and close co-operation between British Rail and its consultants to ensure that solutions of excellence are achieved.

8. To service the Design Policy Committee and to work closely with its Chairman to ensure its successful operation and results.

9. To act as permanent member of the Design Policy Committee and all of the specialist design working groups.

10. To develop and implement procedures that encourage and educate British Rail staff at all levels in understanding the relationship of design to business performance.

11. To advise, at the initial stage, on all design activities being undertaken by the sector directors and executive management of British Rail.

12. To have the right to advise at all levels of the organisation, the right of access to provide advice, and the right of appeal if advice is not taken.

25 February 1987

DOCUMENT V:
MANAGEMENT BRIEF: DESIGN POLICY

The impact of design excellence on business results is well recognised today. The challenge for British Rail, with its unique architectural and design heritage, is to ensure that design contributes fully to the success of its corporate strategies.

A first step towards the new cohesive approach to design on BR was made with the appointment of Jane Priestman in

November 1986 as Director of Architecture, Design and Environment.

The design policy which she was asked to define was approved by the Board at its February meeting and is as follows:

Design Policy Statement

— In line with other major UK service industries, BR will continue to develop and maintain a high standard of co-ordinated design in every aspect of its operation and business.
— Design is seen as fundamental to BR remaining an efficient enterprise and as an essential ingredient of passenger, freight and parcels services and good working conditions for employees.
— In its widest sense, design is seen as a corporate resource such as finance, or personnel, and must have clear central policy and guidance.
— For this resource to be successful the importance of design in the business is a factor which managers must understand, acknowledge and promote. BR will ensure that effective training and education is delivered.

The breadth of design in British Rail encompasses all disciplines. It is not only concerned with appropriate visual requirements but takes proper account of cost effectiveness and maintenance.

Design in British Rail covers four main areas:

1. Architecture
Stations, depots,workshops, office buildings etc, the design of which is mainly the work of architects, design engineers and interior designers.

2. Industrial Design
Locomotives, rolling stock, ticketing, station products and display, which are mainly the work of design engineers and industrial designers.

3. Graphic Design and Communication
Corporate identity, signs, advertising, timetables, promotional literature, mainly designed by graphic designers and typographers.

4. Environment
All areas surrounding railway land and linesides, station approaches, listed buildings and structures, car parks and transportation access — mainly the responsibility of civil engineers, architects, landscape architects and planners.

In addition, the Board's Central Environment Fund encourages community involvement and participation, local government involvement and partnership, and sponsorship of the Arts.

The effective process of management of all these elements will secure a recognised BR identity — recognised by passengers, customers, staff and the media.

The design policy statement ends by saying that design standards are to be kept under regular review by a new Design Policy Committee consisting of no more than five people, chaired by an Executive Board Member, together with the Director of Architecture, Design and Environment. The Design Policy Committee will meet monthly to monitor design projects and ensure that design input is introduced into business projects at an early conceptual stage. Reporting to the Committee will be four or five specialist design working groups.

Details of the implementation of the Design Policy will be given in a future Management Brief.

Micro-encapsulation: The Special Delivery System

Donn Osmon

Donn Osmon's second paper is a specific case of a new invention seeking the skill of the designers to bring it to a range of effective end uses. He describes the first of those end uses in the cosmetics market. He ends with a challenge to readers to provide his company with others!

At 3M we use design to take advantage of the outcomes of scientific and technological research. Our investment in research is high, but we also need to invest in the design of end uses if that research, and so the business, is to derive profit from our investment.

The story of how 3M developed the now ubiquitous 'Post-it' note from research of this kind is well known. Here is the story of another and perhaps more momentous technology looking for end uses. It is the designers who will find uses for it. Have you any ideas?

The product is microencapsulation — a special delivery system — the outcome of a new technology which can put the design profession in the forefront of product development.

We are talking about microcapsules that range from 15-400 microns in size. To give you some idea of their size, you can just barely see a 40 micron diameter capsule with the naked eye. It would need 635 of them, side by side, to extend one inch. So they are very small. But they can deliver real and very special benefits to customers.

They deliver all the real and special benefits of essence, emollient or secret ingredient invented in the customers' own lab and produced on their production lines. The use of this special delivery system has already become familiar in the delivery of fragrance samples known in the advertising industry as 'Scratch and Sniff'. In this application microcapsules of fragrance oils are coated on to paper. When the coated area is scratched, fragrance is released.

A more recent innovation in this fragrance sampling market is the 'Fragrance Burst' sampler, in which encapsulated fragrances are coated in an adhesive system between two plys of paper. When the plys are separated the capsules are ruptured and the fragrance is released. This method eliminates the need for 'scratching' to release the fragrance and has gained widespread use in the promotion of perfume products.

Microcapsules may also be used to create new products and new features. Consider, in this instance, microcapsules as 'new ingredients' where the microscopic capsules help improve the delivery of existing formulae or help offer entirely new formulations.

But what are microcapsules? Basically, they are inert microscopic spheres. Insoluble in many cosmetic and household products formulations, they can be readily added into liquid, cream and dry products. The strength of the capsule is adjustable, depending on the customer's need. It can be strong enough to contain and carry a liquid which will be released when the capsule is rubbed with the fingertips; or it can be so strong as to be unbreakable. Such unbreakable capsules feel smooth and act like micro ball bearings if small (ie less than 40 microns); larger ones have a grainy, mildly abrasive feel, even if they are breakable. When crushed the contents are released — fragrance, moisturiser, reactive agents, secret ingredients, or whatever. The capsule shell is an inert colourless translucent resin through which the colour of the product will show; it readily flecks or washes off.

3M microcapsules have numerous other uses, including cosmetic and household applications. Charles of the Ritz, for example, has the first face powder that makes the skin look polished, not dry and powdery, because it's blended with real beads of moisturiser. This encapsulated moisturiser is our 32 mineral oil capsule filled with 80 per cent mineral oil.

Moisturised eye shadow glides on smoothly and cleanly when the formula blends beautiful colours with millions of these tiny moisturiser beads. Avon Colour Creme — an all over face colour for that fresh healthy look — contains a moisturiser that is delivered intact with these same microcapsules.

Continued rubbing breaks the capsules, releasing oil, and finally giving a smooth feel. This is called the 'indicator effect', going from mildly abrasive to smooth. If the capsules contain fragrance or colour the effect indicates when these are used. Other effects are possible. Used in refining creams for dry skin 180 micron encapsulated oils retexturise skin by the gentle removal of surface cell debris. Pantene revitalising cream conditioners for dry, brittle hair incorporate microencapsulated vitamin mineral oils, 400 microns in diameter, that burst when massaged to release *fresh* vitamins oils to the hair and scalp. Without encapsulation the vitamins would not be stable in such formulas. (These microcapsules must be shipped supported in water at about 30 per cent capsules; the mineral oil capsules mentioned earlier survive shipment dry).

Avon's Tocarra is the world's first replay or renewable fragrance product. When first applied the unencapsulated portion of the fragrance immediately goes to work, and only a fraction of the capsules are broken. Gently rubbing the area of application later in the day opens some of the other capsules and releases renewed fragrance. This idea can be extended to environmental fragrances and household products to deliver fragrance on demand. Similarly the colours required in products can be amended and customised to the precise shade by colouring the encapsulated oil — and the product will arrive at the customer's fingertips that way, without having been oxidised, without fading, or altering on the shelf.

There are a variety of other applications for which microencapsulation might be used. Because the 3M microcapsule can be made essentially vapour tight, aromatic chemicals are retained intact in capsules exposed to ambient atmospheric temperatures over a period of years. Fragrance formulas accentuating the volatile topnotes can now be stabilised in products without hermetic heating.

At 30 microns you can't discern individual capsules either visually or tactually. At 40 microns they are barely distinguishable. At 120 microns they are quite noticeable and have a grainy feel. A product formulation might take advantage of a mixture of different sizes, using some with easily breakable capsules and others for just their ball-bearing properties. Other points of interest include the fact that the 3M microcapsule is almost 100 per cent vapour tight, as well as tight against hydrocarbon propellants and solvents, depending on the particular solvent and ingredient blend. One hundred per cent pure alcohol will cause the contents to leach out through the shell; but 10-40 per cent alcohol solutions may not.

3M offers technical backup, experience, and an eagerness to work with customers to experiment and develop their ideas. Microcapsules afford a special delivery system which provides:

1. protection — of freshness against rancidity, toxicity, photosensitivity, and evaporation — and against other components of the customer's products,
2. extended shelf life,
3. replay — renewable fragrance, emolliency, colour, etc,
4. emollients — liquid oils in dry forms at high levels without emulsifiers, and
5. cost effectiveness — because very expensive and effective ingredients are not lost in transit and are used more efficiently and because inexpensive ingredients can now be used where not previously possible.

In short, microcapsule application is limited only by the customer's imagination. So far the end uses have been mainly in the region of cosmetic fragrances. Where else will your imagination and skills as a designer take you in innovating new end uses for this technology?

Design Management at Ford

Uwe Bahnsen

Uwe Bahnsen is a German designer. He worked for many years at Ford and was Vice President in charge of design at Ford Europe during the period in which the European end of this international company took on the initiative for car design world wide. The present highly successful family of Ford cars were designed under his management. He has recently returned from Ford to Switzerland to take over as Director of Education at the European extension of the US Passadena Art College, the most influential car design school in the world.

His paper is a case history of his projects at Ford. He describes the scope of the company and its design resources in Germany and England, argues the case for strong and effective design management as the key element in business success and, car by car, from the Escort to the Granada, shows how the process works in practice in a highly successful international business where the competition is strong.

In this paper I would like to cover the main design management issues we encounter at Ford and then, after a word on the competitive scenario, to describe the development of the Scorpio car, launched in May 1985, and the design process that led to it.

Design management at Ford is a complex subject because it is involved in practically all our activities — those facing outward as well as internal ones.

Obviously, in a consumer-orientated industry like ours, it is the product by which the company's achievement and its commitment to design is primarily judged. Product design is vital to Ford, and it relates directly to commercial success. This is perhaps best illustrated by the fact that for the past seven successive years our vehicles have not only achieved the first place in sales in Britain, but leadership in Europe for the first time in 1984. I hope to demonstrate that our commitment to design and design management does not end there.

Ford has a strong presence in 16 countries in Europe, with over 40 manufacturing, office and research and development facilities, 2,600 main dealers and approximately 4,000 sub-dealers and workshops. Their visual identification is an important communication link with our customers and it includes, of course, the Ford emblem — one of the world's best-known corporate symbols. Its application and the environment in which it is used follows carefully developed guidelines to protect its integrity. These guidelines are of course frequently reviewed and updated to ensure our corporate identity reflects and supports the product image — a process typical of the care taken by us to maintain the highest possible standards.

It goes without saying that the same attention is paid to all the media through which we communicate with our customers. This includes all printed matter, from letterheads to promotion materials and catalogues. It includes the smallest package for, let's say, a spark plug and extends to the layout, fitting and colour schemes of showrooms and sales offices.

We also plan for a degree of uniformity in our presence across Europe. This uniformity, however, is not allowed to stand in the way of flexible interpretation where appropriate, or of change when the achievement of a particular communication impact is desired — as was the case with the launch of our Cargo truck line. Since the Cargo product design philosophy broke away dramatically from the position and image held by its predecessor, we decided to combine with its launch a total redesign of our commercial vehicle communication platform, including our Truck Dealership and Service Point identification.

We regard our design philosophy as the driving force behind the establishment of a new image for our entire product range. It is therefore appropriate to reflect this philosophy by the external elements of our presence in the marketplace. It is equally important that the internal environment in which this new generation of modern products is designed, engineered and manufactured reflects this commitment towards design excellence as well.

For the launch of the Sierra, Dagenham — Ford's oldest British plant — was redesigned and transformed into the country's most highly robotised car-production facility — no mean feat in a 52-year-old building designed in the days of the Ford Model 'A'. A similar transformation was achieved in our oldest German plant in Cologne for the recent launch of the new Scorpio. This commitment to design in the broadest sense requires the acceptance of design management in all our activities. Design is itself of equal importance to engineering in product development: it has become an integral element of the development process of any new product. It cannot — and it does not want to — exist in isolation.

It would be simplistic to say that there was a time when the designers designed a car, the engineers engineered it, after which the manufacturing people would make it and the marketing people would then sell it. But by comparison with today's highly integrated process that is how it looks in retrospect.

The borderlines of specialisation have become less defined over the past ten years or so, and the process of integration among product development activities — the recognition and interplay with other departments, particularly manufacturing and marketing — is an ongoing process. As a result, design involvement extends over a wide range of parameters which significantly influence a product's final configuration. This involvement begins at the strategic planning phase when internal and external factors are assessed and their effect on our long-term strategy — to remain a trend setter in the industry — is developed. The recognition of the importance of design in this scenario has over the years led to the expansion and strengthening of the design position in Europe.

Ford's European design operations are located in Britain at Dunton in Essex and in Germany near Cologne. In these two design centres we employ more than 300 designers, studio engineers, modellers and specialised craftsmen who support all of the company's European product design requirements, provide occasional assistance to some of the corporation's overseas affiliates, and are involved with specialised design activities — be it for facilities and buildings, or the development of displays and the overall design for trade shows. In this way the product profile remains at the centre of our communication and identification strategy. Design has become highly interdisciplinary embracing most, if not all, visible corporate activities.

For every major product project a design team is established which is led by a design manager. He is automatically a permanent member of the project team which includes representatives from planning, engineering, manufacturing, marketing and finance. The design manager and his team remain with the programme from the conceptual stages through to the beginnings of production. This 'cradle-to-grave' involvement gives every member of the design team periodic exposure and involvement in the various phases of a programme.

Considerable responsibilities are delegated to design management. To achieve this responsibility it is essential that the design manager understands and is able to communicate the commercial and industrial elements of the programme.

Being in charge of the European design operations, I find myself spending about an equal amount of time in either location. But the communication between the two major design centres does not rely upon my travel. We employ in the design studios, and in engineering and manufacturing as well, some of the most advanced computer-aided design equipment, linked to Ford's computer centre through a highly sophisticated satellite communication network. With the introduction of CAD-CAM, design has become further integrated into the total development and communication process. For our designers, graphic stations and computers are rapidly becoming 'new' classic tools of the trade.

Through our involvement with various educational establishments we are communicating our view that design is an interdisciplinary resource and that the recognition of this is not only important to future designers but to future engineers and planners, and to marketing and manufacturing people as well. This recognition is, in my view, essential if design is to be able to function as a major corporate resource, since by its nature it often cuts across many traditionally separate and even potentially adversarial elements within an organisation.

With that in mind let us turn to the design of the Scorpio. But before doing so I want to introduce briefly the background of the European car market, and to identify the competitive scenario in terms of its differences from the North American and Japanese markets. Against this background I will discuss the product strategy and design philosophy that Ford of Europe has developed over the last ten years, and so lead on to the development of our most recent product — the Scorpio — launched in May 1985.

The 'home' market for Ford of Europe consists, as I said earlier, of 16 individual countries. In the north they include Scandinavia, which reaches into the Arctic Circle, while from the southern countries you can see the northern shores of Africa. To cover such contrasting geographical and cultural regions is perhaps not too unusual: what is unique about this diverse market is, however, the fact that over half of these countries can look back at a long history of automobile development and manufacture, and consequently of automobile design, aimed to suit their national individualities and requirements.

Obviously, the number of vehicle manufacturers has reduced over the years. But of some fifteen major manufacturers still active today, the six largest producers — in terms of European market penetration — are separated by less than two percentage points in a market which, incidentially, is very similar in size to the US market, with over ten million cars sold annually.

This neck-and-neck position among the 'big six', with between 11 per cent and 13 per cent market share each, is the reason for the absence of a single dominant manufacturer, as in the United States, or two, as in Japan. It has also prevented the emergence of a dominant car *design* leader. On the contrary, in Europe each national market developed — and to some extent still pursues today — its own individual vehicle strategy, with the result that no single technical concept of design philosophy achieves market dominance.

Some of the reasons can be related to national strategies of vehicle taxation, purchasing traditions, road network and income levels. They were supported by the relative isolation of most European markets through various trade restrictions until the trade liberalisation policies of the EEC started to become effective during the late sixties.

The formation of Ford of Europe in 1967, merging the previously independent, and competing, operations of Ford of Germany and Ford of Britain, was based on the vision that the EEC would eventually provide the basis for full-scale manufacture and trading in all major segments. Much of this vision has come true in the interim and while many of the national characteristics still survive — and will probably continue to do so for some time — the 'big six' producers each offer today a full product range which is competitive in all markets.

In this competitive environment, product integrity and product identity have become two of the key parameters for remaining successful. Each producer offers well built products with state-of-the-art technology — European sourced as well as imported.

In response to the impact of this scenario Ford of Europe, during the past ten years, redefined its product strategy and established a clear design philosophy which is the driving force behind the achievement of a new corporate image through our product range and which started with the development of the 1980 Escort.

The Escort, for which design development commenced in 1976, and programme approval was achieved in 1978, may be regarded as somewhat timid by today's standards, with the still somewhat hard intersection of surfaces and crisp detail execution. But at the time it represented a considerable breakthrough towards the realisation of a new philosophy. Some of our key objectives were to create an easily recognisable identity of the total product that would not have to rely on details or ornamentation, that optimised the usable space within the platform's overall dimensions and also achieved a high degree of aerodynamic efficiency prompted by the increasing demand for improved fuel consumption following the first energy crisis. Our studies resulted in a vehicle architecture which allowed us to optimise those key objectives while giving the car its individual identity which is still highly recognisable today.

The next — and probably most significant — statement

297

of our design philosophy was the Sierra car line, launched in the autumn of 1982. For the basic vehicle architecture, we elected to continue the strategy of '2 ½ volume car concept', while the design can best be described as a 'dynamic sculpture'. Following several generations of hard-edged designs, we recognised that the concept we pursued would be regarded by many as revolutionary — and certainly, coming from a high-volume manufacturer, as quite outrageous. But we were also aware that the statement we wanted to make, signalling a significant change in the corporate strategy, could not be achieved in small steps.

The design of the Sierra clearly identifies it as an object designed for motion; this theme fitted easily into the aerodynamic objectives we set ourselves. In designing the Sierra, we consciously discarded the traditional approach of developing distinct front, side and rear view elevations. All surfaces, in particular surface intersections, were carefully developed to flow into each other and there is no view where one is not aware of the next plane.

Following the achievement of the design, we continued aerodynamic research, although we left the approved vehicle shape unaltered. The result was Probe III which we exhibited in 1981, one year ahead of the Sierra introduction, at the Frankfurt Motor Show. The result was interesting: although Probe III was rumoured to be the shape of things to come from Ford, few of the motoring journalists who saw it actually believed we would have the courage to put such a shape into production. On the other hand, many members of the design community hoped that we would, thus creating a new freedom for their own work. The launch of the Sierra has indeed had such an effect, the results of which are beginning to be seen in the latest generation of new European cars. For us, the Sierra was a satisfying achievement and it certainly has had a significant impact on our corporate design philosophy.

It will therefore not come as a surprise that our latest product — the Scorpio — launched in May 1985, reinforces and expands this product design philosophy. The Scorpio is the largest car we produce in Europe, with an overall length of 184 inches (4.6 m), and it is the flagship of our European fleet.

In the early phases of the programme, around 1980, we concentrated our initial efforts on studying alternative vehicle architecture concepts that would meet the requirements of packaging efficiency, aerodynamic efficiency, and the reinforcement of our product strategy. The configurations evaluated included three volume as well as two volume concepts, and of course the '2½ volume' concept which had worked successfully for us on the Escort and Sierra. These studies were conducted by employing the classic media of sketches and renderings, to explore alternative interpretations. Full-size layouts were used to verify the package opportunities and the potential of different designs. The full-size models we developed were also utilised for extensive windtunnel testing. It goes without saying that excellent aerodynamics and other airflow related parameters, like low wind noise and controlled lift characteristics are vital requirements in a car capable of about 130 miles per hour. To obtain accurate information in the early model stages, full-sized clay armatures are designed to be fitted with a correct vehicle underbody and a fully equipped engine compartment, since these two areas can contribute as much as one third to the vehicle's overall aerodynamic drag.

At the end of the pre-programme phase we elected to concentrate our further development on optimising a similar '2½ volume' vehicle architecture to that described previously, also providing full flexibility of use between passenger and luggage compartment, with a hatchback configuration. Simultaneous wind tunnel tests and design development led to highly sensitive surface executions, including an ambitious piece of glass-sculpture for the rear quarter window as part of the distinctive window treatment of the vehicle's 'greenhouse'. In the execution of a basically soft, flowing shape, it becomes very important that the absence of strong feature or character lines does not lead to a bulbous vehicle. A great amount of attention and expertise is therefore required by designers and model-makers to create the right amount of tension in the surfaces themselves and the surface intersections, to allow the car's design structure to remain

299

apparent. The flush glass panes and the integration of detail components contribute to the feeling of tautness.

In a design that relies extensively on subtle sculpture, the communication of the absolute correct surface details to engineering and tooling activities is paramount. Computer-aided design equipment, employed throughout Scorpio's development, was a significant help.

More than on any previous programme, manufacturing 'friendliness' was one further element we considered in the design of Scorpio. For example, to improve the quality, fit and finish, the door openings are stamped out of a one piece body side, and the doors also are one piece stampings which include the window frames for a perfect match. The design execution has to recognise the effect this method has on the draw-ability of the sheet metal, and it becomes obvious that a designer's understanding of tooling, stamping and manufacturing process is vital for the achievement of the design goal.

Optimised space utilisation, again one of our key objectives, was achieved by the extra dimension created with the rearward extending roof line within the '2½ volume' architecture. It provided the occupants with a very comfortable and generous 'living space' and allowed the incorporation of reclining rear seats.

To make the Scorpio not only a comfortable car, but also an efficient driver's car, particular attention was paid to the ergonomics of the 'working place'. Let's remember we are dealing with a car interior with an active, dynamic environment; it requires a logical and ergonomic arrangment of all function controls. The whole control section of the instrument panel was reduced in size by the use of micro-switches, to place all major operations within sight and easy reach of the driver, with clear function and identification. The principal layout places all light controls and light signals to the left of the steering column and all visibility controls, like wipers, heated windshield, heated backlight and demist function to the right, leaving the centre for installations which can be shared by driver and passenger alike. The overall interior is functional but very 'friendly'; it is designed around the people who will use it, making it a highly efficient yet very 'human' motor car.

In the development of the Scorpio we aimed at achieving a distinctive individual character, while maintaining the car's recognisable identity as a European Ford product. It is total product integrity that is important, with design conducting a significant part of it.

INDEX

Advertising 42, 57–8
Age profiles 156
Ahrends, Burton & Koralek 178
Akzo 121
Albert Embankment 176
Alberti, Leon Battista 196
Aldington, Lord 155
Ambasz, Emilio 199, 200
Amis, Martin 227
Anderson, Sally 86
Ant 107
Apple computer 22, 33
Architectural design 106, 110, 141–4,
    174–90, 198–9, 230, 263
    requirements of 181–2
    team ideals 187–9
    transformation and permanence
    in 182–4
Armchair shopping 159
Arnitel 130
Artec Design 122
Asda 160–1
Audiences of the organisation 60–2
Automatic fare collection systems 99
Automobile industry 28, 155, 292–301

Baker, Kenneth 50
Baker Perkins 31, 41
Barbican 232
Barmag 122, 123
Barnett, Correlli 197
Baskin-Robbins 23
Bathroom design 230
Beaubourg 177–81
Bell, Guy 166
Bellini, Mario 33, 45, 46
Bemberg 127
BhS 139, 244–6
Big Bang 143
Black box 25
Bloomingdales 56
Bloxcidge, John 46, 49

BMW 33
Boilerhouse 155
Bonetto, Rodolfo 33
Bosson, Peter 44
Brain drain 38
Branded structure 59–60
British Airports Authority 41, 162, 165–7
British Rail 41, 99
    background to design 260–4
    corporate identity 261–2
    design management policy 258–87
    design policy 280–7
    design strategy 265–9
    Director of Architecture, Design and
    Environment 284–5
    rolling stock 263–4
    sectorised railway administrations 266–9
    station architecture 263
    station design 269–79
British Rail alphabet 262
Brunel, Isambard Kingdom 92, 199, 260
Buildings *see* Architectural design; Office
    buildings
Burton Group 160
Business & Technician Education Council
    (BTEC) 50–2
Business and Technical Advisory
    Services 222
Butcher, John 36, 154, 233, 236
Butler, Nick 33

CAD-CAM 200, 295
Camborne Fabrics 220
Carter, David 41
Cash-flow relationship with time 95
Channon, Paul 224
Chartered Society of Designers 223
City office buildings 147–52
Clarence Clothing 220
Clark's Shoes 41
Cleaver, Tony 39
Clegg, G L 207

CNAA 50–2, 223
Coin Street 176, 179
Colour-coding system 255–6
Columbia-Presbyterian Medical Center identity programme 247–57
Communications 65, 139
Company failures 65–6, 218–19
Competition 29, 136–7, 144, 158
Competitiveness 12, 221, 224
Computer-aided design 99
Computer industry 45
Computer to computer ordering 80
Concernbureau Vormgeving 15
Concern Industrial Design Centre (CIDC) 15–16, 20
 design awards 18
 design teams 18
 organisation 17–18
Concern Standardisation Department 19
Concorde research design and development programme 88
Conran Design Group 246
Conran, Terence 199, 211
Consumer products 25, 57–8
Consumer reactions 65, 136, 156
Conway, Hugh 205
Coopers & Lybrand 200
Corfield, Sir Kenneth 93
Corporate commitment 35–53
Corporate identity 18, 41, 54–73, 112, 116, 206
 British Rail 261–2
 as corporate resource 70–2
 design 4
 design-based 41
 display of wealth and power 62
 failure of short-term view 69–70
 financial management model 72–3
 and internal state of company 64
 Japanese companies 67–8
 managing 71–2
 mission statements 63–4
 nationalism in 69
 overwhelming need for 70
 programme 61'
 and reasons for collapse 65–6
 role in corporate hierarchy 70
 variations in 62–4
 see also 3M
Corporate image 12
Corporate strategy 9–26

Corporate structure 58–9
Cosmetics market 288–91
Cost factors 97–102
Cost of ownership 98–102
Council for National Academic Awards (CNAA) 50–2, 223
Coventry Panels 41
Coward, Noel 233
Creativity, definition 12
Cultural background 47–8, 195–7, 233
Cuproammonium process 127
Cuprophan membrane 128

Data-processing industry 24, 100, 102, 139
Debenhams 160, 162, 167–71
Deregulation 158
Design
 definitions 194, 203, 217–18, 226
 future of 49–50, 111, 193–201
 map of 195
 use of term 202
Design activities 14–15, 86
Design and the Economy 221
Design appreciation 27
Design attitudes 35, 42–3
Design awards 228
Design awareness 135–40
Design brief 93, 94, 96, 98
Design Centre 155
Design classification 3–4
Design competence 93
Design concept 215
Design consultants 46–7, 49, 268–9
Design Council 220–3, 231, 234–5
Design criteria 12
Design differentiation 29
Design dimension 27–34
Design disciplines 89
Design education 38, 46, 50–3, 155, 235–6
Design environment 215
Design Experience 52
Design for Profit campaign 221
Design function 9–11
Design management 15, 23, 35, 224, 236
 British Rail 258–87
 Ford Motor Company 292–301
 principles of 267
Design mind 202–16
Design mix 30
Design opportunities 24
Design packaging 114–15

Design policy 35, 117–18, 280–7
Design research 44
Design Seminar (Downing Street) 224, 235
Design skills 87
Design specification 93
Design spectrum 90, 92
Design value 136
Designer
  role of 204–16
  status 46
  use of term 227
  see also Design mind
Diabetes mellitus 104
Diagnostic equipment 111
Dialysis 127
Diffrient, Niels 33
Dissing + Weitling 107, 111
Docklands development 232
Dreyfuss, Henry 33

Eames, Charles 211
Eastwood, Paul 205
Edge, Gordon 187
Edison, Thomas 199
Electrical engineering 90
Electronic point of sale systems 140
Electronic typewriter 45
Engineer, role of 13–14
Engineering design costs 88
Engineering designer 87
Enka group 121–2, 128
Entrepreneurial spirit 38
Environment-based identities 56–7
Environmental design 4, 232
Enzyme production 109–10
Ergonomics 25, 43–4
Esslinger, Hartmut 33
Eurorange television 19–20

Fairbrother, Nan 232
False teeth 99
Ferguson TX colour television 219–20
Fermentation plant 108
Financial control 219
Financial management model 72–3
Financial services industry 143, 149
Finland 234
Fletcher, Alan 203, 205, 210
Flexible manufacturing systems 199–200
Floppy discs 79

Folon, Jean Michel 41
Food outlets 170
Ford, Henry 199
Ford Motor Company 21–2, 27–30
  design management 292–301
Foster, Norman 151
Freeman, Christopher 14
Fuller, Buckminister 203, 204
Future of design 49–50, 111, 193–201

Gauguin 203
Gill, Bob 206
Giugiaro, Giorgetto 33
Glaser, Milton 203, 205, 210
Goethe 35
Gooch, Daniel 260
Gorb, Peter 52, 171, 206, 217
Government action 217–37
Government policy factors 80–1
Grandjean, Professor 43
Grange, Kenneth 33, 41, 47, 210, 211
Graphic design 261
Greece 234
Gulf 66

Habitat 155, 160, 241–2
Hansen, Fritz 107
Harmonisation committee 19
Harmonisation-professional equipment
  brochure 18
Harrier aircraft 86
Harrods 56
Heal's 138, 244
Higher education, White Paper on 46
Higher National Diploma (HND) 50
Hodge, David 167
Hong Kong and Shanghai Bank 151
House style standards 17
Household profiles 156
Hunt, John 166

IBM 21, 31, 33, 35, 39, 58
Identification policies 249–56
Identity independence 58
Identity mix 57
Identity programmes 58, 247–57
Independent identities 58
Individuality 157
Industrial design 193–201
  costs 88
  function 11

interdisciplinary nature of 13
Industrial designer 31–4, 87, 91, 213
  role of 13–14
Information design, definition 4
Information processing 24
Information systems 25
Information technology 141–52
  impact of 143
  impact on office sytems 144–7
Inner city centres 156
Innovation 24, 44–6, 229
  definition 12
  design as management tool for 121–31
  see also Novo Industries; Product
  innovation
Insulin
  product development 107–8
  production 105–6
Integration 235
Inventions 229
Irvine, Alan 40
Italy 234

Jacobsen, Arne 105, 106, 108, 109
Jahn, Helmut 143
Japan 234
  corporate identity 67–8
Jobs, Steven 22

Kane, Art 203
Kinneir, Jock 262
Kitchen design 230
'Kitchen of the Future' 20–1, 25
Kodak 33
Kotler, Philip 29, 30
Kuroki, Yasuo 22

Landscape design 232
Lawrence, Peter 203
Lawson, Bryan 209
Le Corbusier 184
Legislation 158
Lethaby, William Richard 50
Levitt, Theodore 29, 33, 76
Lexikon typewriter 45
Lloyd's 151, 185–6
Locomotive design 91, 260
Loewy, Raymond 36, 197
Logotypes 251–3
London 175–8, 195–6
London Business School 155, 236

London Regional Transport 162, 171–2
London Transport 99
London Underground 112–20
  design innovation 115–17
  design policy 117–18
  packaging of design 114–15
  product innovation 118–19
  situation in 1987 113–14
Lorenz, Christopher 204, 211, 213
Louvre system 98
Lucie-Smith, Edward 204

Macmillan, Harold 35
Maintenance 93, 230
Management process 11
Manufacturing costs 97–8
Market globalisation 82–3
Market strategy 76–7
Marketing 29, 33, 60, 96–7
  cost effectiveness 78–9
Marketplace changes 79–80
Marks & Spencer 139
Mass production 200
McAlhone, Beryl 223
Meaningful distinction 34
Mechanical engineering 90–1
Media influence 11, 154, 231
Megatrends 23
Membrane production 126–9
Merchandise development 169
Merchandising range 159
Micro-chip technology 139–40
Microcomputers 45
Microencapsulation 288–91
Mies van der Rohe, Ludwig 41
Miller, Herman, Inc. 15
Miniaturisation 25
Minolta 33
Mitsubishi, corporate identity 67–8
Modern Movement 188, 198
Monolithic identities 58
Morris, William 196, 206
Mothercare 138, 243, 244
Multidisciplinary factors 32, 212

Naisbitt, John 23, 201
Nash, John 199
National Gallery 178
National identities 69
National interest 217–37
  definition 218, 226

New dimension 30–7
New technology 24, 199
Newton's third law of motion 43
Next 139,160
Niche marketing 160
Nizzoli, Marcello 45
Novo Industries
  architecture 106–7, 110–11
  design and innovation 104–11
  diagnostic equipment 111

O'Brien, Jim 41
Office buildings 147–52, 231
  future 151–2
Office design 141–52, 231
  evaluation of 145–7
Olins, Wally 40, 153
Olivetti 31, 33, 35, 38
  co-ordination of visual aspects 39–41
  design approach 36–7
  design programme 22
  design research 44
  early involvement with design process 49
  ergonomics 43–4
  high regard for design 42–3
  high status of designers 46
  innovation 44–6
  relationship with designers 48–9
Olivetti, Adriano 37, 40
Olivetti, Camillo 37
ORBIT-1 145
ORBIT-2 146
ORBIT study 143, 145–6
Over-centralisation 159

PA Technical Science Centre 187
Palmer, Arnold 208
Papanek, Victor 203
Paris 177–81
Pascal 53
Pasteur 208
Payne, Norman 166
Pedersen, Harald 104
Pedersen, Thorvald 104–5
Pegasus vectored thrust turbo fan 86
Penicillin manufacture 108
Pentagram 248, 254
Perceptions management 55–6
Performance requirements 96–7
Petersen, Donald 21, 28, 29

Philips 31, 32
  design activities 15, 16
  'Kitchen of the future' 20–1, 25
  organisation of 16
  special projects 17
Pick, Frank 112–13
Pilditch, James 235
Plastics 129–31
Playfair, Lionel 50
Political economy 197–201
Politics 197
Polymers 129–31
Pompidou Centre 179–81
Pompidou, President 180
Post-It product development 79
Presbyterian Hospital 247
Priestman, Jane 166
Problem-solving 207–8
Product-based identities 56
Product design 28, 29, 57
  checklist of questions 93–4
  consultants 33
  definition 3
Product development 12, 31
Product innovation 112, 118–19
Product intelligibility 25
Product planning 12
Product policy 24
Product strategy 18, 31
Project costs 97
Project management 32
Purchasing department 64
Pyrex 220

Quality assurance 93
Quality of life 157
Quality trends 77–8

R&D 85, 212
Rams, Dieter 206
Regent Street 176
Reliability 93
Retailing industry 56–7, 135–40
  impact of design 153–61
  resurgence in 136–7
Retailing philosophy 241
Richard Shops 138, 244
Robots 201
Rockefeller Center 177
Rogers' Patscentre 186–7
Rogers, Richard 151

Rogers, Richard and Partners 187
Rolls–Royce 87
Rosehaugh Stanhope 147
Ross Electronics 221
Royal College of Art 155, 236
Ruskin, John 201

Saatchi & Saatchi 200
Safety 93, 96
Sainsbury's 139
Sapper, Richard 33
Sebestyen, Charles 169
Segmentation 160
Service industries 162–73
Shopping centres 159
Siegel, Rita Sue 205
Smith, Mike 206
Snow, C P 196, 235
Social class factors 157
Social responsibility 188
Society of Industrial Artists and
    Designers 223
Sociological issues 156–8
Software versus hardware 24
Sony 22, 23, 33
Sottsass, Ettore 33, 214
South Bank 178
Sowden, George 43
Sparke, Penny 214
Special delivery system *see*
    Microencapsulation
Spencer Homes 195
Stellar Components 220
Stephenson, George 92, 260
Stevens, Jocelyn 155
Store design 138
Storehouse Group 241–6
Streamer 100–1
Style 163–72
Styling 30, 198
Subsidiary organisations 58
Sully, Frank 204
Sumner, Tim 219
Sunday shopping 159
Superstores 138–9, 159
Swann, David 169
Swift, Jonathan 35
Symbol connotation research 253–4
Symbols 251–3
Systems approach 25
Systems design 140

Tape drive 101
Taste 12, 195–7
Taylor, Merrick 218
Team design 187
Teamwork 187
Technology 197, 200
Telecommunications 141, 144
Teleshopping 159
Tensabarrier 167
Tesco 139
Textile fibres 124–6
Thatcher, Margaret 153
Thorn EMI 98–100
3M
    changing market place 79–80
    company policy 74–5
    cost-effective marketing 78–9
    current business trends and corporate
        identity 74–81
    floppy discs 79
    globalisation of markets 76–7
    government policy factors 80–1
    Post-It product development 79
    quality trends 77–8
    subsidiaries 75
Time factor 94–5
Top Shop 160
Total environment 25–6
Tradition 196, 234
TV products 19–20
Twenty Companies and Design 220
Two nations 156
Typefaces 255

Undermerchandising 159
Urban decline 156
Urban environment 232
User classifications 4–5

Value chain 34
Victoria and Albert Museum 155
Video systems 31
Visual co-ordination 39–41
Visual design 87
Visual image 139
Visual stimuli 38

Wadkin Vertical Spindle CNC Machining
    Centre 219
Waterloo Station 41, 263
Waterman 214

Watson Jnr, Tom 39
Watson, Thomas 21
Webb, Philip 206
White Paper on higher education 46
Women 157
Wolff, Olins 166
Woolworth 161

Yran, Knut 15

Zukav, Gary 163